IMPOSSIBLE MISSIONS?

NINA BERMAN

Impossible Missions?

German Economic, Military, and Humanitarian Efforts in Africa

University of Nebraska Press

Lincoln and London

Acknowledgments for previously published material appear on page x.

Library of Congress Cataloging-in-Publication Data
Berman, Nina.
Impossible missions? : German economic, military, and humanitarian efforts in Africa / Nina Berman.
p. cm. (Texts and contexts)
Includes bibliographical references and index.
ISBN 0-8032-1334-4 (cloth: alkaline paper)
1. Humanitarian assistance, German – Africa. 2. Economic assistance, German – Africa. 3. Technical assistance, German – Africa. I. Title. II. Texts and contexts (Unnumbered)
HV40.8.A35B47 2004 338.91′4306 – dc22 2003020873

For my parents

CONTENTS

ACKNOWLEDGMENTS

This project was generously supported by grants from the University of Texas at Austin, The Ohio State University, the Kittredge Foundation, and the German Academic Exchange Service (Deutscher Akademischer Austauschdienst, DAAD). Madame Poteau at the Albert Schweitzer archives in Günsbach not only helped me with her expertise but also generously invited me into her home during my research stay. Fieldwork in Kenya would not have been possible without the support of, among others, Raymond Matiba, James Willson, Mrs. Kariuki, Peter Ludaava, David Osiro, Arlette and Nick de Souza, Rama, and Juma. I am indebted to my research assistants, Lucinda Martin, Marike Janzen, and Norm Hirschy, and to Peter Siegenthaler and Rebecca Lorins for their stylistic suggestions. Over the years colleagues and friends were kind enough to share their thoughts with me on the subjects discussed in this book. I would like to thank, in particular, Katie Arens, Sujit Chowdhury, John Conteh-Morgan, Arif Dirlik, Bernd Fischer, Sander Gilman, Kordula Gruhn, Gregor Hens, John Hoberman, Abiola Irele, Peter Jelavich, Marcia Klotz, Sara Lennox, Paul Michael Lützeler, Daniel Mengara, Ruthmarie Mitsch, Christoph Müller, Perry Myers, Alain Patrice Nganang, Ugo Nwokeji, Marjorie Payne, Sara Pugach, Paul Reitter, Werner Ruf, Jürgen Streeck, Janet Swaffar, Nirvana Tannoukhi, Uwe Timm, Lora Wildenthal, Barbara Wolbert, David Wright, Susanne Zantop, and Andrew Zimmermann. The insightful comments made by the readers of the manuscript enabled me to provide some missing links. Additional suggestions and editorial changes by Elizabeth Gratch further improved the text. I owe a special debt to Rick Rentschler, who is responsible for the catchy part of the book's title, conceived one night in a Berlin bar, and who, years later, was good enough to point out that the book consisted of two parts.

Several friendships have motivated much of what is at the core of this study. Many years ago John Thomas and Tseliso Maseela were the first who taught me to pay attention to people and things African. More recently, Zaki Al Maboren's powerful paintings (like the novels and artworks of other African artists) have opened my eyes to expressions of a new humanist vision, not only for Africa. My daughter, Milena, who was a very young and nevertheless meticulous and perceptive research assistant in Kenya, and my stepdaughter, Sara, inspire me in many ways; I am truly grateful to them for their generous support. The book is dedicated to my parents, Karl Fritz and Elfriede Heise; their deep humanism has set a standard that guides my life.

Portions of this book have been previously published. Parts of chapter 2 originally appeared as "Albert Schweitzer: Germany's Alibi and Exculpation," in *German Colonialism: Another "Sonderweg"?* ed. Marcia Klotz, special issue of *European Studies Journal* 16.2 (1999): 69–94. Parts of chapter 3 originally appeared as "Colonization or Globalization? Ernst Udet's Account of East Africa from 1932," in *Africanizing Knowledge: African Studies across the Disciplines,* ed. Toyin Falola and Christian Jennings (Piscataway NJ: Transaction Publishers Rutgers, 2002), 297–313; reprinted by permission of Transaction Publishers; copyright © 2002 by Transaction Publishers. An earlier version of chapter 4 appeared as "Die Bundeswehr in Somalia und die Frage humanitärer Intervention: Bodo Kirchhoffs *Herrenmenschlichkeit,*" in *Schriftsteller und "Dritte Welt,"* ed. Paul Michael Lützeler (Tübingen: Stauffenburg, 1998), 221–42.

IMPOSSIBLE MISSIONS?

Introduction

Am deutschen Wesen soll die Welt genesen. — Emperor Wilhelm II

But their own coming too was not a tragedy as we imagine, nor yet a blessing as they imagine. It was a melodramatic act which with the passage of time will change into a mighty myth. — Tayeb Salih, *Season of Migration to the North*

That's when white people are most dangerous. When they try to make things "better" for Africans. When white people are trying to enslave Africans or rob them, the Africans usually know just what to do. They've dealt with slave traders, invaders, and plunderers for centuries. . . . But when white people come in with a lot of money or "know-how" and try to make things "better," that's when things really go to hell. Why can't white people just visit? Why must they always meddle? — Richard Dooling, *White Man's Grave*

This book is about Germans who went to Africa with "good intentions" but whose interfering in local affairs often had disastrous consequences for Africans. The individuals at the center of this study traveled to and lived in Africa from the mid-nineteenth to the late twentieth century. They spent time in their respective areas for very different reasons but always with a sense of "mission." As engineers, doctors, pilots, soldiers, and tourists, they came to Africa believing their presence and their actions to be beneficial for the respective countries and their inhabitants. In one way or another, they were secular missionaries, promoting modern European civilization in African contexts.

Fortschritt, the German word for "progress," is central to characterizing the mind-set of these individuals, all of whom were part of larger institutional frameworks and historical contexts and helped to establish economic, political, and cultural ties between Africa and Germany.

The idea of *Fortschritt* evokes the Age of Enlightenment, the rise of modernity, and the Age of Discovery. This initial nexus of traveling; the belief in ethical, social, political, and technological progress; and the messianic nature of modernity informs the German relationship to Africa and its portrayals of Africa and Africans in substantial ways. Travel and discovery led ultimately to various forms of intervention and occupation, and a faith in progress legitimized German actions in Africa, which were presented as propelling a process of universal enlightenment and modernization, with benefits for both sides. The missionary fervor and the self-righteousness that distinguished this process evolved from earlier and coinciding Christian practices and persisted as a secular version of Christian culture.[1] In fact, aspects of what Samir Amin calls "religious secularism" are integral to the German stance vis-à-vis Africa.[2] While the definition of *progress* varied from notions of cultural, spiritual, and ethical evolution to economic development, the Germans who brought progress to Africans were convinced of the positive effects of the transformations they offered.[3]

The superior position these Germans claimed for themselves was not based on a belief in a biological superiority of the white race but, rather, inspired by this missionary sense of modernization and development. One of the uniting factors that drew these Germans together is that they all saw themselves as representing the future on the ladder of human development, with Africans stuck in an earlier stage from which they had to be liberated.[4] Nineteenth-century race theory certainly had an impact on the actions of these representative individuals, but racism alone is no explanation for the systemic inequalities that resulted from German involvement in Africa. Clearly, race parameters were developed and mobilized to implement policies after the first European economic and political interventions had occurred. In addition, these parameters can have different functions, including the control of "potentially subversive white colonials."[5] Both the modernizing and the racist frameworks, however, are intrinsically interrelated. By exploring particular case studies, I want to shift the focus to the modernizing mind-set in order to expose a set of motivations that has not been adequately identified in recent discussions and, more important, that persists to this day.

This study seeks to expose forms of domination that derive from a philosophy of progress and "good intentions," from a belief in helping and developing that ultimately can lead to the same structural imbalances that the overtly racist model of intervention produces.[6] Michael Adas has shown how "Europeans' perceptions of the material superiority of their own cultures, particularly as manifested in scientific thought and technological innovation, shaped their attitudes toward and interaction with peoples they encountered overseas."[7] His analysis also confirms that "racism should be viewed as a subordinate rather than the dominant theme in European intellectual discourse on non-Western peoples."[8] The material presented on the following pages corroborates these findings. Taking the German model as a case study, I foreground structures that date back to the days of colonialism but did not disappear with decolonization and that are in fact integral to today's global economy.[9] At a moment when the gap between rich and poor nations is growing, when poor nations are to a greater extent than ever before confronted with war, famine, disease, poverty, and mass migrations, global inequality cannot be understood as a problem of the past.

By focusing on concepts such as modernization and progress rather than issues of race, ethnicity, and culture, this study takes a different route than much current postcolonial and, more recently, transnational and global studies. While the interplay of different mechanisms of domination and oppression has been pointed out by theorists such as Aijaz Ahmad, Samir Amin, Kwame Anthony Appiah, Arif Dirlik, Frantz Fanon, Ranajit Guha, Albert Memmi, and Gayatri Spivak and by writers such as Chinua Achebe, Mariama Bâ, Mongo Beti, Aimé Césaire, Nuruddin Farah, and Wole Soyinka, their works have had a selective reception by the majority of cultural critics who work in the United States.[10] The standard readers on postcolonial studies do not contain sections on "Capitalism", "Christianity," "Development," "Imperialism", or "Technology" but, rather, discuss the subject matter under rubrics such as "Ethnicity," "Feminism," "Hybridity," "Identity," "Language," and "Nationalism."[11]

What accounts for this selectivity? The study of Africa in the context of U.S. academia is to a great extent determined by the specific geopolitical situation of the United States. The focus on race, ethnicity, and questions of cultural identity reflects the concerns of modern immigrant societies and has led many critics to ignore other structures that shape the relationship between Africans and, in this case, Germans. For reasons that are indicative of the immediate social concerns of the United States, questions of heritage and cultural identity are transferred onto situations in which these terms have a different historical meaning.[12] This condition also reflects the ideological vacuum left by the crisis of Marxism in the aftermath of the end of the Cold War and is certainly a response to the only rudimentary critique of racism in earlier Marxist studies of imperialism and colonialism.

As Pierre Bourdieu and Loïc Wacquant argue, "the intellectual confrontations relating to the social particularity of American society and its universities have been imposed, in apparently de-historicized form, upon the whole planet."[13] As a result, interpretive models are employed that are not appropriate for the analysis of situations in Africa past and present and omit the study of other phenomena that are more or equally pressing in the African context. In particular, the focus on race and culture distracts from an analysis of economic and political oppression, or, as Arif Dirlik says, "by throwing the cover of culture over material relationships, as if the one had little to do with the other, such a focus diverts a criticism of capitalism to the criticism of Eurocentric ideology."[14] European scholars, by contrast, tend to treat questions of race and ethnicity (terms that, for historical reasons, have distinct connotations in Europe and are mostly perceived as vocabulary of the political Right) as less relevant for understanding contemporary social and political situations. Just as United States–based scholars focus too much on race and ethnicity, Europeans often underestimate the significance of racist parameters.

The mode this critique of global power relations is taking, in both Europe and the United States, perpetuates, as Johannes Fabian says, a "discourse whose referent has been removed from the present of the speaking/writing subject."[15] Symptomatic of the preponderance of local concerns and the muddling of different agendas is the fact that the field of "postcolonial studies" includes a wide range of subjects and approaches. Two distinct areas of research define the field. The main objective of postcolonial studies in European language and literature departments is to demonstrate the complicity of *European* cultural representations in the colonizing project. In most cases these investigations do not take notice of the histories of those who are the subject of these representations (for example, Africans) but, rather, evaluate the images in their function in constituting European self-images and legitimizing actions aimed at dominating non-Europeans. With regard to Africa, several analyses have pointed out the mechanisms employed for misrepresenting and oppressing African peoples.[16] Certainly, the critique of stereotypes is necessary, but claims made to explain larger historical processes based on the identification of stereotypes are dubious. It does not necessarily take a language of cultural othering to authorize missions of military, political, and economic intervention.

The second focus of postcolonial studies—namely cultural expressions articulated by artists, intellectuals, and other peoples *who are members of colonized and decolonized societies*—constitutes an amorphous field of study, the fuzziness of which reflects the generalizing definition of the term as used by Bill Ashcroft and others. This definition, with its broad temporal and spatial ambition, does not distinguish between literature written before and after decolonization and includes "the literature of the U.S.A," Canada, New Zealand, Australia, and, by analogy, the new immigrant societies in Europe.[17] Yet the primary subject of critique as voiced, for example, in African literature written *after* decolonization has changed: for the most part cultural articulations produced in or about postindependence societies direct their critique not at the former colonizer but at contested areas within these postindependence societies. In addition, countries such as China, Turkey, and Iran were never colonized; should their literatures be termed "postcolonial" because the entire globe is now postcolonial? Or is postcolonialism Western academia's discursive move to colonize the world?[18]

Recent discussions of Africa demonstrate that the current conceptual framework of postcolonial studies is not adequate to address these distinct fields of study. Achille Mbembe's *On the Postcolony,* for example, highlights the intrinsic continuities that connect colonial and postcolonial societies. Mbembe also argues for developing new categories adequate to analyzing the specificity of African situations and underscores the shortcomings of postcolonial visions of Africa, as expressed by what he terms accounts of "developmentalism" and "nativism."[19] He rejects notions of an essentialist African identity in favor of an approach that attempts to consider "practices of the self."[20] While his positions are not entirely new—Abiola Irele and Kwame Anthony Appiah, for example, have also raised these issues—Mbembe's polemical mode and at times obfuscating rhetoric have elicited passionate responses and provoked a necessary debate signaling a new phase of theorizing Africa, the heatedness of which reflects the acute sense of crisis in Africa itself.[21]

Another example that reflects current debates over how to describe contemporary Africa conceptually emerges in the debates of "externalists" versus "internalists." The so-called externalists continue to see Africa's misery as a result of actions taken by Western powers. The legacy of colonialism and the continued interventions of Western states in African affairs since decolonization are considered as the primary reasons for the failure of African development on cultural, economic, and political levels. The internalists, on the other hand, argue that the causes for these impediments are to be found in Africa itself.[22] In the view of these scholars the impact the West had on African societies does not explain the persistence of weak political and economic systems (with corruption as a central malaise) and the explosion of civil wars and other military inter-African conflicts since independence.[23] These debates ultimately challenge paradigms that set the agendas of postcolonial studies in its current form and add new insights to other debates over "alternative modernities."[24]

Scholars evaluating European representations of Africa can learn from these debates. Despite their different trajectories, the premise of both areas of research grouped together under the rubric of postcolonial studies was and continues to be to describe the interconnection between cultural production and various forms of economic, political, and institutional power. Yet, as Mbembe points out, "on the pretext of avoiding single-factor explanations of domination, these disciplines have reduced the complex phenomena of the state and power to 'discourses' and 'representations,' forgetting that discourses and representations have materiality."[25] The lack of historical analysis, the selectivity of readings, and the generalizations we have seen, especially in studies focusing on race and ethnicity, obstructed a more differentiated understanding of the relationship between power, the economy, and culture. The avoidance of the material reality of Africa and Africans, in most of the analyses of European images of Africa, has led to a perpetuation of the old model of Africanism (as well as Orientalism and its brethren). Even though critics have thoroughly unmasked the uses of stereotyping Africa and Africans, ignorance about the political, social, economic, linguistic, and cultural history of diverse African contexts persists.[26] Especially when it comes to cultural representations that are based on an actual encounter with Africa, this ignorance of the African material reality is untenable.

Publications on the German presence in Africa have been slow to emerge over the last few decades, and several scholars have pointed to the reasons for this lacuna.[27] Whereas French and British academics took up the question of colonialism during and after the period of decolonization, West German postwar society and its academics were primarily concerned with arriving at an understanding of World War II and the Holocaust. For West Germans and scholars of German history and culture, the legacy of the German colonial period, which officially ended in 1918, was not as pressing as were the horrors of World War II. In some versions colonialism was seen primarily in relation to Germany's eastward expansionism and to the Holocaust.[28] This focus on World War II also dominated discussion in the United States. Even in the more recent period the theories of Kant, Hegel, and other thinkers of the Enlightenment period are not understood as reactions to three hundred years of slave trade and colonialism but discussed as establishing the foundational discourse that would ultimately result in the Holocaust.[29]

East Germany, however, held a different view of World War II, according to which the antifascist history was claimed by the GDR (while the FRG was seen as inheriting the Nazi legacy), and fascism was understood in the larger framework of capitalism. This approach generated an interest in the history of colonialism and imperialism as manifestations of capitalism and allowed for in-depth investigations of the colonial period; historians such as Karl Büttner, Heinrich Loth, and Helmut Stoecker offered differentiated analyses already in the 1950s.

As a result of both the East German preoccupation with capitalism and the West German and U.S. focus on World War II, colonialism, antisemitism, the Holocaust, and racism (including recent instances connected to immigration) were conventionally not discussed in their interrelatedness, which significantly impeded an identification of the function of racist parameters in German culture. Recent analyses suggest that a shift is under way that contests the resistance of German criticism to discuss both the *longue durée* and the specific instances of racism in German-speaking societies.[30] Susan Buck-Morss's discussion of the influence of the Haitian revolution on Hegel's writings stands out as an excellent example of this contextual approach, which sees German ideas of race in the context of European colonialism.[31]

Another aspect significant in this respect is the relative absence of voices from Africa and Asia in German departments. In recent years an increasing number of critics with roots in India, the Caribbean, and Africa have become members of English, French, and other departments in Europe and the United States. These critics have been able to challenge their respective fields from within by ensuring that their concerns acquired a central place in the scholarly debates. Although there is a considerable number of Africans and Asians who are trained in German literature and culture, these scholars are usually not employed at European or North American institutions but, rather, teach in Africa and Asia. They tend to be geographically and institutionally marginalized within the discipline and, with few exceptions, have not been acknowledged by mainstream German criticism.[32] In a similar way intellectuals from Africa and Asia who live and work in various areas of contemporary Germany are not recognized as significant voices.[33] As a result, German literary and cultural criticism has not been challenged in ways comparable to what we have seen in English or French departments. Whereas the field of German-Jewish studies has succeeded in producing groundbreaking scholarship and in forcing scholars in various disciplines to evaluate their parameters, a similar development has not yet occurred in terms of Germany's relationship to Africa and Asia. Recent discussions inspired by the flourishing minority culture in today's Germany, however, seem to signal the emergence of a different brand of criticism. While bicultural artists gain visibility in the public sphere, academics with bicultural and non-German backgrounds address new areas of concern, in both Germany and the United States.[34]

The first literary critics who discussed Germany's relationship to Africa through an analysis of the textual archive focused primarily on the colonial period and investigated the literature directly related to it. Unlike scholars who analyzed such material under the rubrics exoticism, adventure, or utopia and presented it as reflections of internal German issues, Wolfgang Bader and János Riesz (1983), Sybille Benninghoff-Lühl

(1983), and Joachim Warmbold (1982) acknowledged the historical context relevant to understanding the political import of colonial literature.[35] Their studies brought attention to a corpus of texts previously unknown or forgotten.[36] In addition, several investigations, such as *On Blackness without Blacks* by Sander Gilman (1982), explored representations of Africans in light of social, political, and cultural questions stemming from the specific internal conditions of German societies.[37]

For years these studies did not have a significant impact on the larger field of Germanistik (in Germany) or German studies (outside of Germany). While interest in travel and cross-cultural encounters was increasing, it took almost another decade before *Colonial Space* (1992), the first study on German colonial literature written in English and conceived in the South African institutional context, was published. Its author, John K. Noyes, was also the first German studies scholar to contribute to debates in the emerging field of postcolonial studies, drawing on theories by Homi Bhabha, Jacques Derrida, Johannes Fabian, Jacques Lacan, Edward Said, and others.[38] Nevertheless, in comparison to French and British studies, postcolonial studies did not make significant inroads into German studies until the mid-1990s, and it seemed, as Russell Berman observes, that "Germanists, mimicking postcolonial studies in other literature departments, [were] reproducing the same imitative belatedness that characterized German imperialism of the 1880s, itself always trying to catch up with the British Empire."[39] Panels at conferences, symposia, and scattered articles were the main venues to discuss the articulation of Germany's colonial past and, in particular, the longer history of Germany's relationship to Africa, Asia, and Latin America in fictional and nonfictional texts. The last five years, however, have finally seen the publication of several book-length studies that have advanced our understanding of these texts significantly.

In *Colonial Fantasies* Susanne Zantop presents an extensive archive of fictional and nonfictional texts and demonstrates intriguingly the ways in which fantasies about colonial territories and colonial peoples served to define the German nation. She focuses on the century before the founding of the German nation-state, before the establishment of the German colonial empire. Zantop does not investigate "the colonial reality of the later nineteenth century" but, rather, examines "the formation of a sense of German difference that grew out of specific historical realities in the late 1700s and early 1800s and that manifested itself in Germany's colonial fantasies."[40] Her analysis of the textual material highlights the nexus of tropes of race, sexuality, and nation and describes a universe of imaginations about German superiority and conquest that provided a reservoir of images and beliefs, serving to legitimize xenophobic and racist political action.

While Zantop's study focuses on debates at home, Russell Berman pursues the question of a German colonial discourse in foreign settings. He insists that experience matters and that, in order to arrive at a better judgment of the nature of the colonial encounter, we have to investigate how German travelers articulated their reactions to experiences abroad. Berman's *Enlightenment or Empire* is complementary with Zantop's study in more than one way. While Zantop concentrates on race, Berman argues that the experience of space in travel, exploration, and, finally, colonial conquest is a more significant determinant that precedes colonial ideologies.[41] Berman claims that "a strand of German culture was quite curious about difference, and this interest produced a particular openness."[42] Although he presents textual evidence for this thesis, in particular in the chapter on Georg Forster, Berman does not get around the fact that the curiosity for difference did not preempt but, rather, participated in the development of dominating structures. The many examples of Germans going native, however, from Karl May's heroes to actual cases of Germans adopting foreign lifestyles, provide us with ample material that bolsters Berman's thesis, regardless of the fact that this phenomenon might be explained by various factors. Katrin Sieg's work on *Ethnic Drag,* for example, shows that ethnic drag can do both—destabilize and solidify markers of difference between ethnic groups.[43] There is also evidence that German colonial administrators did not attempt to "Germanize" local populations in ways comparable to the strategies pursued by especially the French; however, as will become evident in this study, the different approach toward local culture did not imply a politics of equality.[44]

The most controversial aspect of Berman's study is his sweeping critique of much of postcolonial and poststructuralist theory, coupled with a passionate defense of the Enlightenment project. Berman insists on the importance of "reason—and by extension, of science, progress, and a normative universalism."[45] His refutation of postcolonial and poststructuralist criticism is reductive at best: he barely engages with specific critics or the range of critics that make up the field. Many, if not most of them, see their critique as solidly standing in the emancipatory tradition of the Enlightenment, and, in line with Theodor W. Adorno and Max Horkheimer's 1944 publication *Dialectic of Enlightenment,* they have indeed elaborated on the internal contradictions of the Enlightenment. As evident from my discussion of postcolonial studies, I identify different reasons for the shortcomings that presently characterize the field of postcolonial studies.

While modernization brought democracy to Europe, repressive traditions were transferred to the colonies.[46] By declaring most non-European societies peoples without history or culture (*Naturvölker*), they were rendered ineligible for the benefits of civilization that were formulated in the political emancipatory movements across Europe. In its extreme forms "civilizationism," as Marcia Klotz calls this ideology, culminated in institutional expressions of racism in Western societies.[47] The paradigmatic cases that exemplify the contradictions Berman glosses over are, for example, the *Code Noir, Apartheid,* and *Segregation,* systems that were legitimized by drawing on seemingly reasonable and scientific theories.[48] In his insistence on science Berman disregards the idea that humanism is an ethical position that may not be verifiable by scientific methods.

An analysis that challenges Berman's generalizing defense of the Enlightenment is provided by Andrew Zimmermann's study on the development of the discipline of anthropology in Germany. In *Anthropology and Antihumanism in Imperial Germany* Zimmermann offers a detailed case study that illustrates the dark side of the Enlightenment and exemplifies how science and reason were used to oppress non-Europeans. Anthropology contains the element of experience that, as Berman argues, has a mind-altering potential. Yet we see anthropologists evaluating the data from non-European areas along the lines of ideologies bolstering European notions of supremacy. During the Wilhelmine Empire, German anthropologists, in contrast to their British colleagues who assumed an evolutionary narrative, "understood nature as a static system of categories that allowed them, in their study of 'natural peoples,' to grasp an unchanging essence of humanity, rather than the ephemeral changes that historians recorded."[49]

Anthropology thus played an important role, offering "Europeans a modern identity as a cultural people whose status depended less on humanist *Bildung*, or self-cultivation, than on the development of the natural sciences—including anthropology as the study of natural peoples."[50] Curiosity about other cultures might be detected in these writings, but the emancipatory side of the Enlightenment was solidly pushed beneath the surface in the taxonomy of non-Europeans who, as the argument ran, deserved and needed to be dominated. As Zimmermann explains, the relationship between anthropology and imperialism was not instrumental (in fact, it was rather complex) but fundamental on a more basic level in that "both anthropology and imperialism were phenomena of a profound shift in global politics, economics, and culture."[51]

The question about the specific impact of anthropological science on colonial policy (which Zimmermann addresses only tangentially) is also relevant when evaluating Zantop's and Berman's studies.[52] Both limit their analyses to discourse: Zantop's interest in "fantasies not action" is echoed in Berman's focus.[53] Similar to Zantop, Berman is not interested in relating the discursive web he identifies to colonial policy or any other form of material action.[54] On that level the books are complementary in that they catalog the archive of colonial discourse, consisting of fantasies concocted at home and articulations based on experience abroad; the impact of these fantasies on actual policy, however, remains obscure.

The many facets of colonial discourse are also explored in contributions to *The Imperialist Imagination,* edited by Sara Friedrichsmeyer, Sara Lennox, and Susanne Zantop.[55] By placing colonialism in the context of the longer history of colonial activities within and outside of Europe and extending the analysis to include cultural representations conceived after the colonial period, articles in the anthology illustrate the pervasiveness of colonialist imagery in German literature, film, and intellectual history to this day.[56] None of the articles on the postcolonial period, however, establishes the connection to Germany's economic and political relation to Africa and other areas.[57]

Other studies, such as Arlene Teraoka's *East, West, and Others: The Third World in Postwar German Literature* (1996) and Konstanze Streese's *"Cric?"—"Crac!": Vier literarische Versuche, mit dem Kolonialismus umzugehen,* have examined postwar texts on non-European areas and shown how "persisting Eurocentric stereotypes of the Third World (representing nature, sexuality, chaos, madness, revolution), especially in the work of well-intentioned, well-informed, politically progressive writers, construct a discourse . . . on Europeanness."[58] This persistence of Eurocentric views is also evident in analyses of texts by postwar writers collected in *Schriftsteller und "Dritte Welt."*[59] Another facet of German colonialism is addressed in a study by Valentina Glajar, who investigates the German legacy in territories of the former Habsburg Empire.[60] Kristin Kopp's analysis of German colonial discourse in Polish territories also opens the door to further explorations of the understudied relationship between German states and Eastern territories.[61]

My overview here is not comprehensive, but it becomes evident that recent criticism has recorded the range of colonial and imperialist images in general and evaluated their functions within the space of the German nation. Two aspects, however, have not been explored sufficiently. First, the connection of colonial and imperialist discourse to modernization has rarely been studied. To a large extent premodern structures of German society were continued in the colonies or in the fantasies about the colonies. While Germans at home discussed the institutionalization of democracy and universal suffrage, the aristocratic past was resurrected and continued in form of a racial hierarchy. As German women fought for equality at home, they became complicit in the subjugation of Africans. This element of transference is touched upon, even if not spelled out, in an article by Noyes, who shows that discussions of nomadism in colonial novels reflect the anxieties of modern, destabilized subjectivity.[62] Lisa Gates's analysis of Leni Riefenstahl's photos of the Nuba also articulates this moment: "What Riefenstahl mourns in these photograph collections is ostensibly the loss of authenticity, the corruption of a pure culture by the modern Western world."[63] As it turns out, however, she mourns this loss because the process of modernization of the Nuba blurs the boundaries between herself and the racial other. Both the creation of a premodern society in the colonies and the celebration of authentic premodern societies reflect the need of the German subject for racial and civilizational boundaries to elevate his or her own status in the modern world.[64]

Second, the relationship of colonial and imperialist imagery to social action and policy in the colonies has been left aside by most critics. This omission raises serious questions, which becomes evident in light of two recent publications about life in the colonies. Lora Wildenthal's *German Women for Empire* and Daniel Joseph Walther's *Creating Germans Abroad* provide relevant details regarding the relationship of colonial discourse to social action. While Wildenthal's study pursues a broader focus in that it surveys the appeal of the colonies for German women and the significant role they played in the colonies, Walther concentrates more specifically on the case of German Southwest Africa, and explores the history of the German community in the area beyond the German colonial period.[65] One issue that provides us with interesting material is the question of miscegenation. Both Wildenthal and Walther demonstrate that miscegenation, in the form of marriage and concubinage, was widespread in the colonies. In fact, colonial officials initially encouraged miscegenation, and here we might detect a prime example that would fit Russell Berman's thesis about the relevance of experience and initial openness toward the culturally different in the colonial encounter (although this interest in the culturally different also took violent forms). Initially, race mattered less to the colonizers than one might assume. This phenomenon can be understood as a response to the fact that in German Southwest Africa, for example, German men outnumbered German women four to six times, and the need for sexual partners was realistically acknowledged. But, regardless of the explaining factors, the frequency of miscegenation shows that, in the early period of German colonialism, racism was not the dominant factor determining relations between Africans and Germans.

Both Wildenthal and Walther state that the discourse of race moved to the forefront in conjunction with wars against the indigenous population. Rather than presenting the wars as a struggle over resources, they were now presented as wars over racial purity and domination. Laws against miscegenation were introduced in the context of these wars: in Namibia they followed the brutal suppression of the Nama and Herero in 1904–7; in East Africa they coincided with the Maji-Maji uprising of 1905–6. Walther shows that in German Southwest Africa notions of German racial identity were also developed in competition with the Afrikaner population, that is, another white population competing for supremacy. Race quite clearly fulfilled a specific function in the unfolding of economic conquest and political domination. It was used at certain moments but did not provide the original impetus for the early stages of conquest. Race became important in building the colonial state, not only as a tool to dominate indigenous populations but also as a means to control white men and women.

What does the relative importance of race in the colonies mean for our evaluation of race in the textual archive, fictional and nonfictional, that was composed for the most part at home in Germany? The tension that is inherent here in the relationship between discourse, social action, and material reality needs to be taken seriously. The behavioral patterns of Germans at home and abroad are not necessarily identical. For the most part critics have applied the insights gained from analyses of German racism in Germany to the situation involving Germans in Africa. Yet, as Christopher Brummer has demonstrated, a "rift between economic and cultural colonial ideologies would appear in countless forms and guises."[66] More research is necessary to understand better the relationship between motherland and the colonies, home and abroad, colonial policies and what happened in the colonies, and the differences among individual colonies. Unearthing oral histories about the colonial period and exploring archives in Africa are of considerable relevance to this endeavor.[67]

Historians have recently revisited German colonialism in comparative studies, discussing the topic in the larger framework of European interventions in Africa. New evidence from these investigations draws a heterogeneous picture of German colonialism in Africa.[68] During that relatively short period substantially different policies toward the local inhabitants were at play in the colonies as well as outside of the colonial setting. While the genocide of the Nama and Herero in German Southwest Africa set a precedent for the Holocaust, German policies in Togo, for example, were often inspired by educational reforms.[69] East Africa saw several different approaches toward local inhabitants, with some governors approaching a more collaborative course and others displaying a greater interest in economic development of the areas.[70] Although no comparative study currently exists that discusses the regional differences in a comprehensive manner, these publications offer a more differentiated understanding of the German presence in Africa.

These recent studies by historians, however, have not yet had an impact on Germanists. In addition, only rarely do critics point to the continuation of the hegemonic relationship between Germany and post-independence countries as a root cause for the persistence of Euro-centric views.[71] The bulk of the abundant fictional and nonfictional writings and the plethora of films about Africa that were produced before and after the German colonial period have yet to be evaluated in the context of global power relations. As a result, the continuous presence of Germans in various areas of Africa since the end of the eighteenth century—as businesspeople, missionaries, bureaucrats, scientists, explorers, nurses, teachers, development aid workers, or tourists—has rarely been acknowledged in relation to the cultural representations produced in and about Africa.

A large corpus of studies exists that comes out of economics, government, history, and political science departments, elaborating on the connection between development and aid theories and the effect these modernization projects have had and have today on African societies. Often critics draw on their firsthand experience, as does Teresa Hayter, who published *Aid as Imperialism* in 1971, and Brigitte Erler, whose *Tödliche Hilfe: Bericht von meiner letzten Dienstreise in Sachen Entwicklungshilfe* (1985) set off a passionate debate in Germany.[72] These studies show that additional mechanisms are at work that are interrelated with racist thought patterns, but the mechanism and repercussions of which have not been explored sufficiently by cultural and literary critics.

The modes of thinking I explore are tied in fundamental ways to German attempts to develop Africa economically, culturally, and politically. As I will demonstrate in the following pages, the impact that the actions inspired by the developmentalist mind-set had and still have can even be constructive, at least in part. More often, however, German interventions in Africa put Africans at a disadvantage. Recent analyses of peacekeeping show that "the influence of external actors has proven to be one source that exacerbated problems left by the colonial powers after decolonization."[73] Carol Lancaster's study of aid to Africa argues that development projects have largely failed because "the aid agencies themselves have often lacked the technical experience, local knowledge, staff, and appropriate processes to manage such projects and programs effectively."[74] Taking additional bureaucratic and political obstacles into account, she suggests that, consequently, a greater involvement of Africans in designing and executing projects is imperative.[75] These observations correspond to results of my investigation.

This study does not concentrate on the period of German colonialism proper but includes both the precolonial period and the time after decolonization, continuing up to the present day. In fact, none of the figures investigated in this monograph was directly connected to a German colonial enterprise. Nevertheless, their pursuits contributed to establishing economic, political, and cultural dominance of Germans over African territories. Broadening the scope of this study to encompass both the pre- and postcolonial eras allows me to highlight continuities that are often neglected in contemporary criticism. Modern Germany's relation to Africa amounts to a form of economic, political, and cultural domination that resembles the colonialism and the neocolonialism of other European powers. Did Germans act toward Africans differently than, for example, their British and French counterparts? Only a comparative study will render a differentiated answer to this question, but the cases detailed here provide new material for such investigations. The type of German presence in Africa investigated in this book was and is driven not by national concerns necessarily (as conventionally assumed in current postcolonial theory) but by the interests of companies, financial institutions, humanitarian and religious associations, and transnational organizations.[76] The way Germans related to Africa was an expression of their self-fashioning as modern subjects. This dynamic was not ended with formal decolonization and, I argue, is still at work today.

Impossible Missions? chronicles a complex problem, the scope of which cannot be underscored enough; millions of volumes are printed annually on various subjects that attest to the persistence of Germany's interest and presence in Africa. The evidence for the extent of this interaction between Germans and Africans that is evaluated in this study offers but a glimpse into what is available for further analyses.

The individual chapters of this study investigate mostly autobiographical German representations of several distinct African societies. Even though autobiographical material displays most of the narrative structures that distinguish fictional texts, the relationship to the subject matter of the account is different and needs to be probed in distinct ways. Each chapter includes an extensive review of the economic and political contexts to which these representations refer. In providing this background, I offer not only an analysis of the German language text in its relevance to German society (that is, images of Africa as reflections of Germany), but in each case I also relate what Germans say about Africa to the particular historical African context. This twofold approach allows me to acknowledge the material reality of African societies and to test the relevance and meaning of the German representation in the context of specific African situations. That is, images of Africa are treated as articulations that refer not only to an imaginary but also to a reality. One of the central concerns of this study is to assert that analyses of fictional and nonfictional images of Africa remain limited in scope if they do not include a more intimate engagement with the actual subjects of the representations. In spite of the potential objection that I propagate a naive realism, I suggest that background knowledge—which naturally may be controversial and heterogeneous—enables us to provide the "thick description," to use Clifford Geertz's term, that is essential for the evaluation of cultural production.

Each chapter explores the notion of "mission" in a different historical period and in a distinct geographical location. Part 1 of the study identifies three paradigmatic situations from earlier historical periods; part 2 makes a leap to the contemporary era and investigates the ways in which the belief systems that were described in part 1 are still with us today.

Chapter 1 begins in North Africa and focuses on the question of modernization by presenting the writings of Max Eyth, an engineer who worked for the Egyptian aristocrat Muhammad ʿAbd al-Halim to help develop the booming cotton industry of the country in the 1860s. Eyth's relationship to Egyptians was deeply inspired by a belief in technological progress. A comparison between his comments on German and on Egyptian peasants highlights the fact that his attitude lacked a culturalist component but, rather, reflected the universalist mind-set that distinguished many proponents of technology and modernization (and continues to do so). The Egyptian case also challenges Edward Said's concept of Orientalism; the local elite believed just as much in *tanwir*, the Arabic word for "Enlightenment," as the foreign investors and specialists who were asked to develop the country. The discussion of Eyth's writings sheds light on this particularly complicated story of modernization.

Albert Schweitzer's presence in Gabon is at the center of the second chapter. While his actual work as a doctor is largely neglected in this analysis, I focus on his motivations for going to Africa and on his basic view of Africans. Schweitzer believed in fundamental differences between civilizations, and both his Christian background and the model he developed in his cultural philosophy deeply informed his notion of progress and the idea of his mission in Africa. While Eyth's passion was technological modernization (which would presumably have social and political ramifications), Schweitzer aimed primarily at "civilizing" and Christianizing Africans. Although Schweitzer rejected biological explanations of the differences between distinct civilizations (and thus cannot be called a "racist" in the strict sense of the word), culturalist thinking and Christianity play a significant role in his interaction with Africans. Christianity's role in the colonizing process is a crucial aspect largely omitted in current postcolonial analyses (which, again, might be explained as related to particular conventions accepted in the United States). Ultimately, the Christian philosophy of Schweitzer emerges as integral to the colonial and neocolonial system and functions to legitimize paternalist German (and other Western) attitudes toward Africa.

The last chapter of part 1 presents an example of what I call the "globalizing mission." The famous pilot and flying ace Ernst Udet's portrayal of East Africa, which was based on his stay in the region in early 1932, reverberates with post-1945 German attitudes toward non-Western cultures. Here Masai and other Africans appear perfectly at ease with modern technology and are presented to the German audience as "friends" who are "beautiful" and "genuine." Progress is again defined by technological advancement, which forms the basis for the cultural compatibility of Germans and Africans. Photographs taken from above by cameras attached to planes feature inviting landscapes with an intact infrastructure. These pictures of an area that used to be a German colony appealed to German dreams of recapturing colonial territory. The representational strategies, however, are a distinct departure from earlier, especially nineteenth-century, descriptions of African space. Rather than depicting Africa as a wasteland of unbounded space that calls for the colonizer to inhabit and structure it, Africa was portrayed as being peopled with cooperative Africans and offering an infrastructure that would allow for further development.

Udet's account of East Africa provides a fitting transition to the second part of the study, exploring the more recent situation. Currently, the German presence in Africa occurs primarily in the realms of development projects, humanitarian interventions, and tourism. The first chapter of part 2 deals with one set of issues by discussing the German army's participation in a humanitarian intervention known as United Nations Operation in Somalia in 1993. The deployment of soldiers was debated passionately in Germany; for the first time since rearmament, German soldiers were sent on a mission that included the potential for combat. The German writer Bodo Kirchhoff took it upon himself to visit the German contingent in Somalia to evaluate whether the participation was justified or not. His account emerges as a paradigmatic example of a contemporary view of non-Western cultures, widespread in German intellectual circles, that is distinguished both by intellectual laziness and racist thinking. Ignoring the limitations of eyewitness reports such as his own (a style of reporting used for most coverage of Africa), he refuses to learn about Somalia's history. Arguing from the position of a seemingly tolerant philosophy of difference, he rejects the idea of humanitarian missions on the grounds of culturalist arguments.

The last chapter is based on ethnographic fieldwork in Kenya and describes the interaction between German repeat visitors and the local population. Views that were integral to the three situations investigated in part 1 emerge again in the actions of "ordinary Germans," who know little about colonialism and do not think about themselves in the context of the *longue durée* of Germany's presence in Africa. The way these Germans relate to Kenyans illustrates that helping Africans has become almost compulsory to contemporary Germans. At the same time these repeat visitors display some qualities that were largely missing from the cases investigated in the previous chapters. The tourists operate along the lines of notions of sustainable development and support Kenyans in areas widely accepted as basic human needs—namely, education, housing, and clothing. The high rate of intermarriage between German tourists and Kenyans, which significantly exceeds the rates of Kenyan intermarriage with any other group of tourists, documents that the relationship between German and Kenyan men and women unfolds in distinct ways.

One of the underlying concerns of this study is to explore the connection of discourse to social action. The conclusion addresses this issue by revisiting the individual chapters under this premise. In all cases investigated here, a tension exists between the actions and the representation of these actions in writings, photographs, films, and oral reports. Common wisdom tells us that people do not necessarily act according to what they say, and the interaction between Germans and Africans is no exception to this rule. At times the actions may be better than the words (as in the case of Schweitzer); other situations make us aware that often people do not anticipate the possible repercussions of their actions (as is the case with the tourists). This study leaves many questions unanswered, but I hope to encourage my readers to rethink assumptions that we have settled into conveniently but that do not stand the test of time.

The case studies presented here document instances in which Germans went to Africa convinced that they knew what was best for its inhabitants. At a moment when we witness large-scale military and economic operations that are presumably intended to better the lives of mostly non-Western peoples, the consideration of previous examples of helping missions may encourage us to approach these situations more thoughtfully.

PART ONE

Prototypes

1

The Modernizing Mission

Max Eyth in Egypt

The concept of progress should be based on the idea of catastrophe.
—Walter Benjamin, *Arcades Project*

A Steam Plow Competition in the Nile Delta

In late April 1864 an unusual competition was staged on a deserted field near Shubra in the Nile delta. The objects of contention were two different models of steam plows, each maker claiming that his was the superior model. On the one side four Englishmen were set to demonstrate the power of a steam plow designed by a man named Howard. The challenging team consisted of a group of Egyptian peasants and their supervisor, the German engineer Max Eyth, who entered the competition with a plow originally designed by another Englishman, John Fowler of Leeds, for whom Eyth had worked before entering the service of an Egyptian aristocrat. The goal of the competition was to establish which of the plows was best suited to work the soil of the Egyptian cotton fields. The stakes were high: the winner of the competition was likely to be chosen by the Egyptian viceroy to deliver a number of the superior plows to Egypt, to help develop the booming cotton industry of the country.

The competition unfolded in a most dramatic way in front of Egyptian aristocrats, European spectators, and Egyptian peasants. Howard's plow was brand-new and technologically advanced; Fowler's plow, however, looked worn-out. It had been used in Egypt for over a year, and Eyth and his team were aware of the possible disasters looming. Nevertheless, Eyth was at an advantage: as the chief engineer of Halim Pasha, son of Muhammad ʿAli and the uncle of Egypt's viceroy Ismaʿil, he had been in charge of developing the cotton fields for his Egyptian employer since early 1863. Having lived and worked in Egypt for a while, he was familiar with the environment. He had adjusted Fowler's plow to meet the challenges of the Egyptian soil, a soil that turned into a seemingly indestructible solid surface once the Nile flooding receded. And, sure enough, Howard's plow was unable to break up the earth, the furrows were not as deep as those created by the plow that was operated by the more experienced Eyth and his Egyptian workers. At the end of the competition Fowler's machine had plowed a significantly larger section than the plow designed by Howard. As anticipated, the result of the competition inspired the Egyptian viceroy to order a large number of Fowler's plows.

How does this scene from the 1860s in Egypt correspond to notions of a nineteenth-century world divided by nation-state alliances and colonialism? How did a German engineer such as Eyth get to be employed by an Egyptian aristocrat? In what ways can Eyth's work in Egypt be understood in the framework of Edward Said's concept of Orientalism?

Eyth was not only a famous engineer but also a prolific writer, and thus we can find answers to some of these questions in his texts. The engineer's autobiographical writings about his time in Egypt shed light on issues such as his motivation for going to Egypt and his self-image as an agent of development, as a German working for British and Egyptian employers, and as a German supervisor to Egyptian peasants. Seen in the context of Egypt's economic and political history, Eyth's story exemplifies the nineteenth-century fervor for development, and it illustrates the process by which economic development of non-European countries, instigated by Europeans and the local elite alike, ultimately created dependency on European investors and even led to colonization. The case of Max Eyth in Egypt, however, challenges widely held assumptions about the mechanisms of European dominance over non-European countries; his work and its representation in his writings demonstrate that Eyth's attitudes and actions were more deeply defined by universalist ideas about progress and modernization than by racist or cultural prejudice. The story of Eyth is a test case for much postcolonial theory; we will see that culturalist explanations fall short of doing justice to the complexity of developments in nineteenth-century Egypt.

In order to understand Eyth's time in Egypt more clearly, we need to get a sense of what it meant to be an engineer at the time in and outside of Germany. Following an overview of Eyth's coming-of-age as an engineer, a closer look at his views of Europe will provide the contrastive framework to evaluate his portrayal of Egypt. A brief review of Egypt's path to modernization situates the German engineer's stay in the country in a complicated tale of development.

A German Engineer

Recounting the early life of Max Eyth and the advancement of engineering in Germany in the second half of the nineteenth century highlights the coincidental development of modernization in parts of Europe and similar processes in parts of the Middle East, Africa, and Asia. Germany industrialized later than England and France and became a nation-state and colonial power only at the end of the century. The shift from the preindustrial to the industrial phase of the German economy is generally dated from 1795 to 1835, while the first phase of industrialization is said to have occurred between 1835 and 1873. A few representative developments highlight the extent of the changes Germany experienced during the transition to the industrial age, which unfolded at a different pace in Germany's various regions. In Prussia the October Edict of 1807 introduced the emancipation of peasants, the freedom to choose an occupation, and the freedom to dispose of land, key factors enabling the process of industrialization. Free choice of occupation was a precondition for the development of existing and new professions and, by granting free movement to workers to wherever they found work, for the growth of the manufacturing sector and industry. The emancipation of the peasants brought about the extension of agricultural land and the introduction of new methods of agricultural production, including developments in the livestock sector. It also led to a stronger social differentiation among peasants, especially an impoverishment among large groups of landless peasants—in Marxist terms, the divorce of the producers from the means of production. With the growth of rural lower classes, their already miserable living conditions worsened: "The farm labourers often lived squeezed together near the animals in fairly primitive, dark, unhygienic shacks with one common room and one bedroom."[1] Life in the cities was not appealing either; sewerage systems were only gradually introduced (in Hamburg in 1848, Berlin in 1852, and Frankfurt in the 1860s), flats were overcrowded, and bathrooms were generally shared by several families. For most of the century the majority of agricultural workers, homeworkers, servants, day laborers, factory workers, and casual workers were noncitizens, without political rights and influence. Petitions and letters of complaint directed at factory owners and at political and legal authorities are moving testimonies documenting the daily struggles and humiliations of ordinary people.[2]

The extent of the changes German society underwent in the nineteenth century is difficult to imagine today. The scale and scope to which the life of the population was altered, for example, by the introduction of the electric light or the development of the railway system, still exceeds any of the developments the twentieth century had in store. Apart from the overall social and economic changes, agricultural crises, increasing public debt, famines, food riots, epidemics, poverty of large groups who moved to the urban centers, high infant mortality, and short life spans characterize the century. People worked ninety hours per week and more, and children and women were used increasingly in the workforce.[3] In the course of the century, especially during its final thirty years, living and working conditions improved for most parts of the society; "hunger and malnutrition were largely overcome in the 1850s, with the end of pauperism and a rise in real wages."[4] The considerable wealth that was produced during the Wilhelmine Empire, however, was enjoyed by no more than a small portion of the society.[5]

As a representative of the new age, Eyth personifies a cultural figure that has come to stand for the overall change German society underwent at the time. The engineer, historically crucial to the development of civilizations, is connected to industrialization and modernization in fundamental ways. Engineering in the modern sense begins in the eighteenth century, with the invention of the first atmospheric steam engine in 1711 by Thomas Newcomen (1663–1729) and its pathbreaking development into the double-acting steam engine by James Watt (1736–1819) in 1769.[6] This machine did for the first time what human beings had always dreamed of: it produced energy that could be used for a variety of purposes. Following the invention of the steam engine, European industries transformed from the domestic or cottage industry to the factory system of industrial capitalism. The new engineering profession designed machines for use in all areas, especially the coal mining, metal, and textile industries. Engineers invented locomotives, constructed roads, railroads, bridges, and tunnels and thus developed an infrastructure that was the motor of industrialization.

As members of a new profession, engineers or technicians, as they were alternately called throughout the nineteenth century, worked in a wide range of positions. While the word *Techniker* "could also refer to a lower species of technologist," the word *Ingenieur* was used as a "generic term for all technical functions above skilled blue-collar work and foreman duties."[7] The engineering profession included factory owners and directors as well as employees, professors, consultants, civil engineers, and others.[8] In the mid-1800s these various occupations reflected substantial differences in educational training; both the wide range of jobs reflecting varying social standing and the discrepancies in training gave the new profession a disorganized and uneven image. This contributed to the fact that engineers had to struggle to gain public recognition. It took several decades before their training was integrated into the higher educational system, and, still today, engineering colleges (such as Technische Hochschulen and Ingenierschulen) do not have the same status as other academic institutions within the German university system.[9]

In early nineteenth-century Germany the development of engineering lagged behind in comparison to the situations in France and England. This was mostly connected to the absence of an educational framework but also to the lack of a central nation-state that would foster trade and development and enable the implementation of the unified educational system. Friedrich List's customs union (Allgemeiner Deutscher Zollverein, 1834) was an important milestone toward achieving all three goals. The lifting of trade barriers in parts of Germany initiated developments, such as the building of a railway system, that were crucial breakthroughs on the road to industrialization. One important event was the founding of the Organization of German Engineers (Verein Deutscher Ingenieure, VDI) in 1856. The organization's foremost mission lay in pursuing the goals of the engineering profession, and its nationalist orientation and interest in unification was a logical consequence. The organization became one of the key players that contributed to bringing about national unity.[10]

The organization acted as a lobbying group that focused on improving educational training for engineers and aimed to raise their social status. It ensured the integration of different types of engineering colleges in the larger educational system. In particular, the society fought for academic recognition of engineering schools. In 1868 the first Higher Technical Institute (Technische Hochschule) in Aachen was recognized in Prussia; until that time only two other schools had academic statutes, the polytechnical school (Polytechnikum) in Karlsruhe (1865) and the Higher Technical Institute in München (1868, founded as a polytechnical school in 1858). The founding of the German empire aided the attempts of engineers to improve the conditions of their profession. In 1879 the responsibility for the Higher Technical Institutes shifted from the Ministry of Trade to the Ministry of Culture. This movement suggests a willingness on the part of the government to treat technical and humanist education equally. Further academic acceptance of the profession was achieved in 1899, when Wilhelm II granted the right to offer doctoral degrees to Berlin's Higher Technical Institute.

Disadvantages for the profession, however, remained an issue. Equality was not yet achieved with regard to positions in state administration, in which recipients of law degrees still held a monopoly. This situation was reflective of the general status of the engineer in German society during the Wilhelmine Era. As mentioned earlier, however, the engineering profession was not a homogeneous group, and especially those engineers who owned factories were in a distinctly different position compared to the salaried engineers.[11] By 1914 the profession of German engineers was "wracked by internal conflict, fragmented into numerous subspecialties and class positions, separated by wide differences in formal education, and locked in bitter combat with industrial employers, social reformers, and the incumbents of the civil-service bureaucracy."[12] In comparison to those working in other European states, the status of the engineer in Germany was still wanting, and laments of discrimination against the profession were frequently voiced.[13] With the founding of the Wilhelmine Empire, the overall social situation of engineers had made measurable advances, but the improvements did not reflect the overall significance of the field and amounted to a discrepancy between status and societal contribution of the group.

In midcentury this gap was even wider than at the eve of World War I, and the bleak opportunities in Germany inspired Max Eyth to leave Germany in the early 1860s to find employment in England, which involved engineers to a great extent in the development of the country and held the most chances in store for ingenious minds such as Eyth's.

To this day engineers are the carrier of ideas about both progress and doom alike. To some they symbolize the future-oriented hopes of modern society, while for others they are responsible for the negative impact of the industrial and electronic age on human social relations, health, and the environment. Disasters of chemical or nuclear plants, climatic changes, pollution, modern warfare, genetically altered foods, and technical failures of all sorts are weighed against the increase in wealth for the general population (in industrialized countries), longer life spans, improved health care, and new means of transportation and communication.

Many fictional and nonfictional texts evolve around the engineer as a nodal point to discuss the benefits and limitations of modernization, in particular the relationship between technology and ethics.[14] The engineer Hans Castorp, the main protagonist of Thomas Mann's novel *Der Zauberberg* (1924), and the mathematician Ulrich, the hero of Robert Musil's *Der Mann ohne Eigenschaften* (1930–43), are vehicles for these authors to voice their views of modernity. From Robert Müller's novel *Tropen, Der Mythos der Reise: Urkunden eines deutschen Ingenieurs* (1915) and Ernst Jünger's novels (*Der Arbeiter,* 1932; *Heliopolis,* 1949; *Gläserne Bienen,* 1957) to Uwe Timm's *Der Schlangenbaum* (1986) central texts of twentieth-century German culture employ the figure of the engineer to discuss issues of economic, social, political, and cultural change.[15]

The literary fascination with the engineer extends back to the beginning of the industrialization process, and German writers documented the transformation throughout the nineteenth century.[16] The bibliographical handbook *Beruf und Arbeit in deutscher Erzählung* (Vocation and work in German narrative) contains invaluable sources that convey the ways in which the industrialization process was discussed especially in popular culture publications. Cataloging German language texts about a wide range of professions published from the Middle Ages up to the early 1950s, the handbook also lists novels and biographies that focus on engineers and technicians. Under the rubric "Industry" the lexicon names titles on 34 different engineering professions and, under the heading "Technology," 26 separate categories.[17] In another entry the handbook lists 60 biographies and novels about famous historical inventors and 76 titles on lesser-known or fictional inventors. Sixty-two titles are given for "Factory Owner," 108 for "Engineer," and 20 for "Technician," with some listed under more than one category. These titles include works by authors such as Alfred Döblin, Heinrich Mann, and Paul Zech, but generally the books were written by authors not familiar to contemporary readers.

Entries for books about engineering and technology do not appear until the 1870s, reflecting the development of the profession. In the following years the number of publications increased steadily, which can also be attributed to the growing rates of literacy at the time. The earliest entry under "Engineer" is Max Eyth's *Wanderbuch eines Ingenieurs, in Briefen* (Travelogue of an engineer, in letters), published between 1871 and 1875. Of the seven titles about engineers published between 1871 and 1900, two are by Eyth, and two of the nine titles listed under "Technics" for the period from 1868 to 1900 are also by Eyth. The bibliography is certainly not comprehensive, but Eyth, along with Max Maria von Weber (1822–81), can be said to be one of the first engineers to write about the life and work of engineers. Others followed in their footsteps and produced popular autobiographies rendering their life stories and views of development and modernization. Prominent examples are Werner von Siemens's *Lebenserinnerungen* (1892), Carl Benz's *Lebensfahrt eines deutschen Erfinders: Erinnerungen eines Achtzigjährigen* (1925), and Eugen Diesel's *Autoreise 1905* (1941).[18] Other engineers also wrote fiction, such as Heinrich Seidel (1842–1906), who constructed the roof for the Anhalter railway station in Berlin and who published popular narratives and poetry. Even with regard to his work in Egypt, Eyth was not the only writing engineer: Heinrich von Stephan and Alois Negrelli Ritter von Molderbe also offered literary reflections upon their work in the country.[19]

Eyth was born on May 6, 1836, in Kirchheim in southern Germany.[20] His father, Eduard Eyth, was a senior teacher at a Latin school, before he became professor at the theological seminar in Schöntal, where the family moved when Max was four. Eyth's grandfather had dedicated his life to the study of classical philology and taught as a professor at a humanist high school in Heilbronn. The future engineer, however, did not follow the humanist model of father and grandfather but developed a fascination with technology at an early age. In his autobiographies Eyth relates a crucial event that is presented as a quasi-religious experience, one that was to clarify for him where his future lay. As a boy of only nine years, he accompanied his father to a hammer mill and, for the first time, saw one of the machines, an *Eisenhammer,* in action: "The thick-headed, industrious hammer, the spouting iron, the mysterious, panting cylindrical airpipe, all the life and clamor in the black workshop filled me with a strange mixture of terror and ecstasy."[21] The encounter shook him up deeply, and, when the boy revisited the site secretly, he again experienced the sense of awe the first encounter had brought on, an almost sexual desire for the movement and sounds of the machine.

In retrospect Eyth presents the experience as a life-changing event: "Whether I became an engineer on the mountaintop above the Kocher valley or only later in the course of that afternoon, I no longer recall with accuracy" (9). As a pivotal encounter, Eyth's *Eisenhammer* episode is comparable to the calling Albert Schweitzer claims to have received in his *Pfingsterlebnis* (Pentecostal experience), discussed in the next chapter. The emphasis given to such events by the authors of autobiographies clearly communicates their desire to endow the story of their life with a "higher" legitimacy and coherence. In Eyth's case a deep fascination with technology informed the course of his life.

As opposed to the humanist gymnasium the father would have preferred, Eyth visited a middle school in Heilbronn and then went on to study at a polytechnic academy in Stuttgart, at around the time when the Organization of German Engineers was founded. He developed a strong belief in the power of natural sciences and mathematics, declaring, for instance, that mathematics teaches "the only truths that can never be doubted" (10). He left Stuttgart after successfully completing his studies in 1856, decorated with a number of awards for his accomplishments. The theoretical education was followed by a year of practical training with the company Hahn & Göbel in Heilbronn, which included hard and mind-numbing labor. The exhausting physical work tested Eyth's stamina and threatened to thwart his ambitions. To balance the demands of the situation, Eyth began to resort to writing, especially to composing poetry. The talent and passion for writing ran deep in the family; his father had translated classical writers, and Eyth's mother, Julie, successfully published a volume of poetry.

The experience with his next employer, Gotthilf Kuhn in Stuttgart, was more productive for the young man. Here his talent was recognized, and Eyth quickly advanced from the position of a toolmaker and fitter to that of technical draftsman. By this time his enthusiasm and determination were unlimited. An excursion to Paris, where the company had sent him to spy on a recently invented gas engine, had invoked in the young man a desire to explore new areas, geographically as well as in terms of his profession. He began to study recent technological inventions in different locations, first in Germany and then in Belgium.

At the time, however, the most appealing country for an engineer was England, the original country of the Industrial Revolution, "on, or rather around [which] an entire world economy" was built.[22] In 1861 the twenty-five-year-old Eyth decided to try his luck on the other side of the Channel. He found employment in Leeds, England, with John Fowler (1826–64), who had just started his own company to build and develop steam plows and other agricultural machines. After quickly learning the basics of steam plowing, Eyth presented his employer with two new designs, which impressed Fowler instantly. Fowler put the ingenious mind of the ambitious young German to work and readily accepted Eyth's suggestions to improve his steam plows. Eyth moved up quickly in the company, for which he worked for over twenty years, until he began to pursue other plans in Germany in 1882.

For the most part Eyth represented the company abroad. In early 1863, on his way to India, he stopped in Egypt to advise one of Fowler's customers. The trip was supposed to be only a short interruption, but Eyth was asked to stay on. He lived in Egypt for over three and a half years, an exciting period in his life, about which he wrote abundantly. As mentioned earlier, Eyth worked as the chief engineer (*Ingenieur en chef*) for Halim Pasha, one of the most powerful and wealthy figures in the country at that time (124). He left Egypt after Halim Pasha lost his standing due to familial quarrels over questions of succession. In addition, the Egyptian cotton boom came to an end when the United States resumed its cotton production after the Civil War. The economic base of Eyth's employer had become eroded on two fronts, and, as a consequence, Eyth handed in his resignation.

After he left Egypt, Eyth promoted his plows and other inventions, such as the use of steal ropes for towing barges, in the United States, Belgium, Latin America, Russia, Hungary, the Caribbean, and other places. Several times he returned to Egypt for short periods. When he was denied an appropriate promotion at the Fowler company, where the atmosphere had changed after John Fowler's death, he left England in 1882 and moved back to Germany. In 1884 he founded the German Agricultural Society (Deutsche Landwirtschafts-Gesellschaft [DLG]), modeled after the British Royal Agriculture Society. In spite of initial impediments, the DLG would become an organization that played a crucial role in Germany's economic development.[23] In 1896 Eyth moved to Ulm to take care of his aging mother. During that period he dedicated himself to writing and continued to work on his drawings and watercolors.[24] He died in 1906, at the age of seventy.

Today Eyth is remembered less for his inventions than for his contributions as a social activist, prolific writer, and cultural philosopher. Soon after his death, he was nicknamed the "poet engineer." His first autobiographical writings were published in 1871, as *Wanderbuch eines Ingenieurs*.[25] A thoroughly revised version of the work was published in three volumes in 1903–5 as *Im Strom unserer Zeit: Aus Briefen eines Ingenieurs* (In the current of our age: From the letters of an engineer).[26] Eyth reworked the material describing his experiences in Egypt in the more novelistic *Hinter Pflug und Schraubstock* (Behind plow and vice, 1899) and *Der Kampf um die Cheopspyramide* (The fight for the Cheops-pyramid, 1902). In addition, the writer-engineer published an epic (*Volkmar*, 1863), a comedy (*Der Waldteufel*, 1878), a narrative about the German peasant war (*Mönch und Landsknecht*, 1881), an historical novel (*Der Schneider von Ulm: Geschichte eines zweihundert Jahre zu früh Geborenen*, 1906), and a great number of professional essays on technology and agriculture. His fictional works were reprinted repeatedly. By 1910, 60,000 copies of *Hinter Pflug und Schraubstock* had been printed, with almost 300,000 copies of the work printed by the mid-1930s. Other novels and autobiographical texts also saw editions of over 100,000 and 200,000 copies within a couple of decades.[27]

Millions of Germans turned to the books by Eyth, who became one of the most widely read authors of German popular culture. Eyth's writings are thus unique documents reflecting the rise of a profession and the overall changes of the period. Informed by the author's humanist upbringing and the spirit of modernization alike, they offer insights into a transforming society from the perspective of one of the active participants and believers in progress and modernization. As an engineer, Eyth expresses the spirit of this era with enthusiasm. At the same time he is also representative of the German *Bildungsbürger,* who believed in progress through education, and exemplifies the emergent middle class that brought about Germany's rise to power after the founding of the empire. In that respect Eyth's accounts express the self-image of this new class by documenting the success achieved by means of technology and hard work rather than through lineage and inherited wealth. The engineer as presented in such writings is a model that remains important today, when the power of representatives of the transnational corporate world, such as Bill Gates and Rupert Murdoch, at times seems to have surpassed that of national political figures.

Eyth's Views of Europe

Im Strom unserer Zeit, the cut, heavily revised, and amended shorter version of Eyth's letters, stands at the center of the following analysis. For reasons of its great popularity and stylistic features, this rendition of Egypt is preferable to the lengthy *Wanderbuch* and the drawn-out *Hinter Pflug und Schraubstock* and *Der Kampf um die Cheopspyramide,* which fictionalize Egypt to a greater extent. Based on the original letters, *Im Strom* still reflects Eyth's initial impressions closely. In addition, the revised and rethought version conveys a sense of the way in which Eyth viewed events that had occurred forty years earlier.

In his introduction to *Im Strom* Eyth looks back at the period he had documented several decades earlier: "Since these days, the world has changed, the young man grown old. Little of what he wrote then would have the appearance of truth today, much of what seemed true to him then he would no longer subscribe to" (vi). Accordingly, Eyth presents the *Wanderbuch* as a historical document and occasionally comments on his rewritten selections from the original *Wanderbuch* letters.

The engineer's humanist education is reflected in his skills and behavior as a writer. Consciously, he introduces himself to the reader as an educated individual who is not only an engineer but also an author of poetry and fiction who gives a learned account of his stay abroad.[28] He is aware of his role as a writer and reflects on the ability to represent his experiences adequately: "But how shall I manage to choose the best from the overwhelming abundance of my experiences? Would a telegraphic style be the best solution?" (29). Much like Alfred Döblin, who years later suggests a *Kinostil* to render the kaleidoscopic and multidimensional nature or modern life, Eyth attempts to invent a new style. After only one paragraph of short or one-word sentences, however, he resorts to the "old tone" and continues to offer a more traditional linear narrative. As in this passage, Eyth often reflects upon the writing process and suggests that writing is the primeval sin of Germans (61). His technical skills are considerable: even though he presents a collection of seemingly independent letters, the structure of the overall result reveals that he carefully crafts his text. He uses such narrative strategies as foreshadowing and flashbacks, recurring motifs, alternating voices and different genres—several poems are interspersed in the text—which allows him to create suspense and tightness in the narrative flow.

Eyth offers an image of himself as an educated individual who appreciates the finer sides of life. He mentions a piano he rented (68), and, in line with the image of the jovial nature of Swabians, the poet/engineer enjoys "wine, women, and song," gives a learned description of foreign cultures, and assiduously works on developing the economy. He is thus distinguished by the key characteristics of an ideal *Bildungsbürger*, namely education, savoir vivre, and hard work. While this deliberately created image betrays Eyth's humanist roots, it also mirrors the self-consciousness of an emerging class that had to emphasize its learnedness and lifestyle vis-à-vis the old elite.

In the introduction to *Im Strom unserer Zeit* Eyth compares his youth to the beginnings of German industry as it was also experiencing a coming-of-age process. He points out repeatedly that the education of engineers was not yet institutionalized when he grew up and explains that he was trained before engineers were able to receive an academic education. The ironic tone of his remarks reflects the engineer's frustration with the resistance that the German academic system put up regarding the granting of degrees of higher education to the engineering profession. This conscious connection to the historical development of the period is key to understanding Eyth: from the beginning he displays an acute awareness for the profundity of the changes he has witnessed.

Several themes that dominate Eyth's account of the period before he left for Egypt chronicle overall working conditions in mid-nineteenth-century Europe and are crucial for evaluating the engineer's move to Egypt. The comparison between Eyth's comments on Germany and Europe and then later on those about Egypt brings to the fore aspects of industrialization and development that were shared by Germany and Egypt at the time. Although Germany was ahead of Egypt in the development of its infrastructure, the ruling class in Egypt was significantly more in favor of large-scale modernization than Germany's elite. From Eyth's perspective the situation in Egypt was more advantageous to his particular projects.

Eyth was convinced that technology is good for the common people. He repeatedly shared his observations about people who lived in poverty and who, he believed, would be helped by the advances of technology. His first excursion as a technical draftsman, for example, took him to a sawmill that was owned by an impoverished man. Eyth is visibly moved by the family's situation: "Even more so I was moved by the man, his wife and four meek children, all of whom would have been bankrupt if the machine would have had to be given up." His task, to repair the machine, has an air of development aid. Reporting on this first assignment to a defunct machine, he calls himself a "pioneer" and even offers a comparison with "Eberhard im Bart" (13). In 1477 this count and later duke founded the University of Tübingen and in 1482 united parts of Swabia, thereby taking great steps toward modernizing Germany politically and intellectually (14). Eyth consciously placed his own work in the context of these societal developments.

In Eyth's description of Germany the situation of people in the countryside was comparable to what he later encountered in Egypt. When, in the episode described here, he finally gets the machine to work, the entire village comes running to watch the fuming chimneys, but the engineer and his coworkers chase the villagers away (14). The curiosity and excitement of the German peasants appears quite similar to the reactions of non-Europeans who encountered signs of modern civilization. When Eyth leaves the village, he admits that the sawmill has become a "matter of heart and conscience," and he is convinced that a good deed was done. At his departure the smallest of the children cries, and Eyth declares that for this child he would have broken his fingers and burned his hands: "Sometimes good deeds are rewarded already in this world" (15).

Often Eyth emphasizes the urgent and at times dangerous nature of his work. When he is called upon to repair a machine, he travels on the fastest trains and renders the emergency of the situations in dramatic words: "Oh my loved ones! I have not even begun to describe my distress, my battle and my victory, and the next disaster is already under way" (16–17). Eyth depicts himself as a self-confident man who is called upon to help and who knows what to do, often making brave and independent decisions (18). In one example the repair work of a large kettle is portrayed as a nerve-racking incident, and Eyth uses strong emotional terms to describe his efforts (20).

Eyth's writings also document another aspect of his profession—namely, how new inventions were copied or spied upon. Again, the vocabulary is rather dramatic in such instances, for example, when he describes an attempt to reconstruct a recently invented "gas machine" on the property of the company he works for: "A windowless shack was built in the court of the factory, to which nobody was given access but me and two mechanics, almost by threat of the death penalty" (26). In his description of the struggle over the construction of the duplicate machine, Eyth resorts to religious vocabulary, calling the process "demonic" and attesting to a "satanic smell" that was exuded by the machine (27). These passages illustrate the increasing competition regarding technical innovations but also the adventurous spirit of the period and the awe and excitement that was felt when engineers came upon groundbreaking inventions.

Eyth articulates the modern nature of the engineering profession, which is independent of time and space: "Spring does not bloom for the engineer, and he knows no hibernation. Sun, moon, and stars shall not stop him" (15). Here Eyth expresses a feeling that Anthony Giddens has identified as one of the defining traits of life in the modern world—namely, the separation of work from time and space.[29] The engineer realizes that an international working culture is evolving (67). He states that Germans will have to learn new modes of interaction crucial to this new culture, for example, the politeness he observes in Britain even toward simple and impoverished people and the generally greater personal freedom he experiences there (53, 97, 98). Eyth also clearly sees the impact that Germany's political unification would have for the development of the economy and laments the lack of German initiative toward achieving this goal (86–87).

Eyth's texts are valuable documents in that he assesses the economic situation in Germany at the time. During his visit to major industrial cities in the Ruhr Valley, he gains a mixed impression. On the one hand, he is fascinated with machines and factories he sees for the first time: "With respectful amazement I approached the four smoking blast-furnaces, the roaring, rushing, pounding puddling furnace and rolling mill" (34). On the other hand he also encounters the signs of economic standstill when he sees "two big, sadly idled factories. . . . warning proof of how bad times are" (35).

Eyth's descriptions of industrializing Germany in the early 1860s paint a picture in which the old agricultural image of the country is still visible even in the new industrial centers. In Oberhausen this encounter between nature and modernity inspires Eyth to label the site as an "almost uncanny place! In the middle of desolate heath, a number of widely scattered palace-like buildings with sky-high chimneys, mines, zinc factories, ironworks. It was too late to do anything useful. An hour-long walk under a beautiful clear sky across heather that was crisscrossed by tracks, through oak forests behind which the furnaces rush, was just as good for me" (35; also 62). The sky above the Ruhr, the pollution of which became a central campaign issue of environmentalists in postwar West Germany, was still blue at the time, but Eyth clearly acknowledges the drastic changes that had already occurred in the landscape.

Eyth was an enthusiastic engineer who wanted to make a contribution to the modernization process (36, 12). Times, however, were hard for engineers in Germany. During his travels through the Ruhr Valley, Eyth met an engineer who had worked for eleven years in the United States and was about to return for another stay (35). Eyth soon followed the example of this migrant engineer.

In his descriptions of Belgium and then England Eyth continued to elaborate on the central themes of his account: the impact of industrialization on the landscape (70–71), the overall economic crisis of the time (38, 59), his own financial struggle (39, 43, 44, 45, 58), his sense of awe for the gigantic dimension of the modernizing process, for the machines, the big cities and the masses of people (43, 50, 57). Eyth was deeply shocked by the poverty and illness he saw in England, by the "pale, sick population, rotten from misery and ill fortune." In his letters he considers the accusation that industrialization itself caused the misery of these people, who make up "three quarters of the whole." Quickly, however, he rejects this thought: "Nevertheless it would be silly to accuse industrialization. . . . It is and will remain the only way . . . to sustain the millions of people in England even at the current standard of living. Industrialization did not create the ugliness that sticks to it. A future can be envisioned in which it will dig its way out of this dirt" (60).

Eyth's excitement about the technological process is most evident in his description of a seven-month period during the World Exhibition in London in 1862, for which Fowler had asked him to design a pavilion (82–100). The engineer gives a glowing account of the technical achievements exhibited, and he considers the time in London the seven most interesting months of his life to that point (99).

The exhibition also gives Eyth ample opportunity to ridicule Germany's backwardness. The engineer pokes fun at the German exhibition booth, where scores of individual territorial states claim their particular spaces and make for an entirely disorganized picture. He talks about plans to promote steam plows in Germany, "to get the young farmers used to the horrible sight of these harmless machines from hell" (93). Mockingly, he remarks that Germans, in contrast to the British, prefer to study technological achievements of bygone periods, rather than to explore contemporary inventions (92). He laments emphatically: "Germany proceeds with steam plowing, as with everything else, extremely slowly. Arabs, Newfoundlanders (not the dogs!), the blacks from Congo, drive our machines happily across their native soil and plant sugarcane, arrowroot and corn in the deeper seedbed of steam-plowed fields; 'for the time being' the German peasant is declared by 'the authorities' unable to be familiarized with the 'complicated' machine. O Germany, Germany! Where are the fruits of your erudition and your intellect?" (96–97).

The German engineer is intent on stressing those aspects of the German attitude toward modernization that compelled him to leave the country in search of employment elsewhere.[30] Later, when he returned to Germany, he attempted to fight Germany's backwardness with clever plots, such as a steam plow competition comparable to the one held in Egypt in 1864.[31]

Eyth believed in the liberating effects of the modernizing mission, and with regard to his own work he attributes redemptive qualities to the steam plows he propagated. The use of steam, he says, promises the "salvation of oxen, horses, serfs, and slaves" (95); here it seems as if inventions such as plows play a role similar to that of the Bible of the earlier missionaries in that they are said to bring "salvation" and a better life. England had given Eyth a chance to display his ingenious mind and put his passion for the new era to work. Egypt was to become the next testing ground for the liberating effect of Eyth's machines. Eyth left a Europe that still showed signs of the old agricultural order, even more so in Germany than in England, where industrialization had been under way for much longer. Eyth had encountered ignorance and resistance toward new machines; he had met naive peasants and inflexible bureaucrats. What kind of conditions did he encounter in Egypt?

Modernizing Egypt

As we have seen, Eyth's story is directly connected to the dire situation engineers were facing in Germany in the 1860s, and his decision to go to England was a response to this dilemma. The move from England to Egypt stresses the profound connection between the booming British economy and the ongoing process of economic expansion.

Eyth's role in Egypt is exemplary, if still somewhat pioneering, for one type of German who worked in areas colonized by other European powers and in territories that invited European investments, such as Egypt and Turkey. German-led construction of railways and bridges and deliveries of weapons and machinery increased in the course of the century, especially after the founding of the German empire.[32] While Eyth viewed his role as that of a modernizer, in his writings he does not discuss the imperialist aspect of his work, which derives first and foremost from the fact that Eyth worked for an Egyptian employer, and Europeans had not colonized Eygpt at the time. The particular historical circumstances of Egypt deserve closer attention in order to comprehend more clearly Eyth's role in the country at the time and also the engineer's portrayal of his work.

Max Eyth came to Egypt during a period of economic transformation and expansion, when the country's leader, Isma'il, pursued modernization with vigor and enthusiasm. Modernization efforts by Egyptian leaders before the advent of the British colonizers in 1882 had begun with the economic, political, and social restructuring under way in Egypt since the early nineteenth century. This process would ultimately lead to bankruptcy in April 1876 and later to the British occupation of the country, in the name of bondholders, a development that was quite different from what the local elite had envisioned.

Egypt had become part of the Ottoman Empire in 1517. As in many other areas of the Islamic Empire, the local structure was barely altered by Ottoman rule. The Ottomans centralized the administration and appointed officials who would facilitate tax collection. The administration focused on the development of agriculture and trade, which led to the rebuilding of the Egyptian economy and restoration of trade with India. Beneath the top level of administration the old infrastructure was not affected by Ottoman rule. Local *'ulama'* and Sufi leaders continued to be powerful forces in the country, acting as intermediaries between the Mameluk elites—the slaves or freedmen in Ottoman military service—and the Egyptian common people. In the first part of the eighteenth century, however, Mameluk households gained in influence to the extent that the changes significantly eroded central power. Some scholars argue that the foundations for the political, administrative, and economic changes of the nineteenth century had already been laid in the period from 1760 to 1775, when 'Ali Bey al-Kabir and Muhammad Bey Abu al-Dhahab ruled the country.[33] Although the Ottomans restored their leadership in 1786–87, however, the country was less unified than before. In addition, Egypt's economy, which had grown and undergone substantial structural change beginning in the seventeenth century, suffered as a result of the European economic expansion and competition.[34] European products, especially textiles, ceramics, and glass, invaded Egyptian markets.

Weakened thus by both economic crisis and internal political strife, Egypt was drawn into the ongoing power struggle between England and France. In 1798 French troops invaded Egypt, mainly because they saw the country as a crucial strategic location in the competition to control trade with India. This led to a British counterinvasion and, in 1805, to the Ottoman appointment of Muhammad ʿAli as governor. Gradually, Muhammad ʿAli, whose family originated from Albania, succeeded in gaining independence from the central Ottoman government and founded a dynasty, which ruled until 1952.

Under Muhammad ʿAli and his successors Egypt entered a period of fundamental restructuring and economic and political expansion. The extent to which Egyptian society was altered during those years led Timothy Mitchell, who describes the changes that occurred in nineteenth-century Egypt in his study *Colonising Egypt,* to forgo a distinction between the efforts of the Middle Eastern elites in power at the time and the later European colonizers.[35] Muhammad ʿAli reorganized the economy drastically. The focus on sugar and cotton production earned money on international markets but also made Egypt more dependent on those markets.[36] Irrigation projects were carried out that allowed for land cultivation during the entire year. For the first time Egyptian peasants were recruited into the new army. An educational system was introduced that included a range of new institutions, from primary schools to universities. Muhammad ʿAli also introduced a new tax system, which resulted in a shift within the economically based power structure.

Muhammad ʿAli depended on foreigners on all levels. His power base consisted of Turks, Kurds, Circassians, and others. The old Mameluk households and the local *ʿulama'* were quickly disabled, by cutting them off from their tax revenues, whereby they lost their economic and political base. In 1811 Muhammad ʿAli had a significant number of Mameluks massacred. He made the economy dependent on foreign markets and imported the machines and technicians that facilitated the restructuring of the economy. On his reforms of the army Muhammad ʿAli was advised by Italian and French military. The reforms were met with resistance on various levels; the conscription of peasants to the army, for example, led to revolts and flight to towns and to Syria, which resulted in depopulation and thus great losses to the agricultural economy.[37]

Muhammad ʿAli's family was granted hereditary rule of Egypt, as Ottoman viceroys, in 1842. After his death Muhammad ʿAli was succeeded for a few months in 1848 by his eldest son, Ibrahim, who was followed after his sudden death by ʿAbbas I, the eldest grandson of Muhammad ʿAli. Under the reign of ʿAbbas I (1848–54) many of the reforms were either halted or reversed.[38] His successor, Saʿid (1854–63), however, embarked on the path of modernization and Westernization. In 1856 he granted the concession for the building of the Suez Canal to the Frenchman Ferdinand de Lesseps, who was also his personal friend. This friendship proved to have "disastrous" consequences, resulting from the "enormous financial obligations" the Suez Canal and other projects incurred.[39]

The modernization efforts were pursued even further with renewed vigor under Ismaʿil (1863–79), the son of Ibrahim. He again improved the transportation system, constructing both the Suez Canal and a new harbor in Alexandria. "He also gave Egypt European-type law courts, secular schools and colleges, libraries, theaters, an opera house, and a Western-type press."[40] Ismaʿil's social, political, and economic reforms had an impact on the entire power structure of the country, creating new social groups of influence and destroying the old order at a breathtaking pace. He was said to be "a man ahead of his time, trying to achieve in the nineteenth century what Mustafa Kemal (Atatürk) in Turkey, and Reza Khan in Iran, successfully achieved at the beginning of the twentieth."[41] The extent to which Egyptian aristocrats identified with European culture might be difficult to fathom today. In 1867 Ismaʿil announced that "Egypt is no longer part of Africa. It is part of Europe."[42] The large-scale reforms and investments, in conjunction with Ismaʿil's extremely lavish lifestyle, which differed from the "general style of government, [which] was rather austere" under Muhammad ʿAli and Ibrahim, threw the country into deep debt.[43] In 1872–73, mostly as a consequence of the harsh conditions under which the loans had been granted, 70 percent of the estimated revenue was needed to pay for the internal and external debt. The Egyptian state was bankrupt and completely dependent on foreign investors and governments.[44]

The dominance of foreign elements that began with Muhammad ʿAli lasted well into the twentieth century; one of the most obvious signs of this foreign domination is the fact that the ruling elite in Egypt spoke Turkish or French until the 1930s. It was not until "1952 that rulers identifying themselves as ethnically Egyptian ruled the country. . . . This did not mean the end of foreign influence in the economic and political spheres, which continued to reflect the ideologies adopted by the Nasserists: nationalism, socialism, Arab unity, and non-alignment, which all stemmed from non-Egyptian concepts."[45]

It is important to understand the significance of these developments; Edward Said's notion of Orientalism as an oppressive tool leading to domination and dependency cannot explain this complicated web of European influences and collaboration by the (only partially Egyptian) non-Western local elite. The extent to which the local elite invited European influence into various countries is often not taken into account in analyses of colonial situations. The black-and-white image that is drawn by the culturalist explanations of current postcolonial theory cannot account for the complexity of the situation and the differences between individual countries.

In the case of Egypt the Europeans kept the upper hand and certainly did not suffer from the failures of modernization reforms the way Egyptians did, mostly on account of their political, economic, and military superiority and, in particular, through debt politics. Egypt's loans were generally obtained on "harsher terms" than comparable loans that went, for example, to Turkey.[46] European influence on the country, however, is unthinkable without the actions of the local elite, who welcomed European involvement in Egyptian economic development. The Egyptian economy grew and raised income, but these trends did not lead to large-scale modernization and the development of industry. The reasons for this evolution lie in a complex set of factors that are not only a result of European economic and political policy, debt politics, and, later, the lack of protective tariffs alone. The resistance to change within the traditional sector, physical obstacles, resource issues, such as the absence of raw materials like iron and coal, lack of a transformation in the social stratification and, with it, the uneven distribution of wealth that did not allow for a broader spread of buying power, as well as internal and external political obstacles all contributed to the situation.[47] These factors are related to the mechanisms of capitalist economies and to the repercussions of differing political and social systems. With regard to Egypt only a few aspects of the botched modernization process can be explained in culturalist terms.

Most important in our context is the development of the cotton industry. As a consequence of the American Civil War of 1861–65, Egypt had seen a spike in demand for its long-staple cotton. During the war prices increased fourfold, setting off a frantic effort at expanding cotton farming. After the war prices collapsed, which nevertheless did not stop the expansion of cotton-based agriculture. It is during this promising period of rekindled economic restructuring, between 1863 and 1866, that Max Eyth worked for Halim Pasha, an uncle of the ruling governor Isma῾il.[48]

In evaluating Eyth's descriptions of his time in Egypt, three main areas emerge that warrant a closer look — namely, his rendering of landscapes and general ambiance, the passages about his work, and his comments on Egyptians and on Europeans working in Egypt. The ideas Eyth expressed by talking about these subjects reveal his general attitude toward the context in which he worked and about the role he played in Egypt. In all three areas Eyth's account gradually evolves from a cliché-ridden rendering of the Egyptian environment to descriptions that reflect a daily interaction with his context.

At the beginning of Eyth's account one of the central tropes of Orientalist discourse emerges on his journey by boat to Alexandria, when he talks about sensing the "sultry breath of the Orient" (109). The Greek landscape he passes is described as a "beautiful scenic corpse" of "brown, bare, lifeless mountains, sometimes a brown, bare, lifeless island," and Eyth states that this region, which holds such a lofty place in the German imagination, is in reality a wasteland: "Everything is dead" (110). The passage to Egypt appears as a journey through a netherworld of death, bringing the passenger to the shores of another world. On the sixth day the lighthouse of Alexandria and the harem and palace of the viceroy come into view, but, because of adverse landing conditions, the ship remains at sea for one more night: "This night was wondrously beautiful. The full moon painted a rose-chafer-green street onto the almost black surface of the sea. Somewhat invisible, the lower shores of the delta lay ghostly white in the nightly dawn of the city. The next morning . . . we were already going full-steam . . . toward the forests of poles and palms that had waved at us yesterday against the yellow evening sky" (111).

On the seventh day of his journey Eyth sets foot onto the soil of a new world. In this first encounter with Alexandria, Eyth continues to speak about the city by drawing on standard topoi of Orientalist descriptions; narrow streets are bothersome, the interaction with locals is hectic and chaotic; sites are portrayed as "shadowless," "mysterious," "half-lit," and "ghostlike." His initial encounter with Cairo is also dominated by the experience of unfamiliarity: "The world," he writes, "gets less familiar every day," all of which is "strange and attractive" at once (114–15; also 113).

When Eyth overcomes his initial disorientation and is able to see beyond the unfamiliar, he begins to describe Egypt in original ways. Most travelers to non-European areas never get beyond this initial stage of culture shock, which accounts for the fact that Western representations emphasize the differences travelers initially observe and express the sense of resistance they feel toward their new environment. Eyth, however, spent a period in Egypt that was long enough to enable him to develop a daily routine and to notice his environment beyond the superficialities of the short-term traveler's experience. Already on his way to Cairo he takes great pleasure in the green and sand-colored landscape and beautifully conveys the breathtaking contrast between the fertile fields, palm tree groves, fig trees, and swamps of the Nile delta and the surrounding desert (114–15). A portrait of Cairo that begins as a description of the stereotypical disorienting Oriental city, with its narrow streets, half-ruined buildings, dirt, scores of screaming traders, donkeys, veiled women, and dozing men, is contrasted with a view of Cairo from a mountaintop: "I was not prepared for such a view," writes Eyth (117). Suddenly he is able to notice the regular patterns of an unfamiliar architecture, the interplay of city, pyramids, and surrounding nature: the Nile, the desert, the fields, exhilarating color constellations of dark blue, golden, sand, green, and silver.

The environment is thus increasingly experienced as appealing and pleasing, and in the course of Eyth's descriptions it serves to highlight the contrast to the vexed political climate the engineer got to know during his stay in the country (118). Eyth renders original portraits of the Egyptian, and later the Syrian and Palestinian, ambiance that are distinguished by images of color, sound, and structures (212–27). Most important, however, the development observable in Eyth's descriptions reflect how his perception changes, from the initial shock he experienced to the gradual appreciation of the country's distinctive features.[49]

This aspect of Eyth's portrayal is aided by drawings and watercolors he made during his stay, some of which are included in the various editions of his writings.[50] Often he includes steam plows or other machines in the pictures, thus foregrounding the process of modernization in Egypt. The result is significant: in one of the most widely read German language accounts of Egypt at the time, Eyth conveys to his German audience the portrait of an agricultural country in transition. In a way Egypt becomes a mirror image of Germany.

Other drawings feature mosques, bazaars, the Nile, and representative sites of Egypt. Eyth's choice in colors reflect his realistic approach and stands in stark contrast to the dark oil paintings of French painters, such as Jean-Auguste Dominique Ingres and Eugène Delacroix, and some of the Viennese artists, such as Hans Makart and Alois Schönn. Several British painters, including John Frederick Lewis, created images of Middle Eastern sites that challenged the notion of a mysterious and inaccessible Orient. Lewis's portrayals of interior spaces, for example, brilliantly convey the effect the light has when it enters the houses through the wooden latticework known as *mashrabiya,* a feature of the Ottoman home that can be found throughout the Middle East. Like Lewis, Eyth chose colors that emphasize the warmth of light, rather than the harshness of the bright sun. And, like Lewis, Eyth wanted to capture the elegance of Ottoman and pre-Ottoman Egyptian architecture, rather than the dilapidated nature of some architectural sites.

The nature of Eyth's comments concerning Egyptians depends on the kind of relationship he establishes with each individual. He does not seem to have learned Arabic, but occasionally he intersperses Arabic words in his account and prides himself on learning how to write the script (211; also 129, 134, 168, 182, 190). People whom he encounters in public places, members of the ruling elite of the country, and the people who work for him are portrayed in distinct ways, suggesting that in Eyth's experience social relations override cultural differences.

On the first few days of his stay Eyth meets Egyptians mostly in public spaces, and these portraits are entirely stereotypical. He talks about feminine features of peasants (111), black hands that greedily examine the white linen of Europeans (112), and the "colorful variety of the oriental street life" (113). In these first letters Eyth employs many of the standard tropes about the Orient; he claims to experience the entire range of the Oriental world, "from the disgusting intrigues at the court of a pasha to the moving prayer of the Arab in the desert" (114). These kinds of images, however, are rare and almost entirely restricted to the first few days of Eyth's stay; gradually, the engineer's views become more balanced, in ways similar to what we have seen with regard to his remarks about landscapes. On his trip back from Syria, which occurs during the end of his stay in the Middle East, he raves about "a half dozen Syrian women of overwhelming beauty" (228); it seems as if he would not have been able to notice these women during the first few weeks of his time in Egypt.

Eyth's portrayal of his employer, Halim Pasha, is a distinct departure from cliché-ridden images of Oriental rulers. Muhammad ʿAbd al-Halim (1831–94), also known as Prince Halim, was educated at the Princes' School in Egypt and then at a military school in France. As a pretender to Egypt's khedivate, commander in chief of the army, director of the War Department, and numerous other influential posts, he was one of the most powerful people of the country at the time.[51] Eyth develops a deep sympathy for this Egyptian aristocrat, who, as Eyth reports, "was supposed to have fought on the barricades for the [French] Republic" (122). Halim Pasha speaks French fluently, dresses according to European customs (apart from his shoes); is energetic, intelligent, likeable; enjoys playing chess with Eyth; and discusses religion and philosophy with his chief engineer. Occasionally, Eyth is frustrated even with Halim, but generally the engineer is full of praise for his employer (146). He admires him for developing an agricultural enterprise that is unprecedented in the world (153).

Eyth appreciates not only Halim but other members of the educated Egyptian elite as well (135). He is fully aware, however, of the political intrigues that plague Egyptian dynastic politics. The ruling viceroy Ismaʿil changed the succession system in favor of his son, and Halim, who would have been next in line to rule the country under the previous system, lost his claim to power. These developments, in conjunction with the changing economic situation, ultimately brought about Max Eyth's departure. He gained firsthand experiences of what were turbulent political times in Egypt, much of which certainly confirmed negative views of Oriental leadership. As we will see, Eyth was able to develop a differentiated understanding of the interplay between local mismanagement, dynastic ambitions, and the actions of foreign investors. Nevertheless, Halim stands out as an enlightened ruler who is not presented as a noble savage but as an individual defined by his education and modern views and actions. Eyth treats Halim with respect and through him enjoys encountering various aspects of Egyptian culture, including hospitality, food, entertainment, and the pleasures of life in a tent.

Eyth's relation with his employees is more ambivalent. One group of comments he makes about them clearly shows Eyth in the role of the authoritarian master, who considers his subjects incompetent and not trustworthy. He never tires of stressing how lazy or weak the Egyptian workers are (121, 123, 143, 190), that they steal and demand bribes (141, 144, 151, 169), and even that he has to use corporal punishment to get them to work (123, 143, 169, 172). In line with the behavior of scores of European colonizers who adopted a violent behavior toward indigenous peoples in the colonies, it seems as if Eyth's willingness to resort to physical punishment increased with the time he spent in Egypt. Peasant workers are depicted as naive and incompetent, especially when they learn about machinery (129–30, 182). It needs to be pointed out, however, that many of the comments are concerned with how Egyptians respond to the introduction of modern equipment and, as such, are reminiscent of remarks Eyth made about the reactions of European peasants when they encountered new machines. One could consider some of Eyth's actions and comments about his involvement in Egypt not exclusively as comments about Egyptians (as members of a non-European culture) but, more generally, about ignorant peasants (that is, members of a social group connected to premodernity). Even with regard to physical punishment, we should not forget that violence of superiors toward their unskilled workers was a fact of life in nineteenth- to mid-twentieth century Europe. Nevertheless, the fact that Egyptian peasants are made to look silly and comical and appear as pawns in the hands of the German modernizer conforms to colonialist practices (170).

Eyth's account of his struggle to teach Egyptians the "proper" attitude toward work is typical of views held by many European secular and religious missionaries. While Germans (as representative Europeans) valued labor as an expression of personal fulfillment, as duty, and as a sign of religiosity, the notion of labor held by members of premodern societies mirrored beliefs that had been dominant in Europe before the

Age of Enlightenment as well: here labor was miserable, toil filled, painful, and certainly not desirable. The work one would do for the community was mostly work for the immediate family; labor for abstract systems, be they a company or a state, and working to improve one's situation outside of the social context of the family or village were new concepts for the Egyptian peasants with whom Eyth worked.[52]

Eyth seems to have held a historical perspective, and for this reason, along with the derogatory comments, he also voices very different views about his Egyptian workers, views that are more in line with his beliefs about modernization and progress. He points out repeatedly that he believes in the intelligence of the Egyptian peasants (121, 123), and he expresses his solidarity even with simple workers: "What is endured by millions of my brown fellow human beings, I can endure as well" (136). At other times he emphasizes the goodness and eagerness of his Egyptian coworkers (137). Eyth's comments are occasionally ironic, and remarks such as his description of "this land of barbarism where I have to represent a piece of civilization" need to be evaluated carefully (141). The longer passage following this comment, for example, at once criticizes notions of German "Kultur" and the shortcomings of his Egyptian domestic workers.

Most indicative of Eyth's programmatic attitude toward his Egyptian employees is the description of the aforementioned steam-plow competition. While the opponent's machines were operated by British workers, Eyth relied on the Egyptians he had trained. In *Im Strom* he recalls the competition: "What I enjoy most is that the victory was achieved by my Arab troops. My colleagues [the Europeans] down here are quite angry at me because I insist that the race [the Arabs] can be educated" (157). This comment clearly reveals the engineer's firm belief in education and the legitimacy of the modernizing mission.

Eyth works closely with his Egyptian employees, including ordinary workers, and his way of interacting is typical of an approach that can be observed to this day on construction sites and in workshops in Germany, with the owner of the business at times working side by side with the workers. This phenomenon has its roots in the patriarchalism that characterized and continues to exist in many sectors of production in Germany, whereby a personal bond between employer and employee was, and is, created through social policies. When Eyth complains about "the somewhat too close association with my brown, puffing, naked-legged fellows" (176), his comment reflects the fact that the engineer does not shy away from doing the hard physical labor he asks of his employees. In this respect he differed fundamentally from other Europeans working in the country, namely, "the British workers, who want to play gentlemen here and do everything to avoid serious work" (118). A willingness on the part of higher-ranking skilled workers, foremen, and owners to get their hands dirty exemplified a work ethic with cultural and social roots in both Christianity and Enlightenment beliefs.

Let us take a look at Eyth's rendering of the Egyptian environment and its people from another angle—namely, the execution of his projects. On a fundamental level Eyth's experience of Egypt is determined by the way his work can or cannot evolve. Ultimately, the climate and natural conditions of the country, the political culture, and the local workers and elites are all seen from the vantage point of the engineer. Here the reader is presented with an evaluation of the country and its people seen through the lens of an ardent proponent of modernization, who struggles with the structures of a premodern society. It is important to remember that Eyth's philosophy was consistent with that of the local elite, who, as Amira El-Azhary Sonbol argues, "embraced modernity as hegemonic discourse. *Tanwir* (enlightenment) became a goal and an ideology of several generations of statesmen, teachers, lawyers, intellectuals, and artists. The socialist and communist movements adopted *tanwir* as much as did the capitalists and industrialists whom the socialists attacked. Believers in *tanwir* looked down on 'traditional' Egyptians who 'kept the country behind.'"[53]

Many passages in Eyth's memoir revolve around the steam plows he supervised and other machinery relevant to his projects. When he first describes the conditions on Halim's large property, he acknowledges with great respect that a great arsenal of machines, pumps, mills, and plows had been in place there for many years but that a supervisor was missing who could ensure the proper maintenance and operation of the machines (127–28). With great pride he lists the machines that were under his supervision and boasts about equipment on the way from England (132, 139, 152, 165). In light of all the impressive machinery at his disposal he calls himself "a monarch" and compares himself to the biblical Joseph in Egypt (160, 124). In Eyth's descriptions Egypt is not a wasteland but, rather, a land of opportunities, waiting for skilled and knowledgeable workers to make use of its resources. At times it seems that the country was flooded with machines that arrived from England in the port of Alexandria, and the lack of expertise and the generally chaotic conditions led to odd situations, with individual parts of machines spread out all over the country (146–47, 175).

Even in light of the abundance of machinery, however, the German engineer encountered numerous obstacles to the execution of his development projects, primarily resulting from a lack of infrastructure, such as adequate roads that would facilitate the transportation of his machines, or from the repercussions of decisions made by inept workers or supervisors. One episode revolves around a plow that had been assembled at the banks of the Nile, rather than closer to its final destination. The real challenge presents itself when Eyth realizes that he has to transport the machine not only across land but also over a canal. He decides to build a temporary bridge, and in a most dramatic scene—"one wrong movement . . . would have hurled people and machine into the murky waters at our feet"—manages to get the plow to the other side (130). Similar scenes are interspersed throughout the text (134, 167–75, 175–76, 177, 182, 190–91, 192–93). The Nile poses another challenge to Eyth's plans; the effect of the Suez Canal and the general power of the river make the engineer's efforts Sisyphus-like (142–43, 146). One of his answers to the multiple problems is the invention of a pump, designed especially for Egyptian conditions, for which he received his first English patent (147).[54] The pump was only one of several machines Eyth designed specifically for the Egyptian context (154).

Eyth's identification with the project in Egypt is also reflected in the use of possessive pronouns to describe events that happen in the country. Not only does he use the word *my* consistently in passages portraying his workers, but, when he talks about his affairs, he also indicates how he understands his relationship to his context by employing the word *us* (143). Whatever occurs does not affect the Egyptians as a separate entity but also concerns Eyth, who presents himself as an integral part of Egyptian society.

These passages also include more general evaluations of the economic situation and the development of a modern infrastructure. Eyth sees himself as cleaning up in a "semi-savage world" (164); when another German engineer arrives, he comments that this fellow German is sent to "clear out the Muslim Augias-stable" (152). He takes great pride in being part of the development of an "agricultural industrial economy . . . the likes of which do not exist anywhere else in the world" (153). To stage a lesson in modern development, Eyth plans an industrial exhibit, which he believes would be "healing for country and people" (156). He boasts about his achievements, for example, when he prides himself "to be the first who plows in Barbaric Egypt successfully at night" (153). While Eyth clearly uses terms that associate Egyptian culture with a premodern uncivilized stage, we should not forget that he did not hold an essentialized view of culture.

He believed in progress through modernization, and he believed that Egypt could modernize. To what degree this modernization implied Westernization is not quite clear; the engineer tolerated cultural difference to a certain extent, but he was clearly prejudiced against the premodern, whether he encountered it in Europe or in Egypt. In his letters Eyth consistently stresses the benefit of the introduction of machines for the development of the Egyptian economy, how much manpower could be saved, and how much the society at large would benefit (154, 195). When a project succeeded, he took great pride in it (195–96). The prospect of participating in the design of a potable water system for Beirut, the only project that took him on an exploratory trip briefly outside of Egypt in those years, obviously excited him (211).

In *Im Strom unserer Zeit* the engineer clearly identifies Egypt's dilemma: the lack of infrastructure impedes the development of industry, yet proceeds gained from industry would provide the funds to build up this infrastructure (174–75). Therefore, he continues to believe in the long-term benefits of his efforts, which do not follow the steps that development had taken in Europe. He laments the lack of personnel and the waste of equipment and energy he encounters all over Egypt (165, 178). Eyth is frustrated but never tires of pointing out how the Egyptian economy benefits from development and how much time and manpower is saved through innovative technology. He never questions the usefulness of his mission, but he acknowledges the adverse conditions in Egypt that, as he understands well, are caused by both local conditions and the actions of foreign investors. Eyth's belief in progress is confirmed through what he experienced in Egypt; he writes that, while he had at times doubted whether progress truly meant a fundamental change for the better, he had begun to imagine the "great truth"; only in the "Orient, especially in those circles that are bedecked with European luxury and European polish, in countries like Egypt, where one bumps daily into a bygone millennium," had the benefit of progress become crystal clear to him (133).

As we have seen, Eyth's relationship toward Egypt was neither determined by beliefs in the superiority of the German race nor by an essentialist view of culture. The engineer was deeply inspired by the conviction that progress and modernization hold benefits for all of humanity. To identify clearly the parameters that motivated Eyth's actions, let us take another look at how Eyth approached non-European cultures.

Before the engineer moved to Egypt, he considered an assignment to India, and his remarks about the country reflect his sympathetic stance toward the area. This appreciation of India, however, does not acknowledge the country on its own terms; rather, the engineer attempts to appropriate India for its relevance to Germans (as their *Urheimat*) and Christians (proximity to biblical sites [103–4]). Nevertheless, we also sense his attempt to build a bridge for his readers that makes his journey to the distant and strange environment more plausible.

Other passages, however, convey a greater recognition of the history of non-European cultures. Eyth is clearly excited when he travels through Lebanon, Syria, and Palestine, yet it is interesting that he does not describe these countries exclusively with regard to their relevance as sites important to Christianity but, rather, embraces the existence of a history shared by Muslims and Christians: "Even for the kaaba in Mecca I feel a certain veneration. . . . Aren't they all humans like me? Should I think less of them because they went or were led a different way than I? Nobody can disdain a stone, but I can respect it because of them, because of millions of fellow human beings who venerate it. Thousands think and feel in different ways. With regard to these matters, however, everybody is allowed to make his own choices and nobody has a right to judge the other" (224–25).

This comment, in particular, reveals that Eyth reflected upon questions of religious and cultural differences and that his basic humanism and universalist outlook determined his attitude toward others. When he left Egypt, he expressed his emotions about the people he had met over the course of several years: “I leave more good male and female friends behind than I would have ever dreamed” (244). The social relations he was able to develop are indicative of the fact that Eyth was invited to carry out his development projects in a country whose elite believed just as much as he did in the benefit of *tanwir*.

Although Eyth’s basic attitude toward Egyptians cannot be described as racist, he does engage in paternalist or colonialist actions (such as corporal punishment) and often depicts Egyptians as comical and incompetent. This behavior, I have argued, is not fundamentally different from that of the ruling elite toward their subordinates in his own country, Germany; in addition, his conduct toward ordinary Egyptians might be seen as more restrained than that of the local ruling class toward its subjects. Eyth’s attitude was primarily determined by a belief in modernization and in the capability of Egyptians for development. He shows respect for the educated elite of the country; while for the most part, he applauds the degree by which they have become Europeanized, he also entertains a remarkable degree of tolerance toward cultural difference.

Eyth regards his work in Egypt as a modernizing mission. Although he comments repeatedly on the backwardness of the country, obstacles to this modernizing mission are not ascribed to the premodern aspects of Egyptian society alone. When the engineer talks about the “Oriental economy,” he includes in this term Arabs and Europeans, the elites in Egypt and the companies in England, bankers and aristocrats (193–94). French and British citizens do not fare well either in the account of the German engineer; his animosity toward the British is tangible throughout his account and surfaces especially in the steam plow competition. Eyth’s contempt of the French is most clearly articulated in a passage about a French manager of an estate, whom he calls “one of the greatest swindlers in the entire country. He combines with the snake-like politeness of his people the barbarism and cruelty of Inner Africa, is accused of bigamy, lets his first wife starve, is involved in Upper Egypt’s slave trade and here, he initiates the most insidious court intrigues” (232).

During his time in Egypt, Eyth had ample time to observe the unholy connections between the modernizing Egyptian society and the machinations of European industrialists and merchants:

> Civilization and barbarism, feverish activities and insurmountable laziness, the old fanaticism which, because it can murder no longer, betrays and steals, and the modern Christian faithlessness, which robs and plunders to an even greater extent wherever it can, all these contradictory elements are lodged in a fraternal struggle. American blue-blooded industrialists and English horse keepers, Greek rogues and French comedians, German drunkards and Italian pharmacists and poisoners, on a broad basis of Arabs and Copts, whose every word is a lie and every action a theft, an attempt to bribe or to be bribed: these are the elements of this society. (148)

Eyth's relationship to and representation of Egypt was inspired by a belief in salvation through modernization. His outlook was neither connected to the interests of the nation-state nor informed by biological racism. As such, Eyth's case exemplifies what Michael Adas has described in *Machines as the Measure of Men: Science, Technology, and Ideologies of Western Dominance,* namely, that Eyth's sense of superiority was based primarily on the power associated with advanced technology and science he brought with him.[55]

Eyth's role in Egypt represents one type of relationship between Germany and non-Western cultures, one that is thoroughly determined by the belief in progress through a very specific kind of education (that is, German/European) and a very specific kind of economic development (namely, modern industrial). Other German attitudes toward non-European countries were and are rooted in racist thinking and existed and continue to exist simultaneously with those exemplified by Eyth. Eyth's good intentions, however, did not prevent him from taking part in a process that ruined the country economically and politically, created dependency on Western states and investors, and is responsible for many of Egypt's problems today.

Studying Eyth's motivations and the complexity of the Egyptian situation allows us to comprehend a paradigmatic situation that is playing itself out to this day. Eyth's modernizing mission failed, but the reasons for this failure are, as we have seen, highly complex. As we have seen, Said's idea of Orientalism offers no explanation for the tangled interplay of internal and external factors. While there is no room here for conspiracy theories that paint the course of history in a Manichaean narrative of oppression, it is possible to identify the factors that brought about economic and political dependency. We look at Eyth in Egypt, however, in hindsight, at a moment when the global expansion of capital is reaching another stage. Once more we are confronted with the repercussions of structural incompatibilities, greed, and political conflict, and once more the temptation is great to resort to culturalist explanations. The story of Eyth in Egypt offers a historical example that encourages us to look again at the complex web of factors that generates global inequality.

2

The Civilizing Mission

Albert Schweitzer in Gabon

> No, my dear Vidal, no! You are not here to implant civilization. Don't fool yourself about that, or, if you haven't already done so, think carefully about it. You are here to protect a certain and precise category of people, that's all. And you will protect them until the others become too strong and throw them out, and you along with them. — Mongo Beti, *The Poor Christ of Bomba*

Albert Schweitzer is undoubtedly one of the heroes of the twentieth century. He appears still to symbolize all that is good about the West: exemplifying Christianity's noblest values through his altruism; Europe's high culture through his eminence as a musician, a specialist in organ building, a theologian, and a philosopher; and modernity's most beneficial achievements through his work as a doctor. His various talents and the ways in which he used them make him a fascinating figure: he held doctorates in theology, music, philosophy, and medicine yet lived under austere conditions in the middle of the African jungle, abandoning the bourgeois lifestyle of his earlier years.

Only a few years after Schweitzer began his undertaking in Africa (he worked in Gabon between 1913 and 1965, with many years between the individual stays spent in Europe), some critics rejected first his philosophical framework and later also questioned the motivations behind his African work.[1] Their analyses discuss Schweitzer as an embodiment of European paternalism and authoritarianism. Yet, regardless of those voices challenging the dominant image of Schweitzer, the doctor and philosopher remains almost uncontested as a symbol of European humanism and Christian charity. Across linguistic and cultural boundaries, the majority of the many biographies and studies of Schweitzer, his medical work, and his writings present only a favorable image of the man.

In German culture Schweitzer plays a role even more significant than in other settings, and he continues to enjoy great popularity. One way to approach the question of his symbolic function is to ask what brought him to Africa and what he intended to accomplish there. Using Schweitzer's self-representation in his autobiographical texts as a starting point and drawing on his philosophical and theological writings from the beginning of the century and from later periods, I will consider Schweitzer's motivations for going to Africa in the context of the "critique of civilization" (*Zivilisationskritik*) prominent in German culture in the period before World War I. I will then investigate Schweitzer's attitudes toward Africans on the basis of writings composed in the 1920s and later. This exploration aims at establishing a better understanding of the significance of Schweitzer in the post–World War II period. The image of Schweitzer created after World War II, I argue, contained an exculpatory function for Germany, particularly in light of the crimes the nation committed during the war, and is still the dominant model for the reception of Schweitzer to this day. On a larger scale the discourse on and by Albert Schweitzer emerges as a paradigmatic site for analyzing the troubled relationship between not only Germany but also, more generally, Western countries and Africa.

The exploration of Schweitzer that follows does not intend to dispute the value of his actual humanitarian work. I want to highlight the tension that exists between his work as a doctor, through which he undoubtedly relieved the pain of scores of Africans, and his views of Africans as he formulated them in his writings. Artists and intellectuals often face criticism because aspects of their personal lives seem to conflict with values they promote in their works. Schweitzer presents the reverse situation: as a European forgoing the comforts of bourgeois existence to spend his life under austere conditions in the tropics, he inspired so many individuals to help others that it may seem pointless to question his motivations. The analysis of writings by and about Schweitzer, however, reveals how these texts are part of the larger corpus of European texts on Africa that, in complex and indirect ways, is integral to colonialist thinking and which functions to legitimate the European domination of Africa.

Missionary or Doctor?

In the epigraph to this chapter Father Drumont, the disillusioned priest in the acclaimed satirical novel *The Poor Christ of Bomba* by the Cameroonian writer Mongo Beti, questions the validity of the "mission civilatrice," a concept central to the legitimization of French, and more generally European, colonialism.[2] After twenty years of missionary service in Africa, Drumont has finally decided to return to France. In a conversation with a French colonial administrator, he recounts what originally had motivated him to come to Africa: "I left France with all the ardour of an Apostle. I had only one notion in my head and one ambition in my heart: to extend the Kingdom of Christ. Rationalist Europe, so full of arrogance, science and self-consciousness, filled me with dismay. I chose the disinherited, or those whom I was pleased to regard as such."[3]

In 1913 Albert Schweitzer left Europe for French Equatorial Africa, driven by similar emotions and comparable thoughts about the state of European civilization. Yet, unlike Father Drumont, Schweitzer appears never to have questioned the legitimacy of his actions in Africa. Initially, the man who would become famous for his work as a doctor in Africa had also envisioned a career as a missionary. In 1904 Schweitzer read an article by Alfred Boegner, the director of the Paris Mission Society, concerning the need for personnel in Gabon.[4] For Schweitzer this request for help became his calling, a revelation resonating with the studies on Jesus he was conducting at the time. Just as Schweitzer's *Geschichte der Leben-Jesu-Forschung* (published in 1906, with an expanded version in 1913) ends with an appeal to emulate the example given by Jesus ("Follow me!"), the article by Boegner effected the experience of an immediate calling.[5] Nine months after he saw the article, on July 9, 1905, Schweitzer sent a letter to Boegner in which he offered his services as a missionary.[6] In the letter he mentions that he was intending to acquire some basic knowledge of medicine in order to be better prepared for the challenges in the tropics, but his initial goal was to serve as a missionary.[7] Nevertheless, the Paris Mission Society rejected Schweitzer, whose religious views seemed too liberal, irreconcilable with the society's missionary goals. Other missionary societies, such as the Allgemeiner Evangelischer Missionsverein, would have accepted him gladly, but Schweitzer was determined to pursue his vision.[8] His father, a Lutheran pastor who held the society in high esteem, was utterly shocked when he learned of his son's intentions to leave for Africa, but Schweitzer's experience of a mystical calling upon reading Boegner's article tied him irrevocably to the Paris Mission Society.[9] His solution was to embark on an alternative route: he resigned his position as the director of the College of St. Thomas in Strasbourg in order to study medicine.[10] Nevertheless, the society continued to harbor doubts about his theological qualifications. After Schweitzer completed the theoretical part of his medical studies, in December 1910, he contacted the society again but was met once more with a rebuff.

The society's negative response in the spring of 1911, however, was based on more than its critical view of Schweitzer's theology. The Second Moroccan Crisis was unfolding that year, and France and Germany had been close to war. By March German policy toward Morocco was changing; politicians, especially Alfred von Kiderlen-Waechters, secretary of foreign affairs, and leading industrial figures, such as Emil Kirdorf and the Mannesmann Brothers, increasingly displayed their concern for Moroccan independence—that is, their intention to protect German access to its deposits of ore. On July 1, in the infamous "pantherleap to Agadir," Germany sent the gunboat SMS *Panther* to the Moroccan city. Yet, while German industrialists were interested in access to Moroccan resources, German politicians hoped to use the crisis to negotiate an expansion of the German colonial empire in sub-Saharan Africa. England, however, did not agree with Germany's push for power; left without support from even allied Austro-Hungary, Germany was isolated. In exchange for acknowledging the French protectorate in Morocco, Germany (among other provisions) received smaller but still considerable territories in the French Congo, thereby expanding German Cameroon up to the Ubangi and Congo Rivers. For pro-colonial Germans, the result of this intervention was a setback; members of nationalist circles felt humiliated and deprived of the colonial empire they had envisioned. Ultimately, the Moroccan Crisis contributed significantly to creating the spirit out of which World War I was born.

The territory Germany had coveted was precisely the area where Schweitzer was hoping to serve as a missionary. In light of the tense political climate and the recalcitrant attitude of the Paris Mission Society, Schweitzer shifted gears. In May 1911 he no longer asked to go to Gabon primarily as a missionary but offered instead to travel to Gabon as a doctor, to build up a medical facility that would be connected to a mission but financed by other sources. The society, influenced by the political developments, nevertheless remained hesitant. Discussions of Schweitzer's religious views, and now of his national allegiance, continued. Schweitzer did not give up; he managed to raise the necessary money by rallying a circle of mostly German donors who supported his endeavor. Indeed, he was more successful than he expected; by spring 1912 Schweitzer had gathered a substantial sum. As a result, he needed only the approval of the society to allow him to stay as a guest at a mission. Members of the Paris Mission Society were now concerned about the doctor's independence. Only the clever maneuvers of Jean Bianquis, who followed Alfred Boegner as the director of the society after Boegner's sudden death in February 1912, ultimately secured the society's support for Schweitzer. On May 13, 1912, the missionary-turned-doctor was finally granted his wish, but a detailed letter limited Schweitzer's work to nonmissionary activities and released the society from any responsibility vis-à-vis the doctor.[11] Now the way was cleared: the decision to go to Lambarene rather than any other place in French Congo was inspired by Schweitzer's acquaintance with Georgette Morel, the wife of the Alsatian missionary Léon Morel, during his internship as a doctor in Strasbourg in 1911–12. Georgette Morel had worked with her husband from 1908 through 1911 at the mission in Lambarene. Schweitzer's contact with the Morels confirmed his wish to go to Gabon and steered him toward this specific location.

It is noteworthy that Schweitzer had close relationships with a number of high-ranking French politicians, some of whom figured quite prominently in the realm of colonial politics in particular, such as Eugène Etienne (deputy of Oran, Algeria, from 1881 to 1919) and Albert Lebrun (colonial minister during the Moroccan Crisis). These contacts ensured the acceptance of Schweitzer's German medical degree by the French authorities. Schweitzer also benefited from the attempts at reconciliation after the conclusion of the Moroccan Crisis, and his connections to influential politicians might have determined the Paris Mission Society's final decision. Its sympathetic attitude toward the doctor, however, would not last long. With the beginning of World War I, Schweitzer and his wife, Helene, were declared "hostile foreigners." In September 1917 they were ordered to leave the area immediately, and—under the supervision of French officers—brought to an internment camp. Until July 1918 the couple was interned in camps in Bordeaux, Garaison, and St. Rémy.[12] These events, which put a temporary end to Schweitzer's activities in Gabon and to the project he fought for over so many years, must have produced a grave disappointment. He fell seriously ill during this period, and he had to undergo several surgeries in 1918 and 1919 before he gradually recovered. But Schweitzer's stamina and determination drove him to pursue his goals relentlessly.

In 1919 Schweitzer and his wife were granted French citizenship. This came as a result of the Treaty of Versailles, and, as Gustav Woytt points out, was not born out of personal convictions or aspirations.[13] (This has not kept proponents of French culture from claiming for French heritage the man whom the French government interned during World War I.) Schweitzer continued to face problems regarding his plans, not only from the Paris Mission Society but also from the colonial ministry.[14] French citizenship would ensure, however, that Schweitzer could return to Gabon.[15] In the end the society's quarrel with Schweitzer resulted in his becoming financially and structurally independent, able to carry out his project according to his own liking. For the rest of his life Schweitzer would move back and forth between Gabon and Europe; fourteen stays in Africa are recorded, amounting to twenty-seven long journeys by ship, which the antimodern Schweitzer preferred to airplanes. During his stays in Europe Schweitzer raised money by going on concert tours, giving public lectures, and inspiring scores of individuals to support his mission in Gabon. The money he had acquired was then used to maintain the hospital, expand and renovate the facilities, and buy medication and other supplies.

Schweitzer, however, did not only work as a doctor in Africa. Contrary to popular belief, his activities included some functions usually performed by missionaries. From the time that Schweitzer arrived in Gabon, in April 1913, local missionaries proved to be more liberal than were the bureaucrats of the French motherland, both with regard to his national allegiance and his theological views. Schweitzer was soon invited to preach and later even to examine candidates for baptism.[16] At the hospital complex in Lambarene he gave sermons daily.

What, then, was Schweitzer's mission in Africa? Considering that he became a doctor to circumvent the skeptical attitude of the Paris Mission Society and given his devotion to missionary activities, we would do well to take a closer look at Schweitzer's intentions. We may grant that his decision to serve the Paris Mission Society was based on the mystical experience of receiving a true calling and that his stubbornness in pursuing his goals drove him on to achieve his intentions—but were there other factors that led Schweitzer to Africa? And, again, what did he want to accomplish, as a missionary or as a doctor, in the tropical forests of Africa?

Why Africa?

Schweitzer was born in 1875 and grew up in Alsace at a time when the area was part of the German empire. Throughout his life he felt more closely attached to this region than to either Germany or France. Schweitzer considered himself a cosmopolitan and was indeed highly critical of nationalism.[17] His cosmopolitanism is comparable to that of the Austrian writer Hugo von Hofmannsthal: both favored a European identity over national belonging, hailed certain aspects of European culture, and strongly believed in the cultural mission of Europe.[18] Schweitzer is thus often hailed as an archetypal European or even a *Weltbürger* (citizen of the world).

At the same time, his roots in Alsace and the changing status of the area after World War I made it possible for him to be claimed by both French and Germans. He was in practice more deeply rooted in German than in French intellectual history and culture. He enjoyed his studies in Berlin and Strasbourg more than the time he spent in Paris, and he often expressed his appreciation of the German language and culture.[19] Most of his writings were composed in German, and his philosophical and musicological studies focused on central figures of German culture. Schweitzer emphasized that, even though he was equally fluent in French, "German is my mother tongue, because the Alsatian dialect, in which I am rooted linguistically, is German."[20]

He remained loyal to Alsace until his death. After his father died, in 1925, the house of Schweitzer's childhood was assigned to the new pastor who came to fill the vacant position. Schweitzer built a new house in Günsbach with the money from the Frankfurt Goethe Prize he received in 1928. The house was finished in 1929, and Schweitzer returned to the village whenever he stayed in Europe. Critics have often focused on Schweitzer's connection to Günsbach in order to emphasize his transnational European identity.[21] Photographs showing him in the circle of his childhood friends are presented as documents illustrating Schweitzer's attachment to the region.[22]

Why did Albert Schweitzer choose Africa as a location for his activities? Answers to this question are provided by his autobiographical, religious, and philosophical writings.

Schweitzer began publishing autobiographical texts in 1921 with the volume *Zwischen Wasser und Urwald.* This early text about his first stay in Lambarene, with his autobiography *Aus meiner Kindheit und Jugendzeit* (1924) and the volume *Briefe aus Lambarene, 1924–1927* (1928), are supplemented by a series of shorter essays and articles in which Schweitzer elaborates on specific aspects of his life and continues to write about his experiences in Africa. Some of these essays appeared in *Aus meinem Leben und Denken* (1931). One of the astounding aspects of Schweitzer's autobiographical writings is the coherence with which the author presents the story of his life: events are presented as evolving in a logical manner, according to a predestined blueprint of his life. In these writings Schweitzer emphasizes events that are identified as turning points in his life and which seem to anticipate future developments. In the more expansive memoir of his childhood and youth, *Aus meiner Kindheit und Jugendzeit,* Schweitzer conveys the sense that the seeds for his future work, especially the African enterprise, had already been planted at an early age.

Schweitzer declares that his first memory was that of an incident that made him realize the possibility of fighting evil through "the word of God."[23] Another episode teaches him that pain and suffering can earn a person attention and empathy. He maintains that becoming aware of the dark side of a desire for attention often helped him to resist the temptation to be in the spotlight (GW 1, 257). Even though Schweitzer is aware of the questionable motivations for consciously solicited empathy, his later life is by far free from this quality. After all, he received attention and empathy because he abandoned the comfort of a European bourgeois lifestyle and exchanged it for a life of hard work under adverse conditions in the tropics.

Most of the incidents that Schweitzer relates are oracular, since there is something almost superstitious about the way everything is presented as predestined. This recounting style reflects in part Schweitzer's mystical inclinations; at the same time it is a narrative strategy that lends coherence to his tale. Schweitzer does not seem to change or develop; it is as if he already carries everything within and succeeds only in revealing his latent potential.

Two childhood incidents are rendered as pivotal for the development of Schweitzer's sense of forgiveness and compassion. He describes how he and other village boys played pranks on a Jewish peddler. In recounting this incident, Schweitzer interprets the passive behavior of the Jew as a superior and exemplary character trait, denoting magnanimity and forgiveness. This episode, Schweitzer asserts, taught him "what it means to remain silent in the face of persecution" (GW 1, 260–61). In Schweitzer's portrayal, Mausche, the Jewish peddler, becomes a role model for Schweitzer, who then begins to treat the peddler respectfully. The development of his relationship to animals figures as another central realization in Schweitzer's portrait of his childhood. He describes how a "voice from heaven" teaches him empathy with all living creatures and motivates him to abstain from torturing animals along with the other village boys. For Schweitzer this event showed not only an inborn and mystically evoked "reverence for life" (to quote the formula he developed later to express the key concept of his philosophy), but it also helped him overcome his "fear of humans," that is, a fear of the judgment of others (GW 1, 276).

While these childhood incidents illustrate Schweitzer's development into a caring and responsible human being, other aspects of his early years point more directly to his choice of Africa as the place to pursue his goals. In a number of scenes Schweitzer describes the tension surrounding his social standing as the son of the pastor in relation to the other, ordinary boys from the village. He describes his desire to fit in and his attempts to not stand out (GW 1, 261–63). Indeed, Schweitzer's position among the Africans in Lambarene mirrors the paradigm of his childhood years: as an educated European, he stands out among the African villagers. The childhood conflict remains unresolved and reappears in a different guise. Just as Schweitzer never becomes an equal among equals in his childhood village (even if he maintains contact with friends from Günsbach until the end), the discrepancies remain, in Günsbach and in Lambarene. In Lambarene, however, Schweitzer's goal was never to be accepted by Africans; in a reversal of the Günsbach scenario, he wants Africans to become like him. Many events and learning experiences of Schweitzer's childhood years are presented in relation to their later importance for his work in Africa. Learning the piano, for example, will help him to raise money for the hospital in Lambarene (GW 1, 279). Schweitzer also mentions a teacher who becomes his role model, teaching him self-discipline and a sense of duty that would eventually enable him to overcome many difficult situations (GW 1, 283–84).

Schweitzer's interest in Africa itself was already awakened during his childhood years. Every first Sunday of the month his father dedicated the afternoon church service to missionaries and their work. The memoirs of the missionary Eugène Casalis (1812–91), for instance, left a lasting impression on Schweitzer (GW 1, 288).[24] Casalis was as a missionary for the Paris Mission Society and served as its director from 1856 to 1882; it was this organization that Schweitzer would later insist on serving. In his memoirs Schweitzer singles out another event that increased his interest in Africa—namely, his encounter with a sculpture by Frédéric-Auguste Bartholdi (1834–1904), who also designed the Statue of Liberty in New York City. Bartholdi's monument of a reclining African wearing a melancholic expression was erected on the Champ de Mars in Colmar, as part of a monument dedicated to Admiral Bruat: "A Herculean figure with a pensive, sad facial expression. This Negro kept me thinking a lot. . . . His countenance spoke to me of the misery of the dark continent." As in the case of the Jewish peddler, it is the expression of suffering and serenity that inspires Schweitzer, who describes his longing to see the sculpture each time his family went to Colmar and writes that he continued to go on pilgrimages to the site over the course of his life (GW 1, 288–89). This African image appears as an omen, foreshadowing Schweitzer's later stay in Africa and emphasizing the mystical aura of his mission.

Other aspects of the young Schweitzer do not seem to predict his future achievements. He had not looked forward to school (GW 1, 259), nor did he develop into an outstanding student (GW 1, 283, 301). But the effect of these details is to make Schweitzer's later accomplishments even more impressive. In a way these seeming shortcomings confirm an important aspect of Schweitzer's African endeavor: his tireless and successful struggles against impediments.

Schweitzer presents himself as frank and self-critical. Just as he describes his inner struggle to overcome the temptation to mistreat animals, he talks freely about his temper and self-righteousness that often created friction with the people around him. He also states that he never really changed in the course of his life (GW 1, 294–95). He came to realize that his enthusiasm for "truth" and "purpose" was an essential part of his identity, and he pursued both with a vigor and determination that at times got him into trouble: "Therefore I am actually still as intolerable as I was then" (GW 1, 296). This remark has an air of coquetry, as if it were intended to obstruct potential criticism. But, indeed, many visitors to Schweitzer's Lambarene acknowledged the doctor's temper; the fact that he slapped and kicked his workers was seen as the all too human side of this otherwise superhuman being.[25] Some biographers excuse Schweitzer's temper and authoritarian demeanor as the sort of behavior that unruly Africans required.[26]

Schweitzer describes the relationship to his parents as ideal and recalls his early years as a "uniquely happy youth." He presents his awareness of his privileged status as another central insight of his life. While the humiliation of the village Jew and the abusive treatment of animals made him conscious of the suffering in the world, his growing awareness of the uniqueness of his privileged youth and childhood, his robust health and emotional well-being, made him feel obliged to share his good fortune (GW 1, 299–300).

Condemning selfishness and encouraging altruistic behavior reflected Schweitzer's Christian upbringing. Accordingly, his epiphany regarding the privileged nature of his existence is presented as a religious experience, in what has become known as *Schweitzer's Pfingsterlebnis* (Pentecostal experience), an obvious allusion to the "miracle of Pentecost." At Whitsuntide in 1896, when only twenty-one years old, Schweitzer decided that—up to his thirtieth year—he would live to enjoy his passions: theology, science, and music. Afterward, once he had given to art and science what he had could, he was going to serve mankind (GW 1, 300).

Schweitzer thus presents the story of his life as a series of events leading up to his work in Africa. This narrative fashions an image of Schweitzer as a selfless and mystically inspired humanist. While some scenes (church services with missionaries, Casalis, Bartholdi's African) clearly point to his future destination, other elements in Schweitzer's development (his compassion, sense of justice, service to mankind, courage, piano playing) are rendered as preparing or qualifying him for the *kind* of work he was going to do in Africa. Schweitzer's biographers generally refrain from questioning the premises of his self-portrait, which they mimic thoughtlessly by treating the information provided by Schweitzer as objective facts. I have no doubt that Schweitzer himself believed that his life possessed a mystical logic and that he was motivated by events he experienced as true callings. A second look at Schweitzer's self-representation, however, reveals aspects that he himself does not grasp. For example, Schweitzer's position among the Africans reenacted that of his youth, where he stood out awkwardly among the village boys. His well-documented temper is also significant: no government agency or church board in Europe would have tolerated his sometimes tyrannical behavior. The colonial context, however, provided Schweitzer with a social world that exercised only rudimentary control over the actions of Europeans and encouraged grandiosity. Africa emerged as an ideal place where Schweitzer could act according to his beliefs and personal predisposition.

Schweitzer's decision to dedicate his life to humanity, in particular in Africa, must also be seen in the context of various intellectual debates before World War I. Schweitzer contributed significantly to central discussions of this era with his theological writings and later with his cultural philosophy, and these texts offer further clues about why he decided to go to Africa. Texts that he wrote later in life are rooted in the intellectual climate of those earlier formative years, during which Schweitzer developed his key philosophical concepts. Throughout his life he continued to produce major philosophical works and to edit earlier writings; his core philosophy, however, can be traced back to the years before 1913, to the period before he left Europe for Africa for the first time.

Like many other intellectuals of this period, Schweitzer struggled to come to terms with the changes caused by modernization. In contrast to the Germany that Max Eyth had left for its backwardness in the 1860s,

German society was now in flux at all levels. Political, social, and economic transformations affected virtually all members of society. At the end of the nineteenth century Germany had gradually developed from an agrarian state with a powerful industry to an industrial state with a strong agrarian base. These changes were accompanied by the emergence of new professions and the decline of traditional crafts. Population growth and shifts in production caused many people to leave the countryside and to move to the new industrial centers. Others became long-distance migrant workers. Women began to join the workforce in increasing numbers, especially in the service sector.

Transportation also changed dramatically during the last decades of the nineteenth century. The railroad system was expanded, and road traffic increased. Horse-drawn streetcars, electric trams, and finally the automobile allowed people to move across space faster than ever before. The modernized version of the bicycle, also introduced toward the end of the century (Schweitzer describes his excitement when he saw a bicycle for the first time in the early 1880s [*GW* 1, 266]), was popular with the majority who could not afford a car. New communications systems reflected the developing needs of a growing and mobile population; the invention of the telegraph and the telephone revolutionized communication. As early as 1910 there were a million telephones in Germany, and the exchanges handled some 1.8 billion calls each year.[27]

Wealth, however, was distributed unevenly. During the period of economic growth preceding World War I, the top 10 percent of the Prussian population increased its share of personal assets to 63 percent.[28] Those who had invested their money in industry experienced the most significant rise in terms of the value of their assets. The number of taxpayers listed as millionaires in Prussia almost doubled between 1896–97 and 1911.[29] The majority of the population, however, benefited only partially from the two decades of economic expansion before 1914: "Well over half of all the taxpayers in Prussia, where two-thirds of the total German population were living, belonged to the lowest income group."[30] The political system did not satisfy the needs of a growing, increasingly more educated, and socially diverse populace. Women and members of the working class began to organize and asked for political representation. Wolfgang J. Mommsen points out that the political system did not adjust to the social changes brought about by the transforming economy.[31]

Changes in gender relations and the structure of the family, moreover, affected not only those who lived in the exploding cities. In one way or another the entire population was in upheaval. These transformations of the economy, social relations, and political structures were interpreted by many as a form of decline. In particular, the rise of the consumer culture and a growing materialism were experienced by many as a deterioration of values. Conditions in the cities brought about a lifestyle that was different from that seen in the countryside, but many of the changes, results of new types of labor as well as the increased buying power of the lower classes, were seen as a form of decay. Mass culture and the demand for greater political representation of the lower classes caused anxiety among members of the privileged classes. Whereas leftists were more concerned with lobbying for political representation for the working class and decried the often inhumane conditions under which the urban proletariat lived, liberal and conservative members of the (mostly Protestant) upper and middle classes reacted to the claims of the working class with indignation and calls for a return to the values of an earlier age. The "Culture War" (*Kulturkampf*, 1871–87) between the Catholic Church and the Prussian state, as well as the state's attempts to suppress socialist and communist activities through the implementation of the "Socialist Law" (*Sozialistengesetz*, 1878–90), aimed at securing the hegemony of Protestant, rationalist, and individualistic middle- and upper-class culture.

The period after World War I saw the emergence of a new attitude toward modern culture and led to a conscious embracing of modernity through an experimentation with new political, social, and economic forms (until fascism put an end to these endeavors through the erection of a rigid order), but the time before the war was characterized by fear and insecurity. As we have seen, in economic terms the prewar period was one of relative prosperity, even though different segments of the population benefited from it to different degrees, but the inadequacy of the political system and a prevailing sense of economic inequality contributed to a climate of anxiety. In addition, the loss of religion as a master discourse and the development since the eighteenth century of the exact sciences coincided with the emergence of nation-states, the expansion of colonial empires, and the development of capitalist economies. The degree and the pace of changes on essentially all levels were decisive factors in the creation of social malaise.

Many cultural critics of the early twentieth century held science responsible for the loss of ethics and for the materialism of the time. Ernst Haeckel's *Die Welträtsel* (1898), for example, a highly popular work in Germany that promoted Darwinian ideas, implicitly raised the question of how ethics were to be reconciled with natural laws of selection and evolution. The impact of science and technology on society was sweeping; it radically altered the physical appearance of the country and the way people thought, worked, communicated, and moved across space. Because of the visible impact science and technology had had on people's lives, it was seen as the cause of all evil by those who experienced the changes in one way or another as loss or disorientation. All members of society were indeed affected by the changes brought about by the ascendancy of rationality, but different groups encountered the changes in different ways. Whereas working-class people and women were lobbying for human rights, political representation, and humane living conditions—demonstrating that there was no lack of values and, in fact, an attempt to forge a new ethics—middle- and upper-class representatives lamented the loss of traditional norms.

Works of art conceived before World War I articulate the central questions of the era. Atonal music by Gustav Mahler, for instance, resonates with the predicament of the individual. In France Cubist paintings by Georges Braque and Pablo Picasso acknowledge both the validity and disorienting effect of multiple perspectives. Literary works by Alfred Döblin, Franz Kafka, Jacob van Hoddis, Georg Kaiser, and Else Lasker-Schüler bring concerns about fragmentation, disorientation, and aimlessness to the fore. Martin Buber, Sigmund Freud, Werner Sombart, Rudolf Steiner, and Max Weber, among others, questioned the compatibility of rational, scientific modern society with the spiritual, psychological, and ethical needs of human beings. Some of these debates focused on a perceived loss of the "spiritual," which was seen in contradistinction to the materialism and mechanistic thinking of the modern world. It is important to understand this concern about spiritual matters as a feature of coming to terms with life in the modern world and with the loss of traditional belief systems. Wassily Kandinsky's text *Über das Geistige in der Kunst* (1911) represents one such attempt to revive the category of "the spiritual" against the materialism of the time.

Until his years in Strasbourg and later in Berlin, Schweitzer experienced modernization from the margins, from his home in the village of Günsbach. Later he lived in cities, including Berlin and Paris, and was exposed to the spirit of change defining this period. He studied philosophy, music, and theology. Both in his studies as well as the experience of life in the metropolis he was confronted with the question of how to bring into accord modern rationality and traditional religion. Quickly, he joined the chorus of voices decrying the state of European civilization.

Schweitzer first approached the question of the relationship between ethics and religion in the philosophical and theological studies that he began in Strasbourg in 1893. He received his first doctorate, in philosophy, in 1899; his dissertation, published in 1899, discusses incongruities in Kant's philosophy of religion. One year later Schweitzer received a doctorate in theology. In his second dissertation (1901) and in another study from that period, Schweitzer approached what he later laid out in great detail in *Von Reimarus zu Wrede: Geschichte der Leben-Jesu-Forschung* (1906; an expanded version was published as *Geschichte der Leben-Jesu-Forschung* in 1913). In this reception study of eighteenth- to twentieth-century research on the historical Jesus, Schweitzer claims that nineteenth-century scholars projected the spirit of their historical period onto Jesus and interpreted his life and teachings according to their own philosophies. Schweitzer argues that Jesus needs to be understood in the context of *his* time; he shows how Jesus' teachings and actions are rooted in the apocalyptic atmosphere of Judaism at the time, and he demonstrates that relevant passages of the Bible indicate that Jesus believed the Kingdom of God to be close and that he saw himself as the Messiah, a thesis that is known as "konsequente Eschatologie."[32] His initial question for the research was Why did Jesus tell his disciples (he refers to passages in Matthew) that the end of the world was near unless he himself believed this to be true? These theses and his attempts at proving them provoked a strong reaction among critics. While orthodox believers dismissed his writings because they seemingly challenged fundamental teachings of Christianity (for example, because of the implied assumption that Jesus erred about the end of the world), liberal believers were enraged by Schweitzer's refusal to reinterpret the Bible in ways that would make the text and Jesus compatible with modern, essentially secular views of the world.

For Schweitzer, however, the reality of the historical Jesus and Christian belief were reconcilable. His provocative writings led to his later problems when he wanted to join the Paris Mission Society. In our context the most important aspect of Schweitzer's work is its conclusion: even if the historical Jesus is understood from within the context of his time, he can still serve as a role model today. In some ways Schweitzer can be considered an unorthodox Christian whose relationship to God and the world is ultimately a mystical one. It is also possible, according to Schweitzer, to be a Christian without believing in traditional transcendental Christian convictions. To understand this aspect more closely, it is necessary to look at Schweitzer's writings on cultural philosophy.

Just as Schweitzer attempts in his theological writings to reconcile scientific thinking and a historical understanding of Jesus with the need for ethics and religiosity, so he aims at balancing these concerns on an even larger scale in his cultural philosophy. He began to write this work in 1915, the year he also developed his central philosophical concept, "reverence for life." He published his extensive study of cultural philosophy in 1923 in two parts. In these works he draws on his theological as well as philosophical training to develop a philosophy grounded in Christianity yet modified in the light of rationalism and science. Schweitzer formulates his philosophy on the basis of historical and comparative studies. After a more general assessment of the contemporary situation in *Verfall und Wiederaufbau der Kultur,* he turns in the more extensive second part, *Kultur und Ethik,* to a description of the development of philosophical thought in Western civilization from antiquity to modernity, at times contrasting Western and Eastern thought (such as Indian philosophy), and finally analyzing the contemporary state of European civilization.

Schweitzer's verdict on contemporary civilization is a gloomy one: "We are witnessing the decline of culture" (*Verfall,* GW 2, 23). This decline, explains Schweitzer, began with the neglect of Enlightenment ethics: "Enlightenment and rationalism had erected ethical ideals that were guided by reason regarding the development of the individual to achieve true humanity, his status in society, society's material and spiritual tasks, the interaction between nations, and regarding their merging into one mankind, unified by the highest spiritual goals" (GW 2, 24). But in the course of the nineteenth century philosophy failed to develop a coherent view of the world: "Finally the natural sciences, which had grown powerful in the meantime, destroyed the palaces built by imagination with plebian zeal for the truth of reality" (GW 2, 26). Schweitzer decries the decline of modern individuals, who define themselves in terms of their work and not in terms of their qualities as human beings. Because of regulations that society imposes in various areas, modern human beings are superficial, only interested in entertainment, indifferent toward others, and no longer independent in their actions and their thinking. Schweitzer differentiates between the ethical and material progress of a culture, and he clearly states that the progress by which the sophistication of a culture should be measured is ethical in nature: "Only an ethical movement can lead us out of this non-culture. The ethical, however, develops only in the individual" (GW 2, 72). Schweitzer argues that only a new *Weltanschauung,* one that is optimistic and ethical, can show the way out of the crisis (GW 2, 85). The dilemma lies in the fact, however, that we cannot know the universe and therefore are not able to develop an optimistic encompassing worldview.

Schweitzer's solution to this problem is to separate *Weltanschauung* from *Lebensanschauung* (view of life). He suggests that we have to accept that we cannot understand the meaning of the universe: "If we take the world as it is, it is impossible to assign to it a significance through which the purpose and goals of humans' and humanity's activities appear as meaningful" (*Kultur,* GW 2, 104). The difficulty of reconciling the findings of natural science with traditional Christian teachings becomes obvious. Schweitzer's solution is to focus on *Lebensanschauung* as a precondition for establishing a *Weltanschauung.* Reverence for life is the solution Schweitzer suggests: "My life carries its meaning in itself. . . . Therefore I give to my life and to all will to live that surrounds me worth, encourage myself to be engaged and create values" (GW 2, 108). Reverence for life is seen as the attitude that defines an optimistic relationship to life, one that may in turn be the basis for an optimistic attitude toward the world, even if the world per se cannot be understood. Based on previous findings from his studies on Jesus, Schweitzer points to the pessimistic aspects of messianic Christianity. Only when the optimism contained in Christianity is applied to the natural world does the Christian worldview develop "an appreciation and interest in the perfection of the organization of society and any contributing external cultural progress" (GW 2, 147).

The logic of this theory has been criticized for its lack of coherency from the beginning, both by sympathetic critics, such as Oskar Kraus (1926) and Werner Picht (1960), and less generous ones, such as Erich Brock (1923–24, 1924–25), J. Middleton Murry (1948), and Helmut Groos (1974).[33] These critics highlight the fact that Schweitzer's ethics does not address the problem of good and evil. Claus Günzler, however, has argued that Schweitzer's principle of reverence for life is an *Ehrfurchtsprinzip* (principle of reference) and should not be equated with a *Wertrangordnung* (hierarchy of values).[34] Gotthard Teutsch also suggests that it is futile to take the concept of reverence for life as an absolute dogma, and he shows that Schweitzer did make adjustments to address the different situations in which distinct forms of life require specific treatments.[35] Nevertheless, Schweitzer's reverence for life is vague to the extent that it remains unclear in what ways this reverence should be paid, what kind of actions are more life preserving than others, and even what represents a responsible humanitarian deed.

In sum, Schweitzer's philosophy, including his central concept of reverence for life, reflects an attempt to come to terms with the challenges of modern life. Schweitzer presents the problem as one of thought. According to his understanding, the materialism of modern society, the importance of ideologies such as nationalism, and an obsession with scientific progress had led to a decay of culture and ethics. The failure of philosophy and the subsequent domination by science of the ideological realm deprived European societies of the tools for ethical progress. Schweitzer's concern is that Europeans have forgotten the importance of ethics and ethical progress, which he claims cannot be achieved through institutions, organizations, or collective actions but only through a renewal of the faith in the power of the individual. Even more centrally, however, Schweitzer sees the solution in a revival of ethical values, such as an optimistic view of life and his principle of reverence for life, a principle that could, he argues, lay the foundation for a new humanism.

An understanding of the internal contradictions and shortcomings of Schweitzer's philosophy is central to an analysis of his work in Africa. The vagueness of his key philosophical concepts—at no point does he define the particulars of his ethics or the concept of "Ehrfurcht vor dem

Leben" — makes it possible for followers from diverse ideological camps to identify with them. But in our context Schweitzer's cultural philosophy is more important for other reasons. His notion of culture is based on a belief in progress and on the preeminence of ethics as the sole criterion for defining a culture's worth. According to Schweitzer, all cultures reflect distinct developmental stages in an assumed evolution of ethics. In a sweeping gesture Schweitzer divides all civilizations into *nonethical* and *ethical* cultures (GW 2, 48). Despite his concern about the demise of ethics in Europe, rather than saving the Continent from further decline, he sets out to rescue African civilization, which falls into this category of the nonethical. Europe remains the representative of the highest form of ethical culture.

Thus, the values expressed in Schweitzer's philosophy privilege a belief in progress and core European and Christian values. We need to remember that Schweitzer wrote at a time during which the right to vote was extended to women, monarchy had come to an end, and democracy became the basis of the constitutional state in Germany. In this light Schweitzer's longing, which he expresses in vague terms such as the spiritual and in poorly defined notions of ethical behavior, emerges as a desire for very specific structures — namely, for an "enlightened" yet authoritarian and patriarchal order, an order existing no longer in uncontested ways in Europe but present in another context: in the colonies.

Given Schweitzer's view of African cultures as nonethical, combined with his belief in progress and the Christian conviction of an entitlement to act as a missionary, Africa emerges as a logical site for his activities. The civilizing mission, maybe the most central concept used to legitimize European colonialism, is quite readily reconcilable with Schweitzer's philosophy. In Gabon Schweitzer found an environment that allowed him to pursue his civilizing mission in largely unrestricted ways. As James Barnes states, "French relations with the Gabonese were based on the French notion of the *mission civilatrice* (civilizing mission), that is, the obligation of the French to instruct Africans (and other lesser peoples) in the ways of French and European civilization."[36] Schweitzer's own approach was quite compatible with those existing structures.

Before Schweitzer chose to go to Africa, he worked with homeless people and released prisoners in Germany and attempted in vain to set up an institution to care for orphans and abandoned children. Bureaucratic regulations and hostile agencies stymied his repeated efforts.[37] In addition, Schweitzer's independent personality and his erratic temperament clashed with the structures of social work; he needed a context that would allow for more personal freedom and minimal control by outside authorities. The colonies granted these conditions in an almost ideal manner, especially after Schweitzer managed to become financially independent, when his work was no longer contingent upon the approval of the missionary societies.

Schweitzer saw Gabon as a fertile ground for his paternalist ideas. In Lambarene he enacted the life of an enlightened ruler, with African serfs, living an agrarian and patriarchal eighteenth-century vision. Schweitzer looked for an empire of his own, and he found it in Africa; here he could be independent and free and could work in ways that were utterly different from the situations he would have encountered in a European clinic, as a social worker or as a priest. Less than a belief in the superiority of a national culture or biological origin, a faith in the legitimacy and redeeming value of European and Christian rule over Africans motivated Schweitzer's enterprise.

The analysis of Schweitzer's cultural philosophy, his theological views, and also his personality, in particular of the formative experiences of his childhood and youth, suggest why Africa was a likely choice for him. Schweitzer's lament concerning the supposed absence of social progress needs to be looked at critically: he did not embrace movements of the period that argued for democracy, emancipation, and equality. Instead, he went to Africa fueled by beliefs of European cultural superiority: the relationship between Europeans and Africans is seen in paternalistic ways, resonating with his experiences as a privileged child among the village boys of Günsbach. He went to Africa as a representative of the upper class, a person easily integrated into the structures of the colonial state. And he went to Africa as a patriarch: his wife and daughter and the female workers at the hospital soon arranged their lives according to his demands.[38] Schweitzer believed in an immediate calling that inspired him to go to Gabon, but this experience more readily explains his insistence on establishing a connection to the Paris Mission Society (instead of joining other, more forthcoming missionary organizations) rather than his choice of Africa in general. The notion of a mystical calling at the heart of his work in Africa has contributed much to fashioning his legend. As demonstrated earlier, other factors explain more convincingly why Schweitzer chose Africa as a site for his enterprise.

Gabon

Schweitzer did not doubt the legitimacy of his mission in Gabon, a situation that becomes evident when we examine his statements about the country and its inhabitants. As preparation for an evaluation of these comments, a look at the history of Gabon provides background material that establishes the connection between the doctor's philosophy and the colonial regime.

Little is known about Gabon during the period before the European presence in the area; uncertainty persists regarding the timing and the conditions of the arrival of the Babongo (Pygmies) and of African Bantu peoples. Since the people of Gabon were illiterate at the time Europeans entered the region, the only written documents available were those of missionaries, explorers, military personnel, and colonial administrators. The recording of oral traditions has contributed to a more detailed knowledge of the people and their histories, but only in the last few decades has data about Gabon been recorded by Gabonese themselves.

The Portuguese were the first Europeans to appear off the coast of Gabon around 1472, naming the area with the terms still used today. Local kingdoms were already established in the area at that time. The advent of European commerce changed the structure of the local societies fundamentally; modes of subsistence, relations between different tribes, and social organization were affected by the introduction of European trade practices and European goods. Toward the end of the sixteenth century Dutch traders began to rival the Portuguese in prominence. Gradually, representatives of other European powers appeared on the coast of Gabon; German, Danish, French, British, and American ships brought traders, who engaged in the exchange of goods with the local population. In addition to ivory, wax, rubber, honey, palm oil, and parrot feathers, slaves were traded, in return for weapons, cloth, metal, alcohol, and trinkets.

It is widely accepted by now that slavery already existed among African societies before the advent of the European influence; individuals were made slaves as punishment for crimes, after defeat in battle, or because of debt. But, as Barnes argues, "slavers from Europe and the Americas exploited this customary practice with their offers of exotic new goods, expanding—and distorting—it into a profitable economic venture."[39] These slavers could also draw on the infrastructure of the Muslim slave trade, although the premodern institution of slavery differed fundamentally from the evolving transatlantic slave trade.[40] In the sixteenth century the Portuguese introduced the large-scale slave trade, which expanded into an active economy by the end of the eighteenth century. By that time the Dutch were also actively participating in the area's slave trade. Both the French and the English began to show interest in the region during the latter part of the eighteenth century. Dyewood and ivory were valued trading goods, but the slave trade continually grew in importance; by 1750 about five thousand slaves were exported annually from the Loango Coast bordering southern Gabon, with many of the slaves captured in Gabon.[41] In the following years these figures increased still more; estimates put the number of slaves exported from the Loango Coast between 1660 and 1793 at nearly one million.[42]

In Gabon proper, merchants from the Mpongwé and Orungu societies were implicated in the slave trade, serving as middlemen by supplying slaves from the hinterland. The Mpongwé leader Antchouwé Kowe Rapontchombo (called King Dénis by the French and King William by the British and Americans) became the leading slave dealer in the area while at the same time also providing forest products.[43] The slave trade had devastating effects on the population of the region; even though it never reached the volume of the trade to the north or south of Gabon, it affected the small population fundamentally, not only decimating the population but also depriving it of its youngest, strongest, and healthiest members. It changed the local economy and pitted different African societies against one another.[44]

Great Britain abolished the slave trade in 1807, and in the aftermath of the Vienna Congress (1815), at which participants signed a declaration abolishing this practice, the British embarked on a crusade against the lucrative trade in humans. The French, who signed the Treaty of Vienna, now increased their interest in the region of Gabon, purportedly aiming at interdicting the slave trade; however, commercial interests and rivalry with the British added other dimensions to the French presence in the area. In 1839 the French established Gabon as a *comptoir* and thus as one of its first territories in Africa (it became a colony in 1906), and by 1846 they had firmly secured their presence in the area. Initially, the French fought slavery only hesitantly, as their actions were carried out somewhat ineffectively during the first years. Yet by the mid-1860s the local slave trade had more or less ceased.[45]

The situation in Gabon after 1845 can be considered protocolonial; indigenous chiefs gradually lost their autonomy to the European nations, and shifts occurred in the power relationships between the local societies. The specialization in trade had eroded the traditional economic structure; alcoholism and disease, often resulting from prostitution, began to decimate the population. In addition to being confronted with the actions of the French colonial regime, Christian missionaries, and European traders, the coastal Mpongwé, among other societies, had to face the Fang people advancing from the hinterland. As Barnes argues, "the arrival of the Fang in Gabon and their subsequent establishment as the single largest ethnic group in the country permanently altered the ethnic balance of power."[46] The French, in particular, favored the Fang and enabled them to overpower the local groups. By the 1860s the Mpongwé population had declined in the course of only twenty years to about a third of its previous numbers.[47] The Orungu likewise had lost their once powerful status by the 1880s.[48]

At the end of the nineteenth century economic activity along the coast of Gabon continued to intensify; while American trade was on the decline and French trade was still insignificant, British and German companies had become increasingly involved in Gabon since the 1860s. The German company Woermann, for example, based in Hamburg, played a decisive role in trade with the area.[49] Germany ranked first in importing the valuable *okoumé* wood until 1939, and it maintains a leading position in trade with Gabon to this day.[50] Germany also participated in the scientific exploration of the area; the Deutsche Gesellschaft zur Erforschung Äquatorialafrikas sent two expeditions to Gabon and the Congo, in 1873–76 and 1874–76.

After the explorer Pierre Savorgnan de Brazza had helped to make the Congo basin accessible from the Gabon coast through his voyages between 1874 and 1882, French interests in the area advanced and efforts were undertaken to strengthen French political dominance in the area.

After the partition agreements of the Congress of Berlin (1884–85), Gabon became part of the French empire in Africa. French colonial rule was especially ruthless in the period immediately following the Congress of Berlin, when "Henri de la Mothe (governor 1898–1901) granted practically unregulated rights to around forty chartered concessionaires over the indigenous peoples of the territory," that is, the Middle Congo.[51] Twelve of these firms were authorized to operate in Gabon. The slave-like labor enforced on the local population, in combination with epidemics and venereal diseases, further depopulated the area. The Colony of Gabon was founded in 1906, and soon afterward Gabon became a part of the French Equatorial African Federation (Afrique Équatoriale Française, or AEF, 1910–60). The implementation of an institutionalized colonial order with a legal and political framework put an end to some of the brutal practices of the earlier period.

Many accounts of Gabonese history do not mention local insurgencies against foreign dominance in the area. These sporadic rebellions against European traders and explorers occurred from 1862 onward. More systematic rebellions followed at the beginning of the twentieth century. From 1903 until after 1913, for example, the Mitsogo fought against the French, who had penetrated their territory. Between 1907 and 1910 the Bayaka attacked Europeans. Likewise, the Binzima, a subgroup of the Fang people, attempted to organize a large-scale rebellion against the French colonizers. These and numerous other, smaller insurgencies were crushed by French military superiority.[52]

As in other countries, colonialism and the founding of Christian missions went hand in hand, although missionaries were occasionally at odds with the colonial state. While French Catholic missionaries have been present in the larger region since the eighteenth century, the first actual missions date back to the 1840s. The first Protestant mission was founded by Americans from the American Board of Commissioners for Foreign Missions in 1842, and a French Catholic mission was founded in Gabon in 1844. The Catholic missionaries were ultimately the more successful: today's Gabon has a significantly larger number of members of the Roman Catholic Church than of any other Christian denomination. Reports show, however, that attempts to convert the population were always difficult. The adverse climate and disease affected the missionaries, and the distrust of the population made the Christianization of

Gabon a Sisyphean task. Even today syncretic religions are widespread in Gabon.[53]

The decolonization process in Gabon, from the Brazzaville Conference of 1944 to formal independence in 1960, was relatively peaceful; this can be partially explained by the fact that France successfully involved members of the local elite who had been raised in mission schools, first including them in the governance of the colonial state and then handing power over to Francophile politicians during decolonization. The first prime minister of the republic, Léon Mba, ruled from 1960 to 1967, gradually suppressing democratic structures until he introduced the one-party state in 1964. A coup in reaction to this measure was put down with the help of French troops, who restored Mba to power. Albert Bernard Bongo (who later converted to Islam and changed his name to Omar Bongo) has ruled the country since 1967 as head of a totalitarian state. In 1990 he undertook the first steps toward establishing a multiparty system. In January 1999, however, Bongo was sworn in for yet another seven-year term as president.[54]

Today Gabon has one of the highest per capita incomes of sub-Saharan Africa because of its large oil resources and its deposits of iron ore, manganese, and uranium. While Gabon was long associated with the timber industry (in 1957, for example, 87% of its total exports were from the sales of *okoumé* wood), the oil industry replaced timber exports in volume by the 1960s.[55] The discovery of oil was a result of French attempts to create its own oil-producing industry in the colonies. The search for oil in French Equatorial Africa began in 1947, and the first successful finds occurred in 1951. Other international companies (Mobil, Shell, and Royal Dutch Shell) soon joined the exploration for oil in Gabon. Today the oil industry is partly nationalized, partly owned by international companies.[56]

France has managed to maintain a secure presence in emancipated Gabon to this day. It holds significant shares in all major sectors of the economy. For example, "the French national oil company, Elf Aquitaine, holds 60 percent of the stock of its Gabonese subsidiary, Elf Gabon, which controls nearly 70 percent of Gabonese petroleum production."[57] Gabon's long-standing ties with France and the country's nondemocratic political structure deprive the population of the benefits of existing resources: the profits go into the pockets of foreign, mostly French, companies and of members of the local elite, who live in ostentatious wealth. In addition, the local economy has not developed alternative sectors, and its dependency on the oil economy makes the country especially vulnerable to external price shocks.

While the economic prosperity of the country has not appropriately benefited the overall population due to corruption, dictatorship, and foreign dependency, the payoff to the larger Gabonese population is visible in some areas. Gabon has one of the highest literacy rates in Africa, estimated at nearly 70 percent.[58] Yet, despite the country's fiscal resources, the medical system continues to be inadequate to fight the special problems of this tiny African nation.

The very recent history of Gabon is not immediately relevant for our excursion into Schweitzer's presence in the country, yet this overview exemplifies the uninterrupted cycle of exploitation observable in Gabon to this day. When Schweitzer arrived in the area in 1913, the country was experiencing a political period that was considered by many as an improvement over the ruthless practices of previous centuries. Yet the local population showed the signs of long-standing exploitation, slavery, forced labor, decimation through disease and alcohol, and general demoralization; it was a people suffering from these afflictions whom Schweitzer encountered as the prototypical Africans. Claude Lévi-Strauss, reflecting in 1995 on his studies of Latin American Indians undertaken in the 1940s, observes that what he had once interpreted as signs of primitivism were actually the result of centuries of colonialist abuse.[59] Schweitzer never arrived at comparable realizations; his thinking was firmly rooted in beliefs about the supremacy of European culture, the progressive nature of historical development, and, of course, the superiority of the Christian religion. Along these lines Schweitzer's hagiographers praise the doctor's mission in Africa and emphasize the presumed benefits of the colonial order, which "saved the Gabonese from slavery."

Schweitzer was fluent in German and French and read Hebrew, Latin, and Greek. But, in the fifty years during which he spent most of his time in Gabon, he never learned any of the local languages. Nor did he ever show any interest in local art or music.[60] He never visited the capital of French Equatorial Africa, Brazzaville, and was generally not interested in Africa per se.[61] This indifference toward African culture is directly related to Schweitzer's assessment of that culture as nonethical and to his belief in his own cultural mission. Convinced that he brings a superior civilization to Africa, he does not even imagine that he might need to familiarize himself with local art and customs. Schweitzer's writings focus on those aspects of Africa that seem to confirm his notion of its nonethical nature. In *Zwischen Wasser und Urwald,* the account of his first stay in Gabon, he mainly elaborates on the characteristics of Africans that emphasize their difference from Europeans and which function to reinforce a sense of the presumably profound distance between European and African cultures.

Especially those forms of behavior that conflict with his reverence for life are seen as indications of an inferior ethical sense. Africans, for example, are unreliable and superstitious;[62] they constantly lie and steal (GW 1, 409; 410–12; 459) and are wasteful (GW 1, 416), irresponsible (GW 1, 437), and cruel to animals (GW 1, 333). He argues that the African, non-Christian sense of justice precludes empathy (GW 1, 385–86). Troubled by what he saw as the lack of a work ethic among the Africans (GW 1, 404; 418–30), Schweitzer explains the need to be hard toward Africans as a result of this lack of discipline and a passion for hard labor (GW 1, 438). In various letters, written during his second stay in Lambarene between 1924 and 1927, Schweitzer restates the concerns he expressed earlier. In *Briefe aus Lambarene* he describes how hard it is to find good workers (GW 1, 491; 546–51). Pointing out how incompetent the workers are (GW 1, 671; 679), he emphasizes their need for constant supervision (GW 1, 493). He portrays Africans as lacking virile vigor and enthusiasm: "The rowers row like a group of ladies on a park's pond" (GW 1, 496). To Schweitzer this lack of a work ethic is a major handicap that delays the building of new additions on the hospital grounds (GW 1, 506–7; 518–21), and it makes supervision and punishment necessary (GW 1, 529–31; 535–37; 550; 626–27; 647; 666). Schweitzer's complaints recall Max Eyth's comments on his Egyptian workers; in both cases European notions of work define the terms of interaction with non-European cultures.

Schweitzer often discusses the superstition of local Africans in contrast to Christian conventions (GW 1, 500–502), and he presents the Africans' perceived lack of empathy and solidarity as tribal ethics (GW 1, 507; 643–44). Schweitzer also describes his daily battle against stealing (GW 1, 509–10; 557; 559; 578), which he explains as a lack of respect for property (GW 1, 557). Africans are easily charmed by valueless objects (GW 1, 553), are generally unreliable (GW 1, 573) and, come hardship, are not resourceful: "Here one doesn't say 'Need makes one ingenious' but 'Need makes one stupid'" (GW 1, 605). A lack of gratitude (GW 1, 515), cruelty toward animals (GW 1, 667), and the absence of ecological thinking (GW 1, 647) are pointed out again and again. Schweitzer considers the absence of ethics (GW 1, 558) as a reflection of the people's state of cultural development: "As true savages they are still quite far beyond good and evil" (GW 1, 555). In Schweitzer's view Africans are still in the realm of the nonethical, but Christianization, Schweitzer argues, will liberate Africans: "Therefore, the native experiences salvation through Jesus as a twofold liberation. He moves from a fearful to a fearless, and from a nonethical to an ethical worldview" (*Zwischen Wasser und Urwald,* GW 1, 457).

How does this view of profound differences between Africans and Europeans compare with the notion of brotherhood often expressed in Schweitzer's writings? "But we, Black and White, sit together and experience it: 'And all ye are brethren.' Alas, if only our donor friends in Europe could be present in such a moment" (GW 1, 402). Such visions of universal brotherhood are a central feature of Schweitzer's public image and explain his broad popular appeal. Yet his notion of brotherhood is qualified; he adds a clause to his vision of harmony: "The Negro is a child. Without authority nothing can be achieved with a child. Therefore I have to define the interaction in a way that reflects my natural authority. For that I coined for the Negroes the term: 'I am your brother, but your older brother'" (GW 1, 435–36). The "natural authority" and "organic superiority" of the European is granted, and, accordingly, real equality is not possible, at least not yet (GW 1, 435, 437). Yet Schweitzer also encourages his readers to look for the human being in the African: "How many beautiful features one discovers in them if one doesn't let oneself be prevented by the many follies of the child of nature to search for the human being in him!" (*Briefe,* GW 1, 685).

Schweitzer's mission in Africa rests on a belief in the predestined role of the European Christian to liberate Africans. Africans are not innately and unchangeably inferior; they are underdeveloped and primitive. Schweitzer grants positive characteristics to Africans that remind one of Rousseau's "noble savage," thus stereotyping Africans through idealization. The "child of nature" is not "spoiled by knowledge" (*Zwischen Wasser und Urwald,* GW 1, 437); he is not lazy but is, rather, a free spirit (GW 1, 420). Africans do reflect upon the world, but they still linger in an "ahistorical view of the world" (GW 1, 455–56). At times, Schweitzer argues, Africans display a potential for ethical rationalism but are still trapped in the realm of a nonethical worldview. Conversion to Christianity is the first step toward acquiring an ethical worldview. Still, the process of conversion is slow: "Through baptism he recants all superstition. But superstition is so grown together with his life and with social life that he will not be free of this for some time to come. . . . Likewise, the ethical conversion remains naturally incomplete" (GW 1, 457–58). The hierarchy that places the European Christian over the African Christian remains as long as the latter persists in the traditional African lifestyle, that is, within African culture, which relegates him, in Schweitzer's view, to the realm of the nonethical. Notions of Christianity are clearly entangled with ideas about culture.

Schweitzer's belief in the superiority of European culture and Christian ethics explains why he never questions the basic structures of colonialism. Although he acknowledges Europe's guilt for its treatment of Africa and sees his mission in Africa as an act of atonement, he believes that Christianity and the right European values will liberate Africans from the realm of the nonethical (GW 1, 472). The colonial state is never questioned; he acknowledges only that it needs to be reformed: "Thus the nations that own colonies need to know that through this [ownership] they have also accepted an immense humanitarian responsibility for their inhabitants" (GW 1, 473). This view, which Schweitzer expressed in 1920, remained basically unchanged throughout his lifetime, even during the decolonization process.

Schweitzer's analysis of the state of contemporary European civilization raises several questions. When Schweitzer speaks of an ethical civilization, he is not thinking about contemporary Europe; after all, he left Europe disillusioned by its failures. He even acknowledges that he might be needed there just as much, because "Europe is ruined and trapped in misery." But he suggests that it doesn't matter where one starts (GW 1, 475). Schweitzer describes how he attempts to hide news about World War I from Africans because the war challenges the image of European Christian culture he would like to convey (GW 1, 440–42;

453). In another passage he voices his anger over con artists who bring European versions of superstition, such as astrology and clairvoyance, to Africa and thereby undermine Schweitzer's image of enlightened Europe (*Briefe*, GW 1, 668–69). These passages demonstrate the contradictions in Schweitzer's approach: in order to view African cultures as irrational and barbaric, he has to suppress those aspects of European culture that would clash with the image of Europe he intends to convey.

Schweitzer's vision of an ideal society amounts to a fantasy of an essentially patriarchal, authoritarian, premodern order, distinguished by blurry notions of reason, rationality, individuality, and reverence for life, a vision that clashes with the violent realities of modern Europe. His colonialist approach to Africa, however, is not based on nationalism or biological racism. In fact, Schweitzer strongly attacked biologists and other natural scientists for attempting to solve ethical questions through their research. Schweitzer criticized biological thinking that attaches ethical values to, for example, Darwin's principle of selection.[63] Especially in opposition to Herbert Spencer's *The Principles of Ethics* (1879), Schweitzer writes in *Kultur und Ethik:* "Ethics when related to processes occurring in nature ceases to exist. This dilemma holds true not only in those situations where ethics is inferred from natural philosophy, but also where ethics is explained through biology" (GW 2, 280). There is a contradiction between this stance and Schweitzer's idea of reverence for life, since he too bases his philosophy on principles of nature, insofar as he sees the will to life as a fundamental "natural" principle that ought to be honored. But reverence for life is incompatible with Darwinism because it implies protection for weaker forms of life and alleviation of the evils of the world through good deeds.

Schweitzer never elaborates on perceived physical differences between Africans and Europeans. While he is aware of specific diseases that exist in Africa, racist claims that depict Africans as being distinguished by differences in blood, size of brain, joints, sexual organs, skin, glands, and so forth never appear in Schweitzer's texts. He quite explicitly rejects the widespread notion that Africans are more tolerant of pain, describing pain, instead, as one of the universals uniting humankind (*Zwischen Wasser und Urwald*, GW 1, 471). The vast corpus of biological and anthropological literature on the physical differences between human beings, such as texts by Buffon, Darwin, de Gobineau, Kant, and Meiners, does not surface in Schweitzer's writings.[64]

Schweitzer's thinking is firmly grounded in his Christian faith and in his belief in the superiority of European culture. He does not discard African culture on the basis of biological racism but, rather, explains the differences through an assessment of the perceived stages of cultural development. At times he even points out the social logic of African customs; for example, he approves of polygamy, because it responds to the perceived needs of African society (*GW* 1, 431–35). Schweitzer explains these customs in terms of the organization of African societies. He does believe, however, that Africans can become "full human beings," "civilized," "cultured." It will take some time and guidance from Europeans, but Africans are not innately different. They are at a different stage in their cultural development, but they are theoretically able to ascend to the higher forms of culture exemplified by European societies. Schweitzer's attitude thus resonates with that of Enlightenment thinkers who brought Africans to Europe to educate them and to demonstrate that they were capable of civilization in the European sense and that only their lack of education accounted for what they saw as a lack of culture and progress.[65]

Schweitzer's reverence for life does not, then, offer unqualified acceptance to all life forms. On the one hand, Schweitzer insists on the equality of all life. But as Gotthard Teutsch explains, this equality does not imply, for example, an absolute ban on killing. Reverence for life has to be understood as "reverence for life based on a duty to be humanitarian."[66] Accordingly, it is possible that life forms that conflict with the humanity of another life could be killed or restricted in other ways. Depending on the definition of *humanitarian,* it is conceivable that the existing differences can result in differentiating, and thus potentially discriminating, treatment.

Whether Schweitzer's belief in superiority was based on biological, theological, or philosophical thought matters only little, since the outcome is the same. Even if he does not use biological racism in his own arguments, the influence of racialist thinking is evident in his cultural superiority complex. Africans can become Christians, but real equality will only be achieved once they give up their African lifestyle and become Europeanized. This explains why Schweitzer never questions colonialism per se. He is convinced that Africans ought to be taught how to work for the benefit of the colonies, because the colonies ultimately bring civilization to Africa: "I do not consider forced labor wrong in principle; practically, however, it is not feasible. One cannot manage in the colonies without forced labor on a small scale" (*Zwischen Wasser und Urwald,* GW 1, 425). Schweitzer suggests that Africans at times need to be coerced to do work from which they will ultimately benefit. In order to put an end to porterage he proposes building roads and thus expanding motorized traffic: "In order to save life, therefore, it may become essential . . . to build the road by forced labour."[67]

Schweitzer wholeheartedly supports the colonial paradigm. He downplays, for example, the commercial benefits of the wood trade: "In this sense, one cannot talk about the wood traders' exploitation of the workers who migrated from the interior, implying that the workers receive too little compensation for their work. What these primitives achieve often stands in no relation to the costs incurred by their nourishment and the wage that they are entitled to receive after completion of the work contract. . . . It may sound strange, but nowhere are workmen more expensive in relation to the actually accomplished labor than in the primeval forest" (*Briefe,* GW 1, 551).

Even though he is critical of extreme abuses and certain practices of rogue traders, his suggestions are directed at *reforming* the colonial system, not abolishing it. W. E. B. Du Bois describes the contradictions between one Schweitzer, who dedicated his life to helping Africans, and the other, who defended the colonial system. He comes to a generous conclusion in his assessment of the doctor by granting that Schweitzer had "no broad grasp of what modern exploitation means, of what imperial colonialism has done to the world."[68]

But how could Schweitzer have missed the connection between economic exploitation, the history of Gabon, and the predicaments of its inhabitants? Schweitzer was blinded by his firm belief in a righteous mission to bring European civilization and Christianity to Africa. Both ideological systems are intertwined, with Christianity's missionary fervor equally present in the cultural civilizing mission. For Schweitzer the right to colonize is legitimate if the colonizers develop a new (and "normal," as Schweitzer puts it) social order for the natives.[69] His vision of a normal society, however, is based on premodern notions of the state, an order closer to the patriarchal feudal system than to modern European constitutional states.

Schweitzer's views did not fundamentally change over the years. The texts quoted thus far were predominantly written in the 1920s, but his later statements confirm his earlier views. Schweitzer pointed out what he considered as the negative effects of higher education for Africans, and he frequently voiced his impatience with Africans who claimed to be intellectuals or wanted to be writers.[70] He claimed that Africans should first be trained in agriculture and handicrafts. These comments express what Chinua Achebe deplored at the 1998 meeting of the African Literature Association in Austin: in the eyes of Europeans, Africa and education do not mix.[71]

Schweitzer's Legacy

Schweitzer believed that Africans first needed to become more culturally evolved human beings before they could be allowed to govern themselves politically: "The task of the whites is to make good and worthy people out of the natives. . . . The chief goal can only be that they should assimilate under the most favorable conditions whatever in civilization is useful and essential to them, thereby becoming people of real worth and humanity. When they have made this measure of progress, they may then decide whether it is imperative that they should govern themselves."[72]

Schweitzer's 1948 comment looks more than awkward in light of the European atrocities of the twentieth century. In two world wars millions of Europeans had slaughtered, exterminated, tortured, mutilated, and raped millions of European and non-European peoples. Germans, in particular, had displayed tremendous cruelty. How is one to explain Schweitzer's blindness, his inability to recognize the shortcomings of European culture, and his condescension and arrogance toward Africans?

Schweitzer was publicly celebrated for his humanitarian work throughout his life. In 1928 he received the Frankfurt Goethe Prize; in 1951 he was honored with the peace prize of the German publishers; and in 1953 he received the Nobel Peace Prize retroactively for 1952, accepting it in 1954 in Oslo. After 1957 Schweitzer was actively involved in an international campaign against nuclear weapons. He was respected by intellectuals and politicians from around the world; his abundant correspondence includes letters to and from Martin Buber, Benedetto Croce, Albert Einstein, Werner Heisenberg, Queen Juliana of Holland, Jawaharlal Nehru, Martin Niemöller, Romain Rolland, Bertrand Russell, Rabindranath Tagore, and Thornton Wilder. In 1947 *Life* magazine celebrated him as "the greatest man of the century," and he became a global symbol of humanism and altruism.

Through it all Schweitzer continued to defend colonialism. In a letter to Dwight D. Eisenhower he urged the American president to support the French position against Algeria's push for independence at a United Nations meeting in 1958.[73] In a conversation with Konrad Adenauer he declared South Africa's system of apartheid the right way to deal with Africans.[74] At the beginning of the century Schweitzer's view of Africans might have been a relative improvement over the racism prevalent in Europe. But by the mid-1950s his attitude had become truly reactionary. To excuse Schweitzer's views simply as a reflection of the dominant thinking of his time releases him from his moral responsibility. Scores of contemporary intellectuals and artists were able to grasp the connections between colonialism and exploitation and challenged the right of Europeans to dominate other cultures.

Schweitzer was born in the nineteenth century, in the same year as Carl Gustav Jung, Thomas Mann, and Ferdinand Porsche; he lived through two world wars, genocides, and fascism and witnessed most African countries' arrival at independence. In the year he was born the first bicycle with a freewheel hub and backpedal brake was invented; he died in 1965, shortly before the first man walked on the moon. In some ways Schweitzer mirrors the contradictions of this century, and his inability to respond to historical changes makes him representative in many ways. Stuck in traditional beliefs and motivated by a zealous faith in the superiority of European Christian culture, he represents the end (one hopes) of an era.

Today Schweitzer, in spite of the views he held about Africa, stands uncontested as a symbol of humanism and selflessness, having survived the criticism that has been voiced repeatedly since the 1920s. The biographical (and mostly hagiographical) literature on Schweitzer that dates back to the 1920s swelled after World War II. Many saw in him a symbol of a reformed Western culture, with particular relevance to the problems of the postwar world. Biographies and studies were published in French, English, German, and other languages, including Japanese, with the most extensive edition of his collected writings published in that language.

How can we explain the persistence of the importance of Schweitzer? I suggest that Schweitzer has provided Germans (and, in somewhat different ways, other Western nations) with an alibi; he has played an exculpatory role, especially after World War II, by offering Germans a role model that seemed to defy ideological constraints by representing a new humanism and a charismatic alternative to the racist ideology of the National Socialists. At the same time, the discourse on Schweitzer served to perpetuate images of Africans as inferior, needy, and incapable of taking care of themselves. It legitimized continued German (and generally Western) presence in Africa and ultimately strengthened the belief in the legality of Western domination of Africa.

Biographies in both East and West Germany written since the 1960s emphasize two aspects of the doctor's story: Schweitzer as a role model providing spiritual guidance and Schweitzer as a representative European bringing culture, religion, and technology to backward Africans.[75] Throughout these works Africa is portrayed as incapable of governing itself. At times Africans rise to the status of noble savages, but, as Schweitzer and his assistants put it, "How nice Africa would be without the savages."[76]

These and other sentiments suggest how Schweitzer lent himself to become Europe's and, in particular, Germany's ideal alibi. Postwar accounts of his work thus function on two levels: on the one hand, they are geared toward the spiritual rejuvenation of a morally bankrupt Germany (and Europe) after World War II. Yet, on the other, they lead also to an exculpation of Germans and a validation of a Eurocentrist and indeed supremacist worldview. Even while the West looked to Schweitzer as a role model, European powers were fighting brutal colonial wars against independence movements in Africa and Asia. These writings divert attention from the horrors occurring in Africa by celebrating the righteous Dr. Schweitzer and by hailing the good that Europe had brought to the continent, thus legitimating colonialism and European hegemony. Far from spurring a reevaluation of colonialism's effects, Schweitzer's presence in Africa resulted in their affirmation.

It is important to note that Schweitzer never went native: he never moved permanently from Europe to Africa but continued to travel back and forth between the two. Schweitzer publicized himself and his project by holding fund-raising events; he went on numerous concert tours, for example, to raise money for Lambarene. The carefully designed public image served to guarantee the financial independence of the doctor, but it is also crucial for understanding his function as icon and alibi. He never learned an African language, and he never bothered to familiarize himself with the African cultural context. In reality and in the European imagination he contained symbolic value as the guardian of colonial continuity: playing Bach, holding Christian services, writing letters to heads of state and intellectuals all over the world, and practicing medicine, he embodied the continued presence of European high culture, religion, politics, and modern technology in Africa.

Since the end of World War II many have seen in Schweitzer the prophet of a reformed Western culture. The vagueness of his ideas and the contradictions they contained made Schweitzer into a protean ideal who attracted followers from every ideological camp. Schweitzer was an eminent theologian, music theoretician, and doctor, and he inspired scores of individuals to help others in need. His notions of culture and development, however, prove to be highly problematic. One wishes he had not written a word about Africans, and one wishes, with W. E. B. Du Bois, that he had set out "to heal the souls of white Europe rather than the bodies of black Africa."[77] In the Foucauldian sense Schweitzer's name stands for more than an author, for Schweitzer, his writings, and his work created a discourse. It is a discourse integral to colonial thinking, a paradigm for the relationship between industrialized and developing countries, a discourse still omnipresent today.

3

The Globalizing Mission

Ernst Udet in East Africa

Piloten ist nichts verboten. — German song, 1932

The Symbolic Power of the Pilot

The history of aviation in the early twentieth century provides a unique entry into understanding the dynamism, energy, dreams, and ambitions of the modern Western world. Aviation most visibly authenticated the developments in technology that allowed people to advance into areas previously the subject of fiction. Flying was made possible by both technological achievements and the personal courage of individuals, and it inspired many to embark on daring endeavors, releasing and producing social energies that extended to all areas of life. The progress that had been made in aviation was crucial in deciding the outcome of World War I, when bombing from aircraft had a devastating impact for the first time. At the same time, "the invention of the airplane was at first perceived by many as an *aesthetic* event with far-reaching implications for the new century's artistic and moral sensibility."[1] Airplanes inspired modernist poets and painters as much as intellectuals and politicians. Aviation and the figure of the pilot became vehicles to articulate the desires and concerns connected to modern life.

The pilots who risked their lives to test the boundaries of human power over nature became the heroes of the modern age. The public followed significant events closely: in 1895 Otto Lilienthal (1848–96), the first true aviator, successfully flew the first of his three biplane hang gliders. Only one year later he died after a crash with one of his monoplane hang gliders. In 1899 the Wright brothers, Wilbur (1867–1912) and

Orville (1871–1948), built their first aircraft, a biplane kite, and began testing their No. 1 glider in 1900, which eventually led them to powered flying. In 1927 Charles A. Lindbergh (1902–74) made the first solo nonstop transatlantic flight. Lindbergh's flight was received with great enthusiasm; it was portrayed by playwrights and filmmakers and inspired further improvements in aviation.

In this early period of aviation pilots were public personas, imbued with an enormous symbolic power. Many pilots wrote highly popular autobiographies, and others wrote biographies about them that led to their further immortalization. Among the pilots were a significant number of women, whose achievements were widely praised as milestones in the struggle for women's rights. Harriet Quimby (1875–1912), Amelia Earhart (1897–1937), Beryl Markham (1902–86), and Elly Beinhorn (1907–36) continue to symbolize this struggle to this day.

In Germany the figure of the pilot was omnipresent in cultural representations: from works by Bertolt Brecht (such as his radio play *Der Flug der Lindberghs,* 1929; and his play *Der gute Mensch von Sezuan,* 1941) to film comedies with Heinz Rühmann (*Quax, der Bruchpilot,* 1941; *Quax in Afrika,* 1945), fictional pilots personified the struggle of the modern individual. The phrase "Piloten ist nichts verboten" (Nothing is off limits to pilots), taken from a song that was presented in the 1932 film *F.P.1 antwortet nicht,* which starred the charismatic Hans Albers in the role of the pilot, is the most enthusiastic expression of this obsession with pilots. But an investigation of the history of aviation and the meaning of its imagery during the first half of the twentieth century offers insights not only into the technological advances and changing social relations of a modernizing society but also into its political dynamic. In an exemplary study of the role aviation played in shaping the German national imagination, Peter Fritzsche explores the impact of aviation on the development of German nationalism from the Wilhelmine Empire through the Nazi period. Taking the Nazi slogan "We must become a nation of fliers" as a starting point, he shows how Germans derived a sense of empowerment from their nation's successes in aviation. Pilots became symbols of a development that tied together technological progress and nation building. The importance of aviation for the national self-image led to further investment in its development and to continuing advances in the field, thus perpetuating and constantly feeding a euphoria that was a great fount for the creation of an empowered image of the nation.

Evoking the figure of Daedalus, "who designed weapons for King Minos of Crete before he fell out of royal favor and constructed wings to flee to Sicily," Fritzsche points out that the story of aviation has always contained the vexed contradiction between the ambitions of the individual and the power of the state.[2] Individual pilots became heroes whose symbolic power extended to areas beyond their actual flying. The success of Graf Zeppelin, for example, contributed to increasing the belief in the might of the Wilhelmine state. In other instances the relationship between the pilot and the state was more direct, which is most clearly demonstrated in the case of World War I flying aces. Stories about heroic figures such as the "Red Baron," Manfred von Richthofen, "are more familiar today than those of World War I generals."[3]

This complicated relationship can also be observed in the case of Ernst Udet, a star pilot since the end of World War I whose attitude toward the different states he served was never quite clear but who, in the end, became entangled in fascism's destructive missions. The following pages explore the ways in which Udet brought the power of the symbolic function of the pilot to the German dream of recapturing a colonial empire. Other famous pilots of the first half of the twentieth century are also associated with Africa and in some cases offered written accounts of the continent: Antoine de Saint-Exupéry (1900–1944) wrote about northern Africa in *Wind, Sand and Stars* (1939); Amelia Earhart reported her views of Africa when she crossed the continent on her way around the world (*Last Flight*, 1937); Elly Beinhorn published *180 Stunden über Afrika* (1933); and Beryl Markham, who had lived in British East Africa since 1906, added *West with the Night* (1942) to this particular type of autobiography. In each of these cases Africa takes on a unique significance.

Udet starred in a movie that was shot in East Africa in 1930–31 and premiered in Germany on April 12, 1932, as *Fliehende Schatten* (Fleeting shadows). The pilot's autobiographical report about this trip to the area, entitled *Fremde Vögel über Afrika* (Strange birds over Africa), was published in the same year. At a moment when Germany was at the brink of entering the Nazi period, both the film and the book take a positive stance toward the native inhabitants of East Africa, presenting them as amiable, even modern individuals. A closer analysis of these two views of Africa, however, reveals quite distinct trajectories. The film, originally conceived by the director Carl Junghans, articulates questions related to the representation of Africa itself. Udet's account, on the other hand, seems more closely to reflect the German desire for the lost colonies. But the dream of recapturing the lost colonial empire is expressed in ways different from the narrative strategies familiar from the early period of colonization and from the racism of the National Socialists. Udet's East Africa emerges as a utopian space; the pilot functions as the harbinger of modernity, introducing modern times to new territories.

At this juncture—the process of bringing and offering modernity to Africans—lays the connection to the concept of mission. What is Udet's role in East Africa? How does he present his encounter with Africans, and what are the implications of that presentation? Does Udet's sympathetic portrayal of indigenous people entail a critique of colonialism? Further, to begin this exploration by situating the text historically, how does his view of East Africa fit into the corpus of German representations of the region, from the time before the establishment of German East Africa to the late Weimar period?

Germans in East Africa

Udet's book and the film he starred in are part of a considerable corpus of fictional and nonfictional literature in German about East Africa, which dates back to the early nineteenth century and continues into our time, when German tourists, doctors, and aid workers offer their views on the region (today particularly on Kenya, which will be explored further in chapter 5). In addition, a vast number of documents exist that cover the period of German colonialism in East Africa.[4] This textual archive reflects the range of ideological components that fed the colonial endeavor: Christianity, the belief in progress, modernization and a civilizing mission, economic motifs, nationalism, and views of cultural and racial superiority.

In the nineteenth century German language fictional and nonfictional texts about Africa became popular in the context of Europe's colonization of the continent. Even before the founding of German colonies in Africa, countless texts were written that document the increasing engagement of Germany in Africa, namely in three areas: missionary activities, scientific exploration, and trade. With regard to East Africa,

Germans focused on an area that formed Deutsch-Ostafrika from 1885 to 1918, and largely reflects the area of today's mainland Tanzania, and later also the territories of Rwanda and Burundi.

The explorer, missionary, and linguist Johann Ludwig Krapf (1810–81) was a key figure inspiring and reflecting the German interests in East Africa. Together with Johannes Rebmann (1820–76), who also conducted linguistic research, Krapf served for the Church Missionary Society and established a missionary station at Rabai, not far from Mombasa. Krapf's autobiographical account, *Reisen in Ostafrika, ausgeführt in den Jahren 1837–55* (Travels in East Africa, undertaken in the years 1837–55), was published in 1858; contemporary biographies by, for example, W. Claus attest to his significance as a public figure who was influential in shaping the collective imagination. The increased missionary activity in the area is well documented in accounts by Gustav Emil Burkhardt, among others. Also in the precolonial period, Hermann von Barth, F. Kurtz, Gustav Plieninger, and Herman Schalow were among the writers reporting on explorations and other scientific expeditions. The fact that many of these accounts were written before the founding of the German colony in East Africa illustrates the direct relationship between scientific and missionary exploration and the ensuing economic and political occupation. At times this nexus of political, religious, and economic interests in Africa was personified in one person, such as Friedrich Fabri, whose 1879 pamphlet *Bedarf Deutschland der Colonien?* became one of the pivotal texts of the German colonial movement. Fabri was a leading figure of the Rhenish Missionary Society, the largest German missionary organization; at the same time, Fabri was also involved in economic and political activities.

Changing attitudes toward a colonial empire surfaced in Germany in the 1840s, especially in conjunction with the revolution of 1848. While the earlier call for colonies had been economically and politically motivated, it now also included arguments rooted in a presumed need for new territories to accommodate the growing German population and also in the national interests of the emerging bourgeoisie.[5] Initially, the main energies of the German colonial movement were directed toward South Africa, South and Central America, New Zealand, North America, and, beginning in the 1850 and 1860s, the Far East. As a goal of German colonialists, East Africa joined this list of targeted territories relatively late. Yet the emergence of organizations promoting German colonies in Africa, such as the Deutsche Afrikanische Gesellschaft and the Deutsche Gesellschaft zur Erforschung Äquatorial-Afrikas, both of which merged to form the Afrikanische Gesellschaft in Deutschland in 1878, was preceded by economic activity in the area. In particular, the large companies of Adolph Jakob Hertz, William O'Swald & Company, and Hansing & Company, all based in Hamburg, had established themselves successfully in Zanzibar after 1844. The island had become a center for trade in the first half of the century, through trade in slaves, ivory, cowry shells, cloves, cotton, and later firearms. As John Iliffe points out, "East Africa was probably the only part of the world where slavery became markedly more common throughout the nineteenth century."[6]

In spite of the strong antislavery movement that had increased in size and influence throughout the nineteenth century, German merchants did not hesitate to establish themselves in an economy still intertwined with slavery. In the 1850s about twenty German ships sailed regularly between Hamburg and Zanzibar. It is interesting to note and reflective of the period before the founding of the German colonial empire that after 1857, in response to an initiative of William O'Swald & Company, German ships and warehouses operated under the protection of the British government in West Africa. In East Africa, where a treaty had been signed between the sultan of Zanzibar and the Hanseatic Republic in 1859, O'Swald was able to expand its position further throughout the 1860s. Already in 1859, Zanzibar exported 16.5 percent of its goods to Hamburg, and 30 percent of its imports came from the German city.[7] By 1864–65 Zanzibar's exports to Hamburg reached 29 percent, and its imports grew to 40 percent.[8] After the founding of the colony in 1885, O'Swald was instrumental in setting up regular steamship transportation to East Africa and a network of trading stations on the coast and in the interior.[9] O'Swald was also responsible for increasing the amount of weapons available in the area, which facilitated the slave trade and internecine warfare between local populations in significant ways.[10]

German companies played a central role in convincing Bismarck to change his mind about colonies. In the scramble for Africa the German chancellor felt the pressure from many sides. The British and French empires were expanding, and, increasingly, German merchants voiced their concerns for their safety and freedom to operate. Especially Adolph

Woermann, whose company dominated the German West Africa trade, helped to convince the chancellor that new measures were necessary.[11] In 1885, one year after the German empire established protectorates in Southwest Africa, Togo, and Cameroon, it responded to the activities of the notorious Carl Peters (1856–1918), one of the leading proponents of German colonialism and a key figure in East Africa. He was infamous for his use of violence and excessive cruelty in dealing with Africans. The German empire gave protection to his East Africa Society, and Britain recognized the German protectorate in East Africa in 1886. Peters had founded the East African Society to accommodate Bismarck's idea of a colonial empire that was mainly geared toward the protection of merchants, an idea based on the model of the British charter company system.[12] But the institution of the East African colony should be seen in relation to the fact that economic and missionary activity was well established in the area, even before the German Africa organization brought these territories to the attention of the German public. In addition, especially companies such as O'Swald were often fundamentally critical of and opposed to the colonial politics of the German state.[13]

Bismarck's idea to leave the colonial regime entirely in the hands of the merchants proved to be unfeasible and was quickly abandoned. A colonial bureaucracy was soon established, and the systematic subjugation of the local population was ruthlessly carried out by administrators and military units. The colonial regime was met with steady resistance in the African territories from the beginning. One of the bloodiest conflicts was the catastrophic war between the Germans and the Herero and Nama in German Southwest Africa in 1904, which reduced the number of Herero by 80 percent and of the Nama by about 50 percent. Lieutenant General Lothar von Trotha, who was in charge of the German army, issued one of first state-supported orders for the elimination of an entire enemy population, extending beyond the goal of military victory. By the time the war was officially over, on March 31, 1907, approximately seventy thousand Africans had been killed in this genocide.

The confrontation between colonizers and native population escalated in East Africa as well, in response to further imposition of taxes and other oppressive regulations. The introduction of cotton farming and forced labor on the fields played a significant role, another chapter in the nefarious history of cotton farming.[14] The actions of the German colonial rulers differed from those of the regime in German Southwest Africa; they "had no intention of 'ethnically cleansing' any region of East Africa intended as a major producer of cash crops."[15] Nevertheless, the result of the war that broke out in 1905 was devastating. According to contemporary German figures, the Maji-Maji uprising, as this war between colonizer and colonized is known, cost the lives of 75,000 Africans, but the real figures are probably far higher. G. C. K. Gwassa and John Iliffe argue that between 250,000 and 300,000 Africans died, approximately a third of the population in the area.[16] In contrast, according to German government figures, Africans killed "15 Europeans, 73 askari and 316 auxiliaries."[17]

After this war ended, the atrocities committed in the colonies led to debates over how to revise the policies toward the native population. The new governor of East Africa, Albrecht Freiherr von Rechenberg, with the support of Bernhard Dernburg, Germany's first secretary for the colonies since 1907, in the newly established colonial office (*Reichskolonialamt*), tried to introduce a more collaborative approach toward the native population. But the new policies were rejected by both the settlers and the colonial administration in Germany, and in late 1911, after conflicts with the next secretary for the colonies, Friedrich von Lindequist, Rechenberg resigned.[18] The memory of the confrontation is well alive today. According to nationalist historians, the Maji-Maji uprising was the first circumstance during which several ethnic groups of Tanzania acted as a unified people.[19] Some scholars stress the significance of this fact for subsequent movements for independence and the development of Tanzanian nationalism.[20] Others have challenged this thesis by pointing to features and events of the revolt that let a more complex picture emerge.[21]

Until World War I put an end to Deutsch-Ostafrika, publications about the region discussed the different trajectories pursued by agencies and individuals in East Africa. The many works written by and about missionaries document the increasing activity after the founding of the colony; by 1912 approximately 171 mission stations had been established in Tanganyika.[22] In addition to book publications, numerous periodicals published by the different missionary societies consistently kept the attention of the German public on East Africa.[23] Exploration and adventure was the topic of many autobiographical accounts by, for example,

Eugen Krenzler, Kapitän Spring, and Wilhelm Wolfrum. W. Brandt's *Mwalimu wa kidachi: Deutsche Sprachlehre für Eingeborene von Ostafrika* (1909), specifically aimed at members of the local population who were encouraged to learn German, documents an element of the German administration's language policy.[24] Economic, historical, and anthropological accounts by, for example, Karl Dove, C. Falkenhorst, Gustav Meinecke, and Karl Weule addressed the different areas of interest in the territory; studies in the natural sciences also abounded. Some texts comment on the bloody conflicts between the German empire and the local population, such as the Maji-Maji uprising. Other publications continued to promote the colony to German citizens as an area for migration, such as Frieda von Bülow's ever-popular novels.

With the end of World War I, the German colonial empire ceased to exist. Togo was the first colony to fall, while East Africa, under the military commander Paul von Lettow-Vorbeck (1870–1964), held out the longest, until it capitulated on November 25, 1918. Nevertheless, German fantasies about regaining the colonies persisted. Autobiographical texts by von Lettow-Vorbeck, for example, were highly popular, translated into other languages and often reprinted over several decades, surviving even beyond the 1950s.[25]

The most important proponent of the colonial dream was Heinrich Schnee (1871–1949), the last governor of German East Africa. His book *Die koloniale Schuldlüge* (1924) was translated into English, French, Spanish, and Italian and was reprinted repeatedly; by 1940, 50,000 copies had been printed.[26] In a similar vein Hans Grimm's *Volk ohne Raum* (1926) became one of the most influential texts promoting colonial ideology. While liberal and leftist circles were increasingly critical of colonialism, the foreign ministry nevertheless reestablished a colonial office (*Kolonialabteilung*) on April 1, 1924. Gustav Stresemann, the Weimar Republic's liberal foreign minister from 1923 to 1929, never vigorously pursued a political course aimed at regaining colonies for Germany, a fact that brought pro-colonial circles closer to the right-wing parties. The responses to a 1927 poll of leading public figures, asking whether Germany should pursue colonial politics, are instructive: while Albert Einstein and Thomas Mann spoke out against the colonial idea, Konrad Adenauer, chancellor of West Germany from 1949 to 1963, supported it.[27]

Some authors, such as Artur Heye, Friedrich Wilhelm Mader, Hans Paasche, and Karl Roehl kept the German passion for East Africa alive by combining a fascination for its nature and wildlife with colonial war stories. Other writers, such as Heinrich Fonck, Wilhelm Rothhaupt, and Hans Walter Schmidt, were less concerned with military confrontations but also continued to appeal to the German longing for a colony in the area. In a similar vein monographs by, among others, Charlotte Deppe and Hans Zache contained general information about the former colony and were aimed at potential emigrants. The era also produced studies in the natural and social sciences. Publications by the Buchhandlung der Berliner evangelischen Missionsgesellschaft and by Curt Ronicke, a well-known writer who continued to publicize the work of missionaries in East Africa from the 1930s well into the 1950s, attest to the continued presence of the missionary societies.

Into this period, which saw a plethora of publications about the former German colony, falls Udet's encounter with East Africa. And, as Udet's case demonstrates, East Africa was not only the subject of German book and journal publications but was also evoked in films and photographs. What brought Udet to the filming of *Fliehende Schatten* and the publication of *Fremde Vögel über Africa?*

Ernst Udet

Ernst Udet was born in Frankfurt am Main on April 26, 1896.[28] Shortly after his birth, the family moved to Munich. Already as a little child, Udet was fascinated with flying, building model airplanes and, together with a group of other youths, founding the "Aero-Club München 1909," which mostly researched and built model planes. While still a teenager, Udet also constructed a small glider, but it got him off the ground only for a few seconds. The euphoria that surrounded the beginning of World War I caught Udet as well; he volunteered to enlist with the army but was rejected because of his height—he was only five foot three inches tall. Udet was determined; using his own money, he had himself trained as a pilot by Gustav Otto in Munich and, after receiving his license as a pilot, reapplied to the army in April 1915. To the great disappointment of the ambitious young man, he was rejected once more, this time because of his age. Unrelenting, he tried his luck in Prussia, where he was accepted but was not immediately allowed to fly. Finally, in September 1915, at the age of nineteen, he began his career as a pilot.

Udet became one of the heroes of World War I. The pilot's great success at downing enemy planes made him the most celebrated German pilot after the legendary Richthofen. Udet shot down his first enemy airplane in March 1916 and by the end of the war had destroyed sixty-two planes. In April 1918 Udet was decorated for his twentieth downing with one of the top-ranking honors of the German military, the order Pour le Merité. For the last few months of the war Udet flew as part of Richthofen's famous squadron. There he also met Hermann Göring, who was put in charge of the unit after Richthofen's death in April 1918.

Several biographers emphasize the chivalrous and pleasant character of Udet, and contrast his civil behavior with the loud, military conduct of Hermann Göring.[29] Udet's behavior in combat was inspired by a heroic code of honor. As Fritzsche explains: "Much of the power of the image of the ace comes from its contrast to that of the infantryman in the trenches. Fliers fought an individual rather than a collective and anonymous war."[30] The code of honor associated with pilots seems to have been predominant among pilots on all sides and is documented, for example, by the funeral that was given to Richthofen after he was shot down by the Canadian Roy Brown. Richthofen was buried with military honors by the British Royal Air Force; six pilots carried Richthofen's coffin, and the procession was followed by over one hundred English and French pilots. Udet recounts another instance of this chivalry in his autobiography *Mein Fliegerleben.* He describes the presence of a British major who had been shot down and stayed in the German camp as a prisoner but was allowed to move around freely. Udet calls him a "gentleman," and the fact that this gentleman later successfully escaped is rendered as a humorous episode.[31] Udet also remembers how one of his pictures, on which the words "As des as" (Ace of aces) were written, was once found with a dead pilot.[32]

After the war the Versailles Treaty largely limited any developments in German aeronautics and ordered the destruction of warplanes, but Udet's passion for airplanes was not to be fettered. Even before the restrictions against the flying and building of airplanes were lifted in 1922, Udet began constructing his first plane. In late 1922 he officially announced the establishment of his own company, Udet-Flugzeugbau. For the next few years Udet built airplanes, participated in competitions, and flew spectacular stunts at air shows that drew crowds of up to 60,000 people.[33] He also made a name for himself with his caricatures, some of which were published as *Hals- und Beinbruch: 100 lustige Karikaturen* in 1928. C. K. Roellinghoff added four-line verses to Udet's comical drawings.

Udet's popularity increased even further when he began to star in films. *Der Alpensegler* (1927) documented his gliding flight from the *Zugspitze,* and in *5 Minuten mit Udet* (1929) he advertised a new razor blade. In 1929 he flew breathtaking stunts that were taken by many as tricks in Arnold Fanck's *Die weiße Hölle von Piz Palü.* The film also starred Leni Riefenstahl, with whom Udet developed a lifelong friendship. In addition, the ace flew and acted in another mountain film by Fanck, *Stürme über dem Montblanc* (1930), in which Riefenstahl also appeared.[34] The next film in which Udet was to star was *Fliehende Schatten* (*Fleeting Shadows*).

Fleeting Shadows—Debunking the *Afrikafilm*

Even though Udet neither wrote the script nor directed the film, the movie has often been described as "Udet's film" or "Udet's Africa-film." This attribution attests to the popularity of the pilot, who had added his symbolic power to the enterprise. In November 1930 Udet arrived in East Africa with a production crew of eleven members that brought together a number of well-known figures from the film industry, many of whom had previously collaborated. The film director was Carl Junghans, who made a series of highly popular films during the Weimar Republic and later combined forces again with Udet for the documentary of the Fourth Olympic Winter Games in Garmisch-Partenkirchen (*Jugend der Welt,* 1936). The camera team consisted of Hans Schneeberger and Werner Bohne. Schneeberger had collaborated with Arnold Fanck in a number of successful films (*Der Berg des Schicksals,* 1923–24; *Der Heilige Berg,* 1925–26; *Die weiße Hölle vom Piz Palü,* 1929; and many others) but also worked for directors such as Josef von Sternberg (*Der blaue Engel,* 1930). After *Fliehende Schatten* Schneeberger brought his creative talents to Riefenstahl's breathtaking film *Das blaue Licht,* which was shot in 1931 and premiered in early 1932. Bohne would go on to work on Riefenstahl's *Triumph des Willens* (1935) and also shot comedies, such as *Amphityron* (Reinhold Schünzel, 1935) and *Hotel Sacher* (Erich Engel, 1939). During the filming of *Fliehende Schatten,* Bohne and Schneeberger were supported by, as Udet phrased it, the "all-round genius Buchholz."[35]

Claus von Suchoky (also Klaus von Suchoki) was hired as a second pilot and actor; he had flown a plane used for the filming of Fanck's *Stürme über dem Montblanc.* (In fact, that project united once again half of the crew of *Fliehende Schatten:* next to Fanck and von Suchoky, Udet, Schneeberger, and Buchholz had been part of the production.) The female actors were Jolly Felsing and Yvette Rodin, who played the role of the female pilot. Neither one of these actresses was a great star; Rodin has a number of smaller parts to her credit, in films such as *Der Mann, der den Mord beging* (1931), staring Conrad Veidt and Heinrich George. Paul Curt (Edy) von Gontard, who brought his wife on the trip to East Africa, and Willi Zietz were responsible for the expedition and production, Udet himself for all matters concerning flying. The supervision of technical maintenance was in the hands of a man called Baier, who had serviced Udet's planes for years.[36]

The filming was completed between December 1930 and April 1931. The movie premiered in the Ufa-Pavillion Nollendorfplatz in Berlin on April 12, 1932. In a tragic aftermath the expedition was to be fatal for Claus von Suchoky and for one of the local German advisors, "Vater" Siedentopf, who lived in Tanganyika and accompanied the crew: Suchoky and Siedentopf never recovered from a crash with one of the airplanes, and both died a few months later.

In the final credits of the film the director of the movie is not mentioned. Carl Junghans, who wrote the original script and directed the filming in East Africa, is referred to as having only "collaborated" on the film. In the process of editing, Junghans got into an argument with the producers and left when they asked for additional footage to be shot in the studio (this is not the only such incident in Junghans's career). Earlier Junghans had made a number of leftist films, such as a feature about the communist movement in Russia, *Lenin, 1905–1928* (1928). He was initially known for his critical films focusing on the social milieu of the underprivileged. Junghans would not remain the Left-leaning social critic he was initially: after a few years abroad he returned to Nazi Germany and gradually advanced to become one of the leading Nazi film directors. For a while he was in immediate competition with Leni Riefenstahl for state-supported commissions. The belligerent and stubborn Junghans, however, got into a number of clashes with Joseph Goebbels and Adolf Hitler over aesthetic and content issues and finally emigrated.

After Junghans left the production of *Fliehende Schatten,* Arnold Fanck, well known for his mountain films in which Udet had starred and for whom cameraman Schneeberger had worked repeatedly, did the final editing. The fact that the film had two different directors might explain inconsistencies that are observable in the film. As will become evident in the following discussion, Junghans had set out to critique the cliché-ridden image of Africa by juxtaposing a superficial melodrama with self-reflective shots of African landscape and life. Udet's autobiographical account of the time in East Africa, as rendered in *Fremde Vögel über Africa,* needs to be seen in the context of this film. Several features of the movie might explain attitudes toward Africans we can observe in his book. The comparison of book and film, however, also highlights fundamental differences in their approach to Africa. Ultimately, Junghans and Udet pursued different trajectories.

The film exists today only in one fragmented copy in the Bundesarchiv in Berlin. The remaining three reels of 35mm black-and-white film, numbered 2 through 4, amount to about half of the original length of 2,278m, providing a running time of eighty-three minutes.[37] The fragment still conveys a sense of the different elements of the film, which combined three narrative threads: an adventure film, the chronicle of an expedition, and an ethnographic document. The plot of the adventure story is related in order to create the impression that the footage is indeed the documentary of an expedition. The actors are addressed by their real names: Udet is Udet, and Jolly is Jolly. Interestingly, in almost all of his films Udet plays himself.

The first of the remaining reels features most of what is left of the melodramatic adventure story. It begins with the departure of a female pilot, Yvette Rodin, who is leaving for Africa on her own, following Udet against the advice of others. She flies over the pyramids, and a map is shown that tracks her route. Waltz music underscores the peaceful and cheerful nature of this flight to Africa, undertaken with great anticipation and in good spirits. Settlements are shown from above; African huts and then African people appear, who look up at the airplane. Women, children, and later a male figure are rendered in close-ups. The Africans, who seem to have been members of the Masai society, watch the attempts of the pilot to land with curiosity and laughter but, as the airplane comes closer, quickly disappear into their huts.

Suddenly, gas spills out of the machine onto the airplane and the pilot, and the plane goes down in a highly dramatic scene. The suspense of the scene is intensified but also slightly ironized by images of monkeys shooting up a tree, the sound of drums, and views of Masai warriors, who seem to get ready for a military attack by forming a row with their spears and shields. While Rodin crawls out from underneath the airplane, animals are shown watching her, again giving a comical air to the scene. In the next shot a different group of Africans (most likely Babati people) find the unconscious woman. Naked men and men with loincloths, surrounded by children, carry the woman away. As the sun sets, she is brought into a hut. The next scene shows her awake, old men are taking care of her, and the entire village seems to be waiting outside, watching the process. Yvette lies naked under a blanket, drinks something, and takes in the people around her one by one. The light falling into the hut from the outside emphasizes the somewhat unreal nature of the situation. Next women are shown washing and oiling the pilot, who shyly covers her breasts. The sexually loaded atmosphere of the scene is accentuated by pictures of two naked men who climb a tall palm tree and whose genitals are clearly visible.

Then the sun rises; the next day approaches. Rodin wraps herself in an African cloth as an African man watches her from the outside and laughs at her. When the woman studies a map, a detail is shown in a close-up and identified as "Udet's camp." Then, in a somewhat unintelligible scene, the African who had watched her comes into the hut, crawls toward her on his knees and hands, and talks to her in incomprehensible speech.

This sequence introduces the central theme of the film, the encounter of different cultures, of Germans and Africans. Although the melodramatic episodes employ clichés about the primitive and strange nature of Africa and its inhabitants, other scenes counteract the stereotyping by ironizing the drama of the encounter. The woman is obviously safe and has nothing to fear. The trope of the white woman who becomes a captive of the "natives," a standard topos of so many novels and movies staged in Africa, is debunked through the exaggeration and exposure of stereotypes. Shots of animals that seem to comment on the situation, close-ups of the faces of friendly Africans, and the use of cheerful music counteract the drama. The remaining fragmentary footage of the film does not reveal the end of this story line, but contemporary reviews of the film indicate a happy ending; in the original version Udet will rescue Rodin.

The next reel shows the expedition setting up camp. African men perform duties traditionally done by women and also by house slaves: they put meat through a mincer, sew, iron, cook, and carry household items. Other African men are involved in physical labor, such as towing a car out of a swamp and setting up tents. Then the camera moves to a paradigmatic colonial setting. The members of the expedition sit down for a meal at a long table, where they are served by an African who wears a long white robe and a fez. A dialogue indicates that they are waiting for Udet, who promptly appears in the sky, creating big commotion on the ground: "Udet, Udet is coming!" Africans look up at the descending plane and begin to play their drums faster and faster in anticipation of the landing. In a small interlude the camera shifts back and forth between the landing and scenes involving the preparation of food and drink. Jolly, one of the German women, tries punch from a big bowl and says to an African: "Excellent, you did that very well, Juma."

This scene is followed by more commotion due to the arrival of Udet. Again, the melodramatic aspect of the scene—Udet the savior appearing in the clouds—is made to seem ironic by the exaggerated activity and the crescendo produced by the drums. To top off the increasingly comical character of the scene, the table that was set and prepared nicely is savaged by monkeys during Udet's landing. When the disaster is discovered, the expedition members react in a most relaxed way: "Oh well, not that bad." Later, Africans are shown sitting peacefully around the airplane. A leisurely conversation takes place between Jolly Felsing and Udet: "And what do you like the best over here?—Kilimanscharo.—Not the women?—No (*laughs*), really not."

This sequence of scenes is choppy and unfocused. The comical aspects determine the atmosphere, and, as a result, Germans in Africa do not emerge as authoritarian and disciplined. Rather, the entire atmosphere is more that of an extended field trip, the interaction with the African world playful. The cross-cultural encounter is not presented as problematic but, rather, ironized by the slapstick character of certain scenes. The ironic commentary exposes clichés about German superiority and African submissiveness alike. The critique, however, is ultimately not entirely successful on its own.

Yet the situation changes when the melodramatic plot is seen together with the ethnographic section of the film, which offers an alternative perspective on Africa. This section documents the life of the Masai by focusing on central areas of their daily routine, on the various activities of the people and the place of animals in their lives: there are shots of herdsmen with their cows and goats, a long sequence follows the building of huts, and Masai are depicted tilling the soil, working in the field, and grinding corn. Women weave and bake, and children play *mancala,* an African bean game. A group of old women is captured drinking from bowls, and the camera conveys their grace and dignity, in stark contrast to the comical characters of the melodramatic segments. The music underlying this scene is quiet, contemplative, explorative.

This footage is remarkable for the method of portraying Africans. The camera takes a deliberately descriptive approach in representing the Masai. Some of the shots of people are frontal and at eye level, bringing the viewer and the viewed on the same level. In other scenes the camera captures a particular activity from different angles. As a result, the camera does not take one distinct point of view; instead, the approach seems pluralistic. In addition, the slow pace of the filming and the gentle music determine the explorative atmosphere of this encounter. By focusing on the daily life of the Masai, the "otherness" of Africans is put into the familiar context of agricultural life. The German viewer thus sees Africans in familiar settings and engaged in well-respected activities. The great value Germans place on work and nature mediates this encounter of different worlds.

In the next scene two German men sit at a table while a woman takes a shower, her silhouette clearly visible. The following sequence of shots is crucial in that it compares a German and a Masai woman in ways that stress commonalities. The German woman (Jolly Felsing) who had just taken a shower puts on her makeup; the camera then shifts to an African woman, who also beautifies herself. Both women look into mirrors and put on necklaces. The back and forth goes on for a while, and only at the end the German woman continues to file her nails, while the African woman puts clay (or cow dung?) on a hut. The end of the sequence could be read in two different ways: for one, it asserts the fact that the white woman does not need to work, while the African woman does. But, given the German emphasis on the value of work, for some viewers this fact might not necessarily disqualify the African woman; it could also be seen as a criticism of the privileged upper-class white woman.

Like the earlier shots from the life of the Masai, this sequence again makes an attempt at bridging the cultural gap by creating a shared framework, in this case a concern for beauty. But, more important, by observing the women looking at themselves, by involving mirrors and thematizing the creation of images, the scene encourages the viewer to reflect upon the question of image making itself. I consider this scene to be the pivotal moment in the film, in which Junghans's original intent—namely, to debunk stereotypes about Africa—is most clearly articulated.

The sequence ends when the German men decide to leave: they want to fly, shoot a lion, and watch a fire in the bush. Their flight begins the fourth reel, which features shots from and about the planes, gliding between high mountains and rocks in a beautiful foggy landscape. A subtitle, "Complete Peacefulness Prevails at Lake Victoria," once more emphasizes the tranquil nature of the African environment. Then the ethnographic trajectory is picked up again. Africans appear in a boat, and the camera moves slowly to take shots of the surrounding reed highlighting the beauty of patterns and structures present in nature. A family of lions majestically parades across the screen. Africans are shown fishing in the lake; crocodiles are lurking nearby. Another series of shots also emphasizes the threat these animals pose for human beings: children play in the lake, and women fetch water, while crocodiles seem to move in closer on them. Nothing actually happens, but the sequence highlights the fragility of life. Shots of hippopotamuses and fishermen round off these views of Lake Victoria, before the camera moves away from the lake and pays tribute to other aspects of African wildlife. Close-up shots of exotic animals such as little elephants who are shown playing and trumpeting must have been an impressive sight for the audience at the time. Shots of giraffes, zebras, and lions complete this tour of African game.

The fourth and last of the three remaining reels ends here. From the footage that survived, however, the individual narrative threads of the film clearly emerge. The love and adventure story, embedded in the tale about an expedition, is a persiflage of the conventional movie about Africa. The ethnographic footage underlines the filmmaker's intention to reflect upon the German (or Western) image of Africa with material that restores humanity to the Africans depicted. This critique can be thought as extending also to the highly popular exotic feature films in general; the 1920s had seen a plethora of such movies staged in India, Japan, Cuba, Algeria, or not clearly defined places of otherness.[38] It should be noted, however, that at no point does the film discuss the colonial context or colonialism. Was the critique of colonialism to be implied with the reflection upon the image of Africa?

A look at the reactions of the contemporary audience might tackle this question from a different angle. As a feature film, *Fliehende Schatten* was not convincing; contemporary critics received the film with both reservation and partial praise. Most of the praise was reserved for the original shots of the African landscape and animals, while the film's narrative was considered simplistic and unnecessarily comical.[39] Two critics accused the film of imitating the central motif of the movie *Trader Horn*, which premiered in 1931.[40] That film, directed by W. S. Van Dyke, was based on the (supposedly) autobiographical account of Alfred Alois Horn, which he wrote down with the help of Ethelreda Lewis, who published the book in 1927. It revolves around the life of Horn, who claims to have lived in blood brotherhood with a "tribe of cannibals" in the Congo. He eventually sets out to rescue a white woman who also had gone native and was revered by her tribe as a "White Goddess." The movie (which was remade in 1973 with Rod Taylor) has been called a landmark in filmmaking, mostly for the stunning footage of African landscape and fauna put together during ten months of filming. It clearly stands in a tradition of fantasies about Africa that center around the threat and desire of white people "going primitive," a central theme in novels and films, from Joseph Conrad's *Heart of Darkness* (1899) to the many books and later films about Tarzan (the first of the novels by Edgar Rice Burroughs was published in 1912). In Germany, where more than 150 films about Africa were made until 1942, several films picked up the motif of the white woman among Africans. Hans Schomburgk's *Eine Weisse unter Kannibalen* (1921), a remake of an earlier version that had premiered in Britain as *The Goddess of Wangora* (1914), was one among many movies entertaining audiences with these fantasies.[41]

Only one critic suggested that the comical elements had been used deliberately to critique conventions typical of the exoticizing German *Afrikafilm:* "Humans and animals unite to prove the absurdity of a certain kind of filmmaking."[42] If we take this remark and the references to *Trader Horn* together, it seems even more likely that Junghans indeed intended to attack the traditional film image of Africa. Another critic appreciated the different representational strategies employed in the film, especially the aesthetic approach toward Africans and their environment, and praises the film for abandoning a folkloristic approach in favor of an aestheticizing perspective: "They [the filmmakers and camera crew] see with different eyes. The naked body of a Negro is captured in its bronze tones, every reflex is registered, curves are explored the way a sculptor would. The beauty of a lion's body becomes visible in the movement of his muscles. . . . This is no longer a folkloristic encounter; a conscious and artistic stylization transforming the material into something greater has occurred."[43] This statement reminds one of Leni Riefenstahl's approach toward African bodies in her films and photographs, an issue that will come up again in the discussion of *Fremde Vögel.*

The critics thus assess that something new had been intended with this film, or they are taken aback by the inconsistencies contained within it. Yet not a single critic mentions the footage about the daily life of Africans or the absence of a discussion of colonialism. The shots of landscapes and animals, or, in this last case, aesthetic strategies, are appreciated in the reviews, but the innovative approach toward depicting the daily life of Africans is silenced. This fact might be proof of the resistance Junghans seems to have faced; if the critics do not even notice or acknowledge one of the central trajectories of the film, then the resistance to the ideas that inspired Junghans—namely, viewing Africa and Africans with respect—might have been insurmountable. Documentaries about Africa had been brought to German audiences before, through films by Carl Heinz Boese, Ernst Garden, Ernö Metzner, and

Hans Schomburgk.[44] For the most part, however, these documentaries either romanticized or exoticized Africa. Junghans's reflection upon representation was unique and, in fact, can be considered a direct attack on Hans Schomburgk, who often mixed documentary footage and fictional elements in his films about Africa but did not employ the self-reflective techniques that distinguish *Fliehende Schatten*.[45]

A dispatch from Africa, which was published in the journal *Film-Kurier* on April 4, 1931, documents Junghans's conflict with the producers and clearly shows the conscious nature of his innovative approach to Africa: "After three months of drudgery many greetings. After a three-months fight producer groggy. Outline of the film secured against all trashy tendencies. . . . Constructed mostly the true Africa. My view of Africa: Everything is very different!"[46] Unfortunately, it remains impossible to know what the film would have looked like if Junghans had had a chance to complete it.

Junghans's way of representing Africa was surely discussed by members of the crew during the production of the film. In Udet's rendition of the African experience, however, the trajectory shifts. Although the photographs themselves reflect the ethnographic approach formulated by Junghans, the captions of the photographs and the introductory text place the encounter between Germans and Africans in the context of modernity and technology. Nothing indicates to what extent Udet was responsible for the photography; the book only acknowledges that the photographs were "taken by the members of the expedition." Nevertheless, Udet presented the book under his name and, through the explanatory texts, added a distinct interpretation to the material.

Strange Birds over Africa

Udet's first-person account of his time in East Africa contains 10 pages of introductory text, followed by 2 maps and 119 black-and-white photographs. The cover of the book features a shot taken from an airplane, capturing a herd of elephants pacing across the bushland. On the top and the lower part of the cover the title of the book is superimposed in big letters diagonally across the landscape, framing the animals visible in the middle section. The letters are printed slightly tilted, so as to repeat the direction of the animals' movement. The author's name at the bottom of the page is placed horizontally, somewhat counteracting the movement of writing and animals toward the left-hand corner of the page. One could read this as a metaphor for the control exerted over the African landscape through the author's act of writing.

The introduction provides background information on the expedition. Udet states the declared goal of this mission to Africa—namely, "to fly in Africa and to film there, in order to catch a bit of the warm sun south of the equator, which we up here in the cold north need so much, especially today, more than ever."[47] But the pilot was not only interested in capturing Africa's sun for his fellow Germans; he also articulates a narrative concept underlying his flying mission. It is noteworthy that Udet does not mention the melodramatic narrative of the movie when he outlines the project but refers to it only as a "frame narrative" that was supposed to provide coherency to the material: "We wanted to give Africa its due and present it in all its beauty and originality, and to underscore the contrast between civilization and the modern accomplishments of technology and an untouched Africa. In order to be able to present our shots coherently, we decided to develop a frame narrative for the manuscript. We agreed that the title, 'Strange Birds over Africa,' most adequately expressed what we had decided to be our task" (3).

The *we* indicates that Udet was involved in creating the conceptual framework of the film, which seems to suggest that both the film and the book are based on shared presuppositions about the image of Africa. But, as opposed to the film, this passage shows that from the start the expedition was constructed along the lines of a dichotomy between civilization and nature, the modern and the traditional. In this passage and throughout the text the premodern and natural are defined as beautiful and worthy of admiration. Yet, and this would reflect the film's intent as well, the contrasts outlined here by Udet do not seem to result in conflict between German and African cultures and peoples. Rather, and in opposition to the narrative concept Udet presents, the compatibility of the modern and the traditional, technology and nature, emerges as the principal narrative thread throughout the book and provides the framework for the text, the illustrations and the captions that comment on the illustrations.

The itinerary of the expedition takes the crew from Mombasa, where they land in November 1930, via Voi to Arusha, and finally to the shores of Lake Manjara, which becomes the headquarters for the filming. Within a few days an "exemplary African airport" is built (4). With the beginning of the rainy season in April 1931, the group splits up and embarks on separate flights. Udet, whose original plane is no longer fit enough for a flight to Europe, flies another plane via Uganda, Sudan, and Egypt. The text ends in anticipation of the landing in Cairo, which is presented as the "return into the grayness of daily life" (12).

In his introduction Udet reports on his encounters with East Africans, the animals he observes, the landscape, and some of the settlements and lodges he and the crew visit. Again, he does not mention the melodramatic film narrative. Rather, he focuses on dangerous episodes that the crew encountered, such as the attack by a lion on Udet's and another companion's airplanes. A crash of Suchoky's plane into a termite hill turns out to be even more serious, and Udet, who rescues the survivors, considers it a "miracle that he and Father Siedentopf got away alive" (7). (As mentioned earlier, both die a few months later from an unknown disease they evidently contracted during this crash.) The result is that Udet's account gives the impression that the enterprise was primarily a scientific expedition that was filmed as a documentary.

Most interesting are Udet's comments about encounters with Africans. The pilot first mentions Africans when "30 blacks" help to construct the airport and a hangar near the film crew's camp. The next reference describes the reactions of several locals who witness samples of Udet's acrobatic flying stunts, which are "admired by the black honorary committee" that had been assembled by a German settler to welcome the members of the expedition (4). Udet also recounts an episode in which an old Masai chief is visibly irritated with the pilot's acrobatic flights and questions Gontard why he did not send an older man on such a dangerous mission (5).

Udet points out repeatedly that the Masai take a strong interest in the airplanes. The old chief is reported to inspect the planes every morning with great curiosity. Another group of Masai observe the maneuvers of the airplanes and approaches the planes after their landing, "running, visibly joyful." Demonstrating their peacefulness, the Masai plant their spears in the soil at a respectful distance from the planes. The encounter is described in enthusiastic terms: "Rarely did we meet such friendly and clever people as these, with whom we became friends in no time."

The Masai inspect the cameras, and the chief and other warriors are allowed to try out the pilot's place and experience the steering wheel. Udet praises the appreciation the Masai seem to have for modern technology: "The Masai people did indeed display an understanding for our modern giant birds, and our friend answered the questions of our white guide De Baer quite appropriately: 'Aren't you amazed that these birds fly?' 'Why should I be amazed if you yourself are no longer amazed?'" (5).

The chief appears also reasonable when he advises other Masai not to take any food from the "bird people" because it will be needed on their future journeys. The conversation continues for a while, until Udet and his crew leave their "black friends." This encounter is representative of the approach Udet takes in his portrayal of Africa and its people: there is no conflict between technology and nature, between civilization and the premodern environment. This image of the Masai is consistent with many of accounts that document their special standing during the colonial era; for example, Masai were used by the German colonial rulers to crush uprisings by other Africans in the region. Masai men will be again at the center of our discussion in chapter 5.

Another group of Africans is praised for their beauty and delightful dances: "The Ufiume-negroes are distinguished by their good stature and grace, and their dances and songs are a pure joy for whoever enjoys beauty" (7). Thus, Africans are generally described in sympathetic ways. Only when Udet leaves East African territory does he meet locals who are either hostile or who cannot be trusted. Just as the climate in Sudan is "unbearably hot and humid," its people are "not hospitable" and attempt to cheat the pilot and his companion (10–11). The enthusiastic reactions to the landscape and the peoples of East Africa are absent in the descriptions of the return flight via Sudan and Egypt.

Notable, too, is the representation of the white settlers and the colonial infrastructure. The British always appear in the most positive light; they are cooperative, chivalrous, and reliable, especially when Udet enters and leaves East Africa (3, 11). The colonial context is not only not criticized, but it is not even acknowledged as such. Germans do not appear in competition with other European powers, nor do they want to save "Africans who have been mis-treated . . . by the power-greedy British colonizers," as Susanne Zantop has argued in her interpretation of the Nazi film *Germanin.*[48] Udet consistently eschews criticism and avoids confrontation; the entire stay in East Africa is presented in a spirit that seeks to convey an air of cross-cultural respect and understanding.

Most important, however, the travelers can count on the support of Germans in the area. Father Siedentopf, who joins the crew as a guide, is referred to as an "old Lettow-Vorbeck-warrior" and thus connected to one of the key symbolic figures of German colonialism (7). When Udet needs repair work done on his plane, he finds two German carpenters in Arusha, Master Glaser and Master Bleich, who prove to be of great help to the crew (8). The fact that an infrastructure of German craftsmen could be said to exist in East Africa at the time highlights the continuous German presence in the former colonial territory, a presence uninterrupted by the change of colonial ownership. In fact, since late 1925 Great Britain had allowed for the return of Germans into areas of the British mandate. German settlers and merchants began to move back into the area in increasing numbers, supported by substantial loans granted by the German government, which displayed great interest in promoting and enabling resettlement.[49]

Following the introductory text, two maps are inserted (13). The map on the top of the page renders the entire African continent, but no nation-states or colonial state borders are identified. Geographical references are rivers (such as the Niger, Congo, Zambezi, Orange, and Nile Rivers) and lakes (Lake Chad and Lake Victoria) and the names of places important to Udet's excursion (for example, Mombasa, Voi, Arusha, Khartoum, and Cairo). The slightly smaller map at the bottom focuses on East Africa and features mostly Tanganyika, Kenya, a part of Uganda, Rwanda, Burundi, and a small slice of the Congo. The area of today's mainland Tanzania at the center of the map is referred to as "Tanganjika-Territory, formerly German East Africa," while Burundi and Rwanda are not identified as part of the former German colony. Beneath this, in smaller print, the words *British Mandate* reveal the current status of the region. Thus, the area is first and foremost presented as former German territory, while the reference to British ownership is only added secondarily.

This map most clearly reveals the subtext underlying Udet's narrative. The excursion does not venture into just any African territory; it focuses on an area known to Germans from the days of empire when it was one of Germany's most attractive colonial possessions. Placing his trip to East Africa in the framework of German colonial history, Udet brings his symbolic power to rekindle the lingering German dream for a colonial empire, resonating with many contemporary publications and films that shared this vision.

The black-and-white photographs make up the largest part of the book (over 80 percent of the pages) and underscore the difference between the ethnographic intent of the film and the ultimate message of the book. While the film articulates the issue of representation through scenes that convey a message of self-reflexivity, Udet's account presents the reader with a different conclusion. The photographs include such general subject matters as animals, Africans, settlements, landscapes, the airplanes, and the crew; however, the material is presented in distinct ways. In particular, the specific angles, foci, contrasts, and points of view employed by the photographers, in conjunction with the captions that comment on the images, turn the photographs into interpretative messages. Here the contrast between film and book is again substantial: whereas Junghans uses the juxtaposition of fictional film and documentary to reflect upon the issue of representation and to make an attempt at an alternative and more descriptive portrayal of African daily life, Udet stages the photographs in a way that conveys a message about the German presence in East Africa that is imbued with colonial desire.

Two groups of photographs are most relevant in this context—namely, images that amount to a survey of the former colonial property and shots that depict Africans in their responses to modernity. What Simon Schama said in *Landscape and Memory* about the general value of engaging with landscape imagery holds true for these portrayals of African landscapes as well and in fact stresses the utopian character Udet's images conveyed to the German public at the time: "Instead of being yet another explanation of what we have lost, it is an exploration of what we may yet find."[50]

Many of the pictures were taken from above, by cameras that had been attached to the outside of the airplane.[51] This photography from above is emblematic of the political and cultural power structure existing between Germans and Africans. The former colonizer surveys the space from a privileged position, overseeing the land he imagines to recapture, and thus literally occupies what Edward Said has termed "*positional* superiority."[52] Moreover, because a single wide-angle shot taken from above can capture a vast geographical area, these photographs emphasize structures and patterns that would not be visible otherwise.

In *Colonial Space* John Noyes, drawing on Homi Bhabha, argues that in colonialist literature African territory was often at first presented as boundless and devoid of quality, which entailed a promise of freedom but also implicitly seemed to call for the presence of the colonizer to introduce order.[53] The first step in taming the wilderness was achieved through the description, categorization, and classification of space and the subsequent drawing of boundaries. Space was made accessible and manageable, preparing it for use by the colonizer.

In Udet's portrayal of East Africa the region is either already under control because it bears the marks of civilization, for example, through settlements and roads, or African space is represented in ways that amount to an appropriation of the territory. In many of the photographs taken from airplane, either a structuring shadow falls onto the landscape, often in the shape of a cross (at times even resembling the Christian Cross; see 9, 24, 25, 26), or part of the airplane itself is seen on the picture (38). Two pictures show jeeps parked against the backdrop of a beautiful landscape (52, 61); others combine animals, landscape, and airplanes (39). Some shots of airplanes or of other examples of modern technology are set against the background of a landscape that includes Africans (34), and other pictures combining several topics again feature a cross cast over the scene (28). A number of pictures focus on animals in the landscape (58, 67).

In summary, most of the photographs of landscapes contain evidence of modern life and of African people, settlements, and animals; only five pictures of landscapes depict neither animals nor European or African people (20, 21, 23, 57, 65), and four of them are portraits of mountains. Cars and airplanes indicate the presence of Western technology and civilization in the African space. The shadow cast by the airplanes over African land is the most subtle image confirming this presence.

In a similar vein photographs that feature settlements convey an image of Africa that is already developed. Again, the photographs taken from above indicate the existence of controlled and planned development. Arusha (5), Umbuque (32), Nairobi (68), and game park lodges ("The Fig-Tree-Hotel," 62) are distinguished by wide, linear streets that follow regular patterns. A Masai village ("Typical Masai-Kraal," 33) emerges as an orderly settlement, and the view from above emphasizes its recognizable structure and architectural design. The one settlement that makes the least structured appearance is a coffee farm, which includes the house of an official who checks travelers coming from the north for tsetse flies (59). Several streets connect the various buildings on the compound, however, and lead to larger roads, thus showing the connection of the settlement to a larger infrastructure. Only one shot is included that does not bear any signs of modern development and is reminiscent of colonial representations that emphasize the "uncivilized" nature of African settlements—namely, that of a hut that is nestled into the surrounding vegetation (57, bottom).

The captions commenting on the two images of Nairobi reveal Udet's enthusiasm for pointing out evidence for modernization in Africa. The picture at the top presents a wealthier neighborhood: "Nairobi is developing. In the foreground the new English church. Notable are the many cars, which are parked along the modern and spaciously designed roads." The focus on a symbol of Christianity in this picture connects modernization to Westernization. The picture at the bottom of the same page shows a neighborhood inhabited by Africans: "A Negro settlement in Nairobi. The roofs are covered with the metal of Shell gas-containers. From many kilometers afar one can see the shine of this practical and cheap roofing" (68).

These buildings, which are all approximately the same size and situated on streets that run in consistent patterns horizontally and vertically, reflect an air of regulated development and urban planning. In Udet's description the shining roofs appear as harbingers of modernity. In essence both photographs and their texts point out to the German audience that Africa is modernizing and progressing. Similarly, the caption introducing the settlement of Umbuque makes a point of connecting the place to the larger infrastructure: "Umbuque, one of the largest Negro settlements in Tanganjika, extends over many kilometers. The road at the top of the picture leads to Arusha, and is part of the famous Cairo-Cap-road" (32). Consistent with previous photos, this one is taken from above so that the buildings appear as elements of larger regular patterns.

This emphasis on an intact infrastructure emerges as the most important aspect in most of the images focusing on settlements. That is, Udet's visual account of Africa emphasizes the accessibility of the East African territory and its potential for development. This is not in line with the spirit of the early phase of colonization, in which the call to conquer Africa was put forth to potential settlers through images of supposedly unclaimed land, thus encouraging Germans to fantasize about ownership. Here the appeal conveyed through the shots of settlements taken from above emphasizes possibilities for development and the general accessibility of the country. This African territory is no longer a wilderness but, rather, a region with a potent infrastructure, a region open to further modernization. Both modes of fantasizing about Africa are ultimately about mastery and colonization, but the approach taken toward Africa in each is fundamentally different.

The many photographs taken of Africans during Udet's expedition also diverge from other portrayals of African peoples as they were known especially from ethnographic photography. In contrast to the sometimes more sympathetic representation of peoples from the South Pacific, for example, ethnographic pictures from the late nineteenth century onward predominantly portrayed Africans as mysterious, uncanny, and unappealing.[54] It is important to note that, up until the middle of the twentieth century, many of these pictures were not taken by anthropologists but in studios or by amateur photographers, such as missionaries, colonial administrators, or different kinds of travelers.[55] As Derrick Price has pointed out, "Photography grew up in the days of Empire and became an important adjunct to imperialism, for it returned to the Western spectator images of native peoples which frequently confirmed prevailing views of them as primitive, bizarre, barbaric or simply picturesque."[56] With regard to textual representations of African territory during the period of German colonialism, Africans were often denied their existence altogether. As Noyes argues in his analysis of several German colonial novels, writers employed a range of strategies to erase the presence of the native Africans, in order for the colonizer to claim the territory more readily.[57]

Udet's portrayal differs from these earlier conventions of depicting, or erasing, Africans. For one, the photographs were taken by professionals, not by amateur photographers, who were responsible for much of the ethnographic photography of the period. Schneeberger and Bohne were some of the best cameramen working at the time and brought their technical and aesthetic knowledge to the photography as well. In terms of content, the photographs contained in Udet's book also do not reflect the widespread patterns that have been discussed by Malek Alloula, Frantz Fanon, Anne McClintock, and others, who highlight the dehumanizing strategies employed in visual representations of Africans.[58]

We have already seen that locals are rendered in a sympathetic light in Udet's text, and a similar approach can be observed with regard to the photographs. Among the one hundred photos of East Africa included in the book (nineteen additional pictures document the journey home, through Sudan and Egypt), twenty photos focus on Africans centrally; eight depict Africans and Germans together; sixteen show Africans in contact with symbols of European technology or civilization, such as airplanes, cameras, and mirrors; and eight focus on African settlements. Four of these pictures bring together Germans, Africans, and technology. Excluding the pictures of settlements that do not feature African people visibly, about two-fifths of the images present the viewer with images of Africans.

Again, the captions introducing the pictures are interpretative and clearly geared at controlling the reactions of the audience. Two groups of pictures are distinguishable. The captions of the more conventional images comment on the beauty of Africans, their traditions (such as dance), character, and physical features. The photographs of dancing Masai (13, 17, 19) or of specific customs (such as scarifications [48 top] or bridal hairstyles [49 top]) address standard areas of anthropological presentations of other cultures, and the captions are, for the most part, merely descriptive. Some of the photographs comment on Africans with condescension: a picture featuring an old man who wears a cooking pot on his head and sports little bells as earrings particularly stands out (12). One photograph shows a man with twelve fingers, a feature guaranteed to generate feelings of revulsion in the German audience, and is in line with nineteenth-century traditions that presented members of distant cultures as freaks (64 top).

These conventional anthropological images emphasizing cultural difference are countered, however, by photographs that stress shared notions about character and beauty. Four comments on pictures explicitly praise the beauty of African bodies: a shot from below of a naked torso and shaved head of a young woman is presented as "Strength and

Beauty in Africa: Babati Girl" (10), and the text commenting on the picture of a naked upper torso of a young Masai warrior reads, "Strength and Beauty in Africa: Proud Masai Warrior" (11). In two other instances the textual comment refers to the beauty and exquisite build of the Africans depicted (43, 47). Another image of a broadly smiling young Masai woman, who is decorated with bracelets and necklaces and whose head is shaven, features the woman from above the navel, partially covered with a cloth, leaving one breast bare. The text reads, "Would you like to fly with us?" (42).

The photographs stressing the beauty of African bodies are informed by aesthetic and formal considerations. The images of young women focus on the interplay of light and form to stress the well-balanced nature of physical proportions. In spite of the fact that these images depict naked or half-naked bodies, the focus on form and beauty and the relaxed way with which these young women interact with the camera gives their expressions a charm that does not resemble the staged lasciviousness of Orientalist photography.[59] In a similar way images of men convey a proud but not aggressive masculinity (11). The light placed on their bodies stresses regular features and balanced proportions, reminding one of the comment made by L. H. Eisner, one of the critics of *Fliehende Schatten* who praised the film's aesthetics.

The concept of beauty these pictures articulate combines physical strength, youth, and regular features and is reminiscent of aesthetic parameters that distinguish classical Greek and Roman sculptures. The bodies described as beautiful are those of young people, who are tall and slender, with firm and muscular bodies and immaculate skin. Apart from the aesthetic notions embodied by these Africans, the individuals portrayed also seem to express certain values. Pride, strength, friendliness, genuineness, naturalness, and modesty are the dominant characteristics, all of which were highly priced values in German society at the time.

This association of beauty and worth, beauty and character, has its roots in ideas about physiognomy as developed, for example, by Johann Kasper Lavater (*Physignomische Fragmente zur Beförderung der Menschenkenntnis und Menschenliebe,* 4 vols., 1775–78) and Christoph Lichtenberg (*Über die Physiognomik,* 1778). Racist traditions used this approach aligning beauty and character to discredit Africans; by declaring

African bodies ugly and not compatible with European ideals, the character of Africans became automatically suspect. Udet's approach thus transcends these racist traditions by presenting African bodies in ways that highlight their comparability with European norms.

This view of African bodies as beautiful is typical of an approach that only a few years later became crucial to one kind of Nazi aesthetics. In Leni Riefenstahl's documentary films about the 1936 Olympic Games, *Olympia: Fest der Völker* (*Festival of Peoples*) and *Fest der Schönheit* (*Festival of Beauty*), for example, the sense of beauty conveyed crosses cultural boundaries and includes individuals from different cultures. The emphasis is on muscles, proportion between height and weight, gestures, mimicry, and gait, and in the focus on form the individuality of the athlete evaporates to become part of a larger message of strength and surrender. Riefenstahl is also famous for her images of the Nuba, who live in the Nuba Mountains in the Kordofan region of central Sudan. Her two volumes of photographs, published as *Die Nuba* (1973; *The Last of the Nuba,* 1974) and *Die Nuba von Kau* (1976; *The People of Kau,* 1976), focus on areas of the Nuba culture that are exotic (though in many ways not unfamiliar) to a Western audience, such as their cult surrounding nakedness and physical strength. A large section of *The People of Kau* deals with the Nubas's exquisite artistic way of decorating and scarifying their bodies. Yet Riefenstahl's aestheticizing focus on youth, strength, blood, pain, and nakedness blocks out other aspects of Nuba life, such as older people, clothed people, and the considerable agricultural activities of the Nuba.[60] This focus on specific aspects and her glorification of these aspects through the use of distinct aesthetic strategies has earned her strong reproach from critics, who chide her for creating a "fascist aesthetics."[61]

Riefenstahl's books, among other publications, are partially responsible for the great deal of interest in the Nuba that has subsequently led to a destruction of many of their traditional ways of living. The Sudanese government has attempted to change Nuba customs with often violent means, which have had devastating effects on the people. Interestingly, Nuba organizations do not necessarily reject Riefenstahl's representation of their culture; in fact, Suleiman Musa Rahhal's book *The Right to Be Nuba: The Story of a Sudanese People's Struggle for Survival* takes an approach very similar to that of the German filmmaker and photographer.[62]

Riefenstahl's focus on youthful beauty and strength is also present in some of the photographs in *Fremde Vögel;* her Nuba, however, remain enigmatic and exotic and express a message of exclusion. In contrast, the photographs included in Udet's book follow a range of aesthetic approaches and generally attempt to build bridges emphasizing commonalities between Germans and Africans.

Other images of Africans contained in Udet's book that do not focus on the beauty of bodies also stress the agreeable character of the people. Some photographs feature Africans and Germans in contact with modern civilization in ways that point out the nonconfrontational nature of this encounter. Much like some of the passages in Udet's introductory text, Africans are presented as friends (8 top, 34 bottom, 39 top). The captions to such pictures not only emphasize the personal aspect of the friendship between Udet and the Masai but also imply intimate conversations, as if the two parties spoke the same language. Other captions commenting on the encounter between Africans and Germans and modern civilization employ words such as *trust* and *joy* to describe the locals' reaction to airplanes or to other tokens of modern civilization (6, 7, 16 top). Africans are "well-mannered" and "peaceful" (34 bottom, 35 top); they enjoy playing with the cameras and mirrors (36 top, bottom 16).

The juxtaposition of photographs that stress the beauty of Africans and those that focus on the ability of Africans to behave as moderns, while adhering to a traditional code of honor, seems to suggest that a certain sense of beauty and character predisposes Africans toward an appreciation of technology and modernity. Africans thus appear as noble savages, naive, but perfectly capable of meeting Germans on account of an honor code adhered to by both sides and on account of a value system shared by Germans and Africans alike. Udet, who was often praised for his chivalry, mediates this appreciation of Africans. His Africans are able to value the blessings of modern civilization: The reaction of an old man to the airplanes is described as expressing amazement but also "genuine joy" (7). Especially the Masai come across as a group of people at ease in their encounter with modern civilization. Several images show Africans working on the airplanes or collaborating with Germans in other ways (2, 3, 6, 22 top and bottom; 39 top). Only two photographs depict Africans as porters or servants, roles familiar from traditional colonialist representations (31; 37 top).

The message conveyed through these representation of Africans is clearly informed by a tradition that portrays members of premodern cultures as noble savages. This tradition was only rarely part of German portrayals of Africa; one would have to go back to Wolfram von Eschenbach's medieval epic *Parzival* (1200–1210) to find possibly the most positive black characters German literature ever created, the African queen Belakane and her biracial black-and-white spotted son, Feirefiz. As mentioned in the previous chapter, a forthcoming (though not unproblematic) attitude toward Africans also emerges during the Enlightenment period, when a number of Africans were brought to Germany and educated, in order to prove the point that the state of African civilization was a matter of "nurture," not "nature."[63] Although this civilizationist line of thought existed in German culture consistently from the Enlightenment period onward, racist theories—which also had their roots in the Enlightenment era's attempt to understand, categorize, and master global history—were equally and at times more pervasive in discussions from the days of German colonialism into the mid-twentieth century.

Similar to what we have seen in the cases of Schweitzer and Eyth, Udet's account is not informed by biological racism but draws on other traditions—namely, the notion of the noble savage and the Enlightenment ideal of progress and cultural development. But this kind of seemingly appreciative attitude toward Africans is neither a sign of an emancipatory stance, nor is Udet's approach unique. For example, in an early documentary from 1911, entitled *Die Fortschritte der Zivilisation in Deutsch-Ostafrika: Eine staatliche Fachschule in Tanga,* Africans are presented as able to be educated, learning about masonry, carpentry, and printing.[64] As Alain Patrice Nganang has shown, even films shot during the Nazi period employ the image of the "nice African." Here Germans appear as the better colonizers in comparison to the British or the French, and Africans are portrayed as hoping for the return of the Germans. That is, the dream of a German colonial empire is additionally legitimized through its correspondence with the desire of Africans themselves.[65]

Along these lines the superior position of Germans is not questioned in Udet's account. On the one hand, Udet's portrayal of Africa and Africans stresses the compatibility of German and African cultures. Areas of commonality include ideas of physical beauty, a shared code of honor, and a common positive relation to modern inventions. On the other hand, racial and cultural difference does not amount to a challenge to the German position of superiority. The appropriation of landscape and the ownership of technology clearly indicate who is in charge. Germans appear and leave (and might return again) with their airplanes in the fashion of a deus ex machina, foreshadowing the appearance of Adolf Hitler at the beginning of Leni Riefenstahl's documentary of the 1934 Nazi Party rally in *Triumph des Willens*. But domination is achieved without drawing on the vocabulary of racism.

The message sent to the German readers is one that encourages the presence of Germans in East Africa in the context of modern development. Africans are not hostile but, rather, friendly and open to modernization and development. By not acknowledging the British colonial context, German dreams about return to the territory are more easily expressed. The land already has an infrastructure to offer that allows for further development. With this focus on modernization, race appears as a secondary element structuring the encounter between Germans and Africans. This outlook was common to many films and texts of the era, whose main trajectory was the dream of regaining a colonial empire. Whereas Junghans's original project differs from those films, Udet's book ultimately feeds the colonial dream.

At the center of Udet's encounter with East Africa are specific ideas about development, civilization, beauty, ownership, and modernity. The views he expresses are on a continuum of attitudes about modernization and progress that originated with the Enlightenment and have determined German representations of non-European cultures since the late 1700s. While biological racism emerged in the late eighteenth century as a belief system dominating views of and later actual policies toward African cultures, the nonracist approach toward cultural difference coexisted throughout the centuries. Depending on the area and the time period, one or the other of the two models prevailed, but to this day both models are factors facilitating the control of African societies and peoples from the outside. Udet's approach to East Africa appealed to Weimar Republic sensibilities. Technology and modernization were at the heart of this period of classical modernity in Germany. Although the Nazis would incorporate technology into their vision, notions of cultural and social modernization developed during the Weimar period were rejected by the Nazi ideologues. Within a period of only a few years, previously dominant paradigms were replaced by other ideologies.

In our current historical context Udet's account of East Africa encourages us to reflect upon the vocabulary of globalization. Even if contemporary agents of globalization refrain from using a racist vocabulary and employing racist policies, attention needs to be paid to questions of agency and to the actual results of the encounters between Africans and, in this case, Germans. While Udet's images of Africa reflect a then novel approach to colonization, his approach is comparable to strategies that can be observed today in the latest push for the global expansion of capital.[66]

Once the Nazis came to power, publications that rekindled the dream of recapturing the colonial empire soared. One of the figures symbolizing the bygone era was Carl Peters. He remained an inspiring figure to many Germans who hoped to regain the lost imperial glory. Peters, often represented in leather boots and holding a whip, demonstrated ideal führer figure qualities admired during the Nazi era. Novels and films about Peters that were published in the Nazi period speak to the significance of this key figure of German colonialism. Numerous films and book publications glorified the period of German colonial rule in East Africa. Texts that were popular during the Weimar period were reprinted, such as books by General von Lettow-Vorbeck, Friedrich Wilhelm Mader, and Ludwig Weichert, and accounts of the works of missionaries document the continued presence of missionary and medical workers in the area.

In the political climate following Hitler's ascension to power, Udet's 1935 autobiography, *Mein Fliegerleben,* renders the African experience in stark contrast to the account offered in *Fremde Vögel.* The chapter on Africa, entitled "Four Men in Africa," is comparable in length to the introduction to *Fremde Vögel* but reads like a chapter out of a novel by Ernest Hemingway. Being a radical departure from Udet's previous account, it focuses mostly on hunting and the mastering of dangerous situations. In fact, the entire expedition is presented as a journey undertaken by Schneeberger, Siedentopf, Suchoky, and Udet. The filming is mentioned briefly, but the other members of the crew and the original reason for the stay in East Africa are completely erased. The women who were part of the expedition and filming are entirely absent from the text and the illustrations.

Of the ten illustrations not a single one features an African person. Two photos focus on Udet, two on animals, and one shows his travel companions Schneeberger and Suchoky. Five pictures included within this chapter on Africa are not related to the African journey and feature an air show in Los Angeles and scenes from the Greenland expedition during which the movie *SOS Eisberg* had been filmed. Just as Africans are missing among the visual representations, they are hardly mentioned in the text. After five pages of text and four illustrations, the reader learns about the presence of Africans for the first time. "We move our base to Babati in the area of the Ufiume-negroes."[67] The Babati, or Ufiume, who figured so prominently and positively in Udet's *Fremde Vögel,* are now "negro females" (*Negerweiber*), who are acknowledged as "slender" but whose gait is described as "strangely floating" (140). The next reference seems initially appreciative. Babati women are again described as slender, the men as proud. But this image is quickly interpreted by Schneeberger: "They are so nice . . . because one does not see the dirt on them." White settlers emerge as the genuine natives of the area (142). Other episodes have Africans burst forth screaming out of the bush, or let them assault a dead buffalo with their long knives (144). In another scene Babati girls are said to be jumping around the airplane, with "bouncing breasts" (149). The encounter with the Lau in southern Sudan (151–53), already a problematic scene in *Fremde Vögel,* is dramatically blown up in this later account. Only a story involving hunting techniques of the Masai vaguely recalls the appreciative image rendered in *Fremde Vögel* (146–47).

Udet's text from 1935 clearly aligns itself with the new ideology. An epilogue of two pages expresses Udet's association with Nazi beliefs: "My own life has become insignificant, it has merged with the current of our common German fate. We were soldiers without a flag. Now we raised it again. The Führer gave it back to us. For the old soldiers, life has become worth living again" (176–77). This epilogue, which most explicitly expresses his nationalist orientation, is followed by a list of Udet's downings of airplanes during World War I. While the erasure of the film crew and the transformation of the time in Africa into an adventure story can be explained as a reaction to the negative reception of the film, the rewriting of the image of Africa is clearly ideological. (Most likely, the elimination of the women from the account occurred for the same reason.)

Udet died on November 17, 1941, from a self-inflicted gunshot wound. The official explanation issued by the Nazis claimed that he died accidentally while trying out a new gun. Friends and biographers seem to agree, however, that he committed suicide. Carl Zuckmayer eternalized Udet in his play *Des Teufels General* (1945; first draft 1942); General Harras, who dies in the play in a suicide mission because of the disenchantment with the political system he served, is molded after Udet.[68] The discrepancies between *Fremde Vögel* and *Mein Fliegerleben* most clearly demonstrate the abrupt change that Udet underwent and are indications of the tension that might have driven the pilot to suicide. Like Junghans and Riefenstahl and many others, Udet was opportunistic and pursued a path that proved to be beneficial for his own career. Ultimately, however, he might not have been able to reconcile his worldview with that of the Nazis.

PART TWO

Successors

4

Humanitarian Interventions

The German Army and Bodo Kirchhoff in Somalia

Grievous times are now upon us, times of death and woe.
The sky has turned to smoke,
There is uproar and shrieking, columns of dust, attacks—
In truth this world is smouldering with strife
And with forebodings of war.
Friends part and head their different ways,
Close kinsmen align themselves in rival factions
And pierce each other's flesh with spears.
Loyalty to one's kin, and respect for the parents of one's spouse,
Are ways of life which are now dead.
—Maxamed Cabdille Xasan, "Perhaps the Trumpet Has Sounded"

UNOSOM: A Test Case for the New Germany

In the course of 1991 the world became aware of an unfolding disaster in Somalia. As a result of political disintegration and an extreme ecological crisis, hundreds of thousands of people had already died, and the lives of millions of Somalis were at stake. Beginning in January 1992, the United Nations decided on various measures, grouped under a mission called United Nations Operation in Somalia (UNOSOM, later UNOSOM I), designed to further the peace process in Somalia.[1] Mohamed Sahnoun, special representative and head of UNOSOM until his resignation on October 26, 1992, led a fact-finding mission to the affected areas in March of that year. He describes the extent of the crisis: "At least 300,000 people had died of hunger and hunger-related disease, and thousands more were casualties of the repression and the civil war. Seventy percent of the country's livestock had been lost, and the farming areas had been devastated, compelling the farming population to seek refuge in remote areas or across the border in refugee camps. Some 500,000 people were in camps in Ethiopia, Kenya, and Djibouti. More than 3,000—mostly women, children, and old men—were dying daily from starvation."[2]

While the steps taken by the United Nations were initially along the lines of a classical *peacekeeping* mission (that is, designed to provide humanitarian aid, to attempt to negotiate a cease-fire, and to impose a total arms embargo), the operation gradually developed into a *peace-enforcing* intervention involving military actions. Facing the reality of an increasing crisis in Somalia, the Security Council of the United Nations voted in its third resolution on Somalia on April 24, 1992, to launch UNOSOM. Following the breakdown of a cease-fire and the further disintegration of Somali society, the United Nations decided to expand the scope of the operation. Resolution 794, adopted by the Security Council on December 3, 1992, went farther than any preceding UN mission.[3] It "authorizes the Secretary-General and Member States . . . to use all necessary means to establish as soon as possible a secure environment for humanitarian relief operations."[4] The Somalia resolutions of the Security Council are also exceptional in that they all attribute the need for intervention to a perceived "threat to international peace and security."[5] This reasoning indicates a shift from preventing strife between states to interventions aimed at restoring order within a state—that is, for the first time it allows UN involvement in a civil war by identifying it as a threat to world peace. Under the leadership of the United States, UNOSOM I developed into UNITAF (United Task Force, generally known as Operation Restore Hope), an operation aiming at peace enforcement.[6] After a large portion of American troops left Somalia in the spring of 1993, and UNOSOM II was launched by the United Nations, new contingents were needed in order to secure a fragile stability in the war-ridden country.[7]

Among the new contingents arriving in Somalia in 1993 were German troops. The decision by the German government to join this UN operation was the result of a long and passionate debate that did not cease even when the first German soldiers were already on their way to the Horn of Africa. The question of the German army's participation in UN military operations had been increasingly discussed since unification, and German participation in UNOSOM became a test case for defining the foreign policy of a unified Germany. UNOSOM provided Germany with an opportunity to redefine its new role on the international scene; in that regard, the debate is comparable to West Germany's postwar discussion leading up to rearmament. Particularly relevant in this context, and predating the heated controversy over UNOSOM, was the debate over the German stance in the First Persian Gulf War.[8]

Regarding its participation in UNOSOM, the German government ultimately reread its Constitution (which originally defines the mission of the German army as "defense") to allow for the army's participation in the Somalia operations. The developments leading up to this newly conceived purpose of the German army occurred over the course of several years. Beginning in 1991, German soldiers had participated in a number of UN operations: apart from German participation in enforcing the no-fly zone over Bosnia-Herzegovina, German soldiers had provided humanitarian aid in Turkey, Iran, Cambodia, and the former Yugoslavia. Expert military personnel had taken part in a mine-clearing mission in the Arabian Gulf, and the Bundeswehr facilitated UN flights in Iraq by providing airplanes and helicopters. In particular, Germans were discussing whether the German army should be allowed to join *out-of-area* military operations not brought about by a need to defend German territory.[9]

Several historical events made it possible for Germany to justify the participation of its army in out-of-area military operations.[10] Because compatibility with the postwar German constitution was at stake, the debate was structured in the form of a "debate of principles" (*Grundsatzdebatte*). Article 87a, paragraphs 1 and 2, of the Constitution contain guidelines for the use of troops and limit the purpose of the army to "defense." As a reaction to the lessons of the two world wars, this provision was intended to preclude the option of engaging in aggressive foreign policy through constitutionally specified guidelines. Article 24 of the Constitution is also of relevance: it describes the transfer of "sovereignty to international institutions." In addition, compatibility with Article 59, paragraph 2, which regulates parliamentary endorsement (*Zustimmungsgesetz*), played a significant role in the debate. In sum, several factors were important in resolving the issue: the definition of *defense* (*Verteidigung*) and *defense situation* (*Verteidigungsfall*);

the definition of the term *operation* (*Einsatz*); whether the Constitution regulates geographical or political areas of operation; whether membership in alliances obliges Germany to participate in operations larger than strictly national ones; and whether especially the membership in the United Nations (but also in NATO, KSZE, and other international bodies) necessitates a redefinition of the existing state order in terms of international scenarios. As Wolfgang März points out—and he summarizes the consensus existing among the leading voices of the debate—historical developments have made it possible to understand Article 87a GG differently today from when it was written.[11] These developments—that is, the interpretation of these developments that was endorsed by a majority of Germans—ultimately enabled the German army to participate in UN operations without requiring an actual rewriting of the Constitution.[12] The reinterpretation of the Constitution was clearly a political endeavor; a different understanding of unified Germany's role in the international arena would have allowed for the continuation of West Germany's former foreign policy.

A first attempt to codify a new vision of an expanded German role in the international arena were the "Guidelines for Security Policy," published by Secretary of Defense Volker Rühe on November 26, 1992, in which he set the parameters for German security policy and for German military actions, including in areas outside of territory comprised within NATO. On December 17, 1992, the German government decided to send a contingent of up to fifteen hundred soldiers in support of the United Nations operation to Somalia, a decision that immediately set off a heated debate. Beginning in August 1992, the German air force had already been participating in an airlift to bring medicine and food from Kenya to Somalia, but the German government wanted to get involved on a larger scale. Reaffirming its principle decision from December, the government restated its determination to send a contingent of seventeen hundred German soldiers to support UNOSOM on April 21, 1993, even before the question of constitutionality was clarified. Originally, the German soldiers were to be stationed in Bosaso, a coastal town in northeastern Somalia. For a number of reasons it was decided that the Germans would be more useful (and safer) in Belet Huen, approximately three hundred kilometers north of Mogadishu. It seems that the decision to send the Germans to Belet Huen originated with Maj.

Gen. Thomas Montgomery, deputy commander of UNOSOM II military forces and senior U.S. forces commander during UNOSOM II, who figures negatively in German reports about Somalia and, as certain problematic aspects of the German mission unfold, develops into a scapegoat responsible for the distress of the Germans.[13] The mission of the German soldiers was to provide humanitarian aid and to solve logistical problems but most of all to support a contingent of forty-five hundred Indian troops (ironically, these Indian troops never arrived). Because of possible attacks by local Somali groups, the German soldiers were equipped with armored vehicles, in order to be able to defend themselves.

An advance detachment left Germany for Somalia on May 12. In mid-June, when only 240 German soldiers had arrived in Somalia, the Social Democrats (SPD) put in a request for a legal order (*einstweilige Anordnung*) to stop the mission until the Supreme Court had come to a decision regarding its legality. In its ruling on June 23 the Supreme Court stated that the House of Representatives was eligible to decide the matter and therefore worked out a clever compromise, ruling in favor of the SPD's request yet setting the stage for legalization through the Parliament. This move indeed led to a legalization of German participation in UNOSOM II through a positive vote of the Parliament on July 2. The debate had been heated once more. The following exchange between two members of parliament might not be representative of German parliamentary debates, but it does reflect a distinct linguistic and intellectual ignorance toward Africans. The Christian Democrat Joachim Graf von Schönburg-Glauchau, speaking in favor of German intervention in Somalia, reasoned that "for example a village can be terrorized by a horde of monkeys and no woman will be able to fetch water or till the fields if nobody keeps the monkey horde in check."[14] Konrad Weiß, a member of the Left-leaning Bündnis 90, at whom Schönburg-Glauchau's comments were directed, answered—without reflecting upon the count's questionable comparison—that it was not the duty of "soldiers from Pirna or Pirmasens to keep the monkey hordes in Africa in check."[15]

The Supreme Court ruling and the parliamentary vote were important in determining the new status of unified Germany in the international arena, and they are indicative of the direction the German government wanted to take. The debate over the mission of the German army, mirroring those over the peacekeeping and peace-enforcing role of the United Nations, continues to this day.[16]

Intellectuals and Artists: The Moral Conscience of a Nation?

German intellectuals and artists have a long-standing tradition of intervening in debates over foreign policy; especially since the confrontations of the 1960s, German writers and other public figures have consistently voiced their opinions about the repercussions of global capitalism, imperialism, military conflicts, development aid, and, in this case, humanitarian intervention. Often mostly liberal intellectuals have projected their own dreams of a just society onto the non-European countries at the center of the debates. Arlene Teraoka has shown how postwar German writers employed the Third World as a vehicle to "envision a nonhegemonic mode of encounter with non-German others," in the course of which they nevertheless perpetuated "Eurocentric, sexist, and racist images."[17] Texts by Hans Christoph Buch, Hans Magnus Enzensberger, Günther Grass, Franz Xaver Kroetz, Christoph Peters, Martin Walser, and others reflect this tension.

One feature that distinguishes many of these texts is the gap between the writers' lack of knowledge about the countries they discuss and the scale of the claims made.[18] Often writers were invited to spend several months or weeks in one of the Goethe-Institutes located in Africa, Latin America, and Asia and, more or less as a by-product of this circumstance, published a firsthand account of the country they encountered. Many of these texts take the form of eyewitness accounts, a version of the autobiographical genre and one that holds a particular appeal. A special claim to truth is often attributed to reports by eyewitnesses. Eyewitness testimony is essential in the legal system, although it is interesting to note that it is weighed differently in different cultures. While the legal system of the United States places a relatively high value on such testimony, the German judicial system assigns a higher credibility to circumstantial evidence.[19]

Eyewitnesses themselves are very charismatic; they stimulate the imagination, become objects for identification, and serve as proxies through which a situation can be experienced. Eyewitnesses seem to be most believable if they are outsiders, if they appear to observe from a neutral, unbiased perspective. This apparently neutral perspective endows their views with a potential truth value; it seems to raise subjective statements to a level of objectivity. We assume that the gaze of the outsider is innocent, that it is more truthful than the reports of the media, the government, or the scholar, who might have consulted many books but has him- or herself never encountered the actual object of study. And who would be more predestined to assume the role of the eyewitness than the artist, the paradigmatic outsider?

The eyewitness takes on a special significance when involved in current events. Coverage of Africa often appears in the form of eyewitness accounts, such as essays by Ryšzard Kapuściński, some of which are published in *The Shadow of the Sun: My African Life* (2001). In Germany Peter Handke's firsthand accounts of Serbia (1996), which appeared amid the continued political strife in Bosnia, provoked an intense and controversial discussion.[20] Another such example arose in the context of the Somali crisis, which inspired the German writer Bodo Kirchhoff to evaluate the UN operation in the country.[21]

Kirchhoff undertook the journey to Somalia primarily in order to write an account of the German participation in UNOSOM. The writer spent fourteen days during the summer of 1993, from June 19 to July 2, in a German army camp in Belet Huen and in Mogadishu. Kirchhoff became an eyewitness to the events in Somalia, and his experience is documented in his travel diary, *Herrenmenschlichkeit* (*Humanity of the Masters,* 1994). What led him to undertake this potentially dangerous mission?

Kirchhoff went to Somalia to see for himself whether this intervention, and particularly the German participation in it, was legitimate: "I opt for finding out whether this operation can be meaningful or not" (28).[22] In this search he reflected the desire of many Germans to have access to information not mediated through government sources or reflecting governmental and party politics but which comes from an unbiased outsider. Apart from assessing the role the Germans were playing in the operation, Kirchhoff raises more general questions about humanitarian interventions and regarding the role of the United Nations, which, as already indicated, is in a process of reassessing its function since the end of the Cold War.[23]

Kirchhoff seemed a qualified candidate for the kind of adventure that awaited him in Somalia. Many of his novels (*Zwiefalten,* 1983; *Mexikanische Novelle,* 1984; *Infanta,* 1990; *Der Sandmann,* 1992), short stories ("Olmayra Sanchez und ich," "Der Badeanzug," "Desire," and Tschakwau," among them, published in 1987 with other short stories in *Ferne Frauen*), and essays center around questions regarding cultural difference and the complex power relations between rich and poor nations. Some of the texts are based on extensive travel in Africa, Asia, Latin America, and the United States, which the writer has undertaken since the early 1980s.

It is important to note, however, that Kirchhoff is generally less interested in understanding other cultures than in the portrayal of what he calls the "German abroad" (8). For the most part the other serves to elucidate and mirror the self; the goal is not to engage with the other as a distinct subject. This perspective is especially evident in Kirchhoff's essays. "Skat in Addis Abeba: Eine gesamtdeutsche Auftragsarbeit" (1981) is more a commentary on the German Democratic Republic, on the relationship between East and West Germany, and on some aspects of development aid than about Ethiopia.[24] "Im Reich der Ungeliebten: Deutsche Szenen aus Bangkok" (1982) describes the adventures of German sex tourists in Bangkok.[25] The aspirations and dealings of German right-wing expatriates in Paraguay is the topic of "Der Mantel des schönen Konsuls: Neue Flüchtlingsgespräche in Asunción" (1982).[26] "Nach Abzug der Scham" (1982), again ostensibly looking at German sex tourism in Bangkok, turns out to be a cynical commentary on the West German intellectual scene of the early 1980s.[27] "Zeichen und Wunder: Ein Reisebericht" (1982), referring once more to the trip to Ethiopia, reflects upon the author's struggle in relating to other cultures.[28] And in "Dem Schmerz eine Welt geben," originally presented as a lecture at the university in Frankfurt, Kirchhoff recounts his stay in Somalia in order to develop his views on the function of writing in contemporary society.[29] Kirchhoff also wrote the screenplay for Romuald Karmakar's film *Manila* (1999), which revolves around German tourists in Thailand.

In Kirchhoff's work writing about non-European cultural contexts is an exercise in attempting to understand the self. The alienation from home enables the German narrative voice, be it fictional or autobiographical, to bring out concealed aspects of Germanness; the displacement makes possible what is impossible at home: to talk about anxieties and desires, fears and dreams. This by itself legitimate dimension of Kirchhoff's writing, that the other functions to highlight aspects of Germanness but is not thematized for his or her own sake, plays an essential role in Kirchhoff's account of UNOSOM.

While the German subject is always at the center of Kirchhoff's narratives, this self is highly problematic. Whether his texts deal with Germans abroad or at home, the identity of the protagonist—a constructed, inauthentic, alienated, modern, and male German individual—is always contested. For the most part Kirchhoff narrates his texts from a singular first- or third-person perspective (in contrast, the novels *Infanta* and *Schundroman* [2002] are told by an omniscient narrator). Throughout his oeuvre, Kirchhoff's male German narrator raises questions about the impossibility of human interaction and of communication; of sexual exploitation, sex tourism, materialism, the impossibility of authentic experience, and the interrelatedness of fantasy and reality. His protagonists are often detached, enigmatic figures; they frequently appear as cold, emotionless narcissists who have lost the ability to engage in human interaction.

Yet, as Benjamin Henrichs points out in an analysis of Kirchhoff's first published prose text, "Ohne Eifer, ohne Zorn" (1979), it seems that, more than Narcissus, "the crabby Onan . . . [is] the symbolic figure" in Kirchhoff's text.[30] In this early analysis Henrichs quite appropriately names the gesture of self-absorption that is a central motive of so many texts by Kirchhoff. The author pursues these themes in his plays, novels, and narratives, such as *Body-Building* (1978, 1980), *Die Einsamkeit der Haut* (1981), *Dame und Schwein* (1985), "Der Ansager einer Striptease-nummer gibt nicht auf" (1994), *Katastrophen mit Seeblick: Geschichten* (1998), *Drei Fische für zwei Paare* (first performance 2001), and *Parlando* (2001), Kirchhoff's most accomplished novel to date. The protagonists are unable to establish human contact, to find fulfillment in and through another. The incarnation of these Onan-like figures is the first-person narrator in the short story "Der Mittelpunkt des Universums" (1980), who masturbates sitting in front of a mirror and, as a logical conclusion to this self-absorbed ritual, finally licks up his own sperm.[31]

Women and the culturally different in Kirchhoff's work serve to articulate the self-centeredness and materialism of the modern world, in which social relations are transformed into business transactions and the human body becomes fetishized. It is this aspect of Kirchhoff's texts that distinguishes them as critical commentaries on modern existence: the absence of questions about happiness, ethics, and communication let the reader contemplate this omission. His masturbating protagonists are the mirror image of an alienated world and bring to the fore that which is lost. Kirchhoff's detailed description of his heroes' thinking and feeling provoke a desire for that which is absent from their world. In perceiving what is missing, the reader is asked to develop an alternate vision. It should be added that Kirchhoff masterfully creates a suspenseful and captivating atmosphere in his novels and short stories, which often contain elements of mystery writing.

Kirchhoff is a visible figure in contemporary Germany's cultural scene. The extensive discussion of "Der Ansager einer Striptease-nummer gibt nicht auf," for example, documents the attention critics and readers pay to his publications.[32] His provocative writings about sexuality and gender relations, in particular, have made the author a contested public figure. Kirchhoff's celebrity is attested to by his participation on juries and committees for literary prizes, such as the Bettina-von-Arnim-Literaturpreis, sponsored by the women's magazine *Brigitte*, and the Gratwanderpreis für erotische Kurzgeschichten, sponsored by the German *Playboy*. Yet Kirchhoff's daring excursions into the world of human (especially male) fantasies have also turned the author into an icon of machismo, and critics treat him as the embodiment of an overload of testosterone. Kirchhoff himself is largely responsible for this image; provocative public appearances and statements (including an interview with the German *Playboy*) have influenced the reception of his literary texts. The conflation of the life of the author with the characters and message of his works leads to a reductive reception of Kirchhoff's powerful writing and cultural critique.

To escape his image as the paradigmatic macho writer, Kirchhoff submitted the play *Mach nicht den Tag zur Nacht* under the pseudonym Odette Haussmann for the 1997 Autorentheatertage at the Schauspiel Hannover. Haussmann introduced herself as a German-French writer from the island of La Réunion, presently living in a psychiatric clinic in London. Jury member Wolfgang Höbel selected it as the best play from among 193 submissions. When the identity of the author was revealed by the journal *Focus* shortly thereafter, critics reacted overwhelmingly with diatribes against Kirchhoff, possibly out of solidarity with Höbel and in fearful anticipation of having to face similar embarrassments. Unfortunately, Kirchhoff did not know how to capitalize on these reactions: instead of advertising the selection of his play as an indication of the literary and intellectual strengths of his writing and as proof of his ability to write about gender relations in ways that transcend a perspective bound to his own gender, he pouted. He claimed that the revelation of his identity was detrimental to the play and that he now found himself in the situation he had hoped to avoid—namely, that the play was dismissed on account of knowledge about his authorship.[33]

The author's public persona and the characteristics of the literary texts outlined here—chiefly, the narcissism of Kirchhoff's materialistic, alienated protagonists and their inability to communicate with others—are important for an understanding of Kirchhoff's Somalia account. While the cynicism and provocation contained in Kirchhoff's literary texts succeed in highlighting problems of human existence in the modern world, these stylistic means are perceived differently by the reader when it comes to autobiographically inspired essays or, as is the case with regard to *Herrenmenschlichkeit,* the autobiographically inspired diary. And here the person Kirchhoff and his views need to be taken into consideration. In light of Kirchhoff's intention to contribute to the discussion about the meaningfulness of German participation in UNOSOM and about the general legitimacy of the intervention ("I opt for finding out whether this operation can be meaningful or not"), his text deserves to be taken seriously. Whereas a literary account has manifold options to develop a differentiated narrative, involving different voices and multilayered perspectives, and is thus potentially able to describe many of the contradictions and complexities of reality, the eyewitness report, through its one-dimensionality, is naturally limited. This limitation does not have to be a shortcoming, however; a limited but unique perspective may be invaluable for the understanding of a particular situation. On the other hand, an eyewitness report cannot replace a multidimensional investigation into a problem, and here is where Kirchhoff's account, which is stocked in bookstores' sections devoted to political rather than literary books, becomes pretentious. Rather than sticking to his initial presentation of the account as subjective and limited, he ends up generalizing and drawing conclusions that bear no adequate relation to his actual experiences. Generalizations, a lack of self-reflexivity, and an even stronger lack of knowledge of historical conditions lead to a perpetuation of cultural prejudices, especially about African cultures. Why did Kirchhoff's project ultimately fail? Why did the text not contribute to the establishment of a more differentiated assessment of the situation in Somalia and the question of humanitarian intervention?

Humanity of the Masters

Five days after the Supreme Court ruling and only a few days before the parliamentary vote allowing the dispatching of troops to Somalia, Bodo Kirchhoff's upcoming visit to Somalia was announced for the first time in the June 28 edition of the weekly *Der Spiegel*.[34] Four weeks later excerpts from Kirchhoff's diary were published in the magazine.[35] The longer book version, *Herrenmenschlichkeit,* on which my discussion is based, was published a few months afterward, in 1994. The dust jacket of the book deserves some attention: it uses the photograph of a smiling African child, dressed in blue sweatpants, adorned with the Adidas logo, a T-shirt with the design of the German soccer team, and green rubber sandals. The child seems to be dancing or attempting to skip over his own shadow. The background color of the dust jacket is beige, evoking desert sand: the child seems almost forlorn, accidentally dropped off in the void of the desert. The letters of the book's title cover a part of the child's head. Thus, the words "Humanity of the Masters" encroach on the child's body, which is dressed in German clothing. This allegorical depiction of the relationship between the ideology of humanism and Somali bodies, however, does not express the critique voiced in this text but, rather, reflects Kirchhoff's project itself.

Herrenmenschlichkeit, like the original excerpts in *Der Spiegel,* is presented in diary form, although no longer organized strictly chronologically. It is divided into various sections that recount Kirchhoff's time in Somalia and includes a smaller number of interspersed sections covering the author's stay in a German hospital in Frankfurt. The past and the present finally converge on the last pages, which document his stay in an Italian hotel where the author recovered from hernia surgery. This illness began on the second day of his stay in Somalia, eventually forcing Kirchhoff to end his trip prematurely and to return to Germany for surgery. The text about Somalia is thus also the story of an illness. This feature, namely the way in which Kirchhoff intertwines the journey and the illness, points to the constructedness of the narrative voice. Although the narrative voice of the text is not fictional, as the first-person narrator of a novel would be, the conscious narrative embedding requires us to analyze this autobiographical first-person voice in much the same way as we would a piece of fiction.

The presentation of the narrator's illness demonstrates this fictionlike quality most vividly. On June 19, his first day in Somalia, the narrator notices "pain in the loins while carrying" (10). Repeatedly, he mentions the increasing pain resulting from his hernia (13, 15, 18, 20, 50), and he is worried about his inability to run: "Me, on the other hand, nervous, knowing that I can't run" (31; cf. 38). Additionally, the narrator has to deal with the repercussions of a stomach flu and take medication. Regarding the malaria pill Paludrine, Kirchhoff suspects that it is also prescribed to the German soldiers to weaken their sex drive (49). Furthermore, the narrator is annoyed with the desert sand and a gigantic spider, infamous for its painful bite.[36] The reader thus encounters the narrator as a vulnerable person, wounded among soldiers, journalists, and Somalis. It removes him, the civilian, even more from the military and from the media personnel, and it highlights his awkward position. The illness marks the writer, who lives with the troops as a kind of "army chaplain," as a marginal, displaced figure.[37] In fact, the illness gives him an air of heroism: he stays on even though he is wounded so that he can make his observations and report to us. Kirchhoff casts his narrator as a classic antihero, whose weakness is bound, or at least meant, to earn him sympathy.

The narrator announces self-reflexivity with the very first sentence of the account. The phrase "The Somalis, as far as I was able to observe them" indicates subjectivity and subtly excuses the narrator from the responsibility of knowing about things he has not seen (7). He directly addresses the limitations of his own project—namely, that his writing about Somalia is based on a rather brief encounter (56–57). Such disclaimers appear repeatedly in the text, the narrator often commenting on his statements with interjected phrases such as "I believe" or

"I think."[38] His account, therefore, stresses "observation" and was not composed after consulting background materials. It is the admittedly subjective, yet disengaged, report of an eyewitness who relates information acquired by observation and through hearsay: "As I was told" is one of the phrases the narrator uses to describe how he gathered information (7). Such reflexivity seems to bolster his position as a neutral, unbiased observer. This is further enforced through the structure of the extended diary: the passages referring to the time in the hospital and in the Italian hotel indicate a thought process, a continued reflection about the experiences in Somalia. They signal the writer's attempt at gaining distance, apparently in order to present and comprehend the events objectively.

The predicament of his limited subjective view, however, appears to be counteracted by the writer's marginal existence in the camp and in Somalia. He identifies himself as an "outsider" (9), a "foreigner" (48, 50), and the "only civilian" (48). The narrator often emphasizes that his goal is honesty: "I don't think I write in order to expand my circle of friends; when it seems appropriate I make myself vulnerable, systematically. It would seem shameful to me to hide any conflict with myself—a conscious difference to the heroes of modernity (whom I as well once honored) who seemed to live the way they wrote" (27). He thus promises a great deal of sincerity, even if that means acknowledging ambivalences and paradoxes for which he has no solution: "Question: What would you advise? Answer: I am clueless" (62–63). The narrator cannot resort to easy, reductive answers: "Of course I would prefer to be, crazy thought, one-dimensional, an Orwell, and write my Homage to Catalonia, but for me, for us, because we are well informed about the horrors committed by all sides, remains only a nomadic existence between good and evil" (36).

Both factors—physical vulnerability and the marginal, self-reflexive status—seem to qualify the narrator as a neutral observer, an ideal eyewitness to the events in Somalia. Yet a closer look at the diary reveals that this form of self-reflexivity and marginality is in many ways akin to the narcissism of Kirchhoff's literary protagonists. The narrator's goal to write about the German abroad is reflected in the content of the narrative itself, which is in fact an account of a German abroad, and ultimately reveals more about this German than about the situation in

Somalia. To be sure, the narrator foregrounds questions regarding the ethics and motives underlying humanitarian aid and intervention. But the diary tells us more about the views the German narrator holds about cultural difference than about the Somalis themselves; it tells us more about the writer's subjective ideas regarding the relationship between Germany and Africa than about the concrete situation in Somalia.

This becomes evident in every aspect of the text: in the narrator's critical view of the role the media plays in reports about war and famine, in his descriptions of homosocial life in the military, in the portrayals of soldiers from different nations, and, finally, in those passages in which he discusses the Somali people and their war-ridden country. A closer look at the text reveals that the narrator, in his act of witnessing Africa firsthand, falls back on stereotypes instead of bringing historical knowledge to bear. In the following discussion I focus on Kirchhoff's portrayal of soldiers, journalists, and Somalis to demonstrate how these images reflect German clichés about Africa and about other nations. I suggest that historicizing the situation in Somalia could have prevented Kirchhoff from reproducing stereotypical views and racist thought patterns and from lapsing into a lament about the inaccessibility of cultural difference and feelings of helplessness in the face of human suffering.

Among the German soldiers the narrator feels "less uneasy than [he] had expected," and he contemplates whether the reason might lie in the fact that he himself "had once been a soldier." The narrator remembers how he had joined the German army voluntarily, in contrast to "the friends who lived a good life in West Berlin and Frankfurt" and who had forgotten him quickly after he enlisted (17). He presents himself as a political activist who, in contrast to the aforementioned friends, lives rather than theorizes his convictions. His time in the army emerges as a turning point, leading up to the artistic career of the writer. The reader thus learns that the narrator's service in the army resulted in a reversal of his initially negative opinion of the military; while he no longer aspired to change the army, the change occurred within the narrator himself. At the same time, he developed an aversion to armed rebellions in the cities—that is, to anarchistic, guerrilla tactics, as had been propagated and practiced by members of the Red Army Faction in the late 1960s and early 1970s (17–18). Both aspects are influential for the narrator's evaluation of the events in Somalia: a critical yet appreciative relationship to the Bundeswehr and a strong dislike for armed rebellions.

The narrator renders the atmosphere in the German camp in a sympathetic, at times even tender, way. He strikingly describes the different symbolic dimensions of this excursion to Somalia for the average soldier: “Their first big trip, they say; their world up to now: Saarbrücken, Schalke, Majorca, Gottschalk; one had once been to Paris. And now this! They seem like carnival princes and, as the inspection drags on, they teach the children *Alle meine Entchen*” (11). The mission to Somalia is thus related to tourism, sports, and entertainment, areas of German life that are distinct from the work sphere. The military intervention is likened to a carnival parade; tanks turn into floats upon which the German soldiers are seated, like carnival royalties, engaging playfully with Somali children. The narrator succeeds in highlighting dimensions of the mission that stand in stark contrast to its seriousness: that German soldiers are called upon to save people from starvation and that they could potentially get involved in deadly battle.

Repeatedly, the soldiers, passing out ballpoint pens and gummy bears (11, 54), are shown in an affectionate vein: “On the way to the tent a soldier, apparently lost in thought, humming the theme song of *Sandmännchen*” (59). This generally positive portrayal of the German soldiers continues in the descriptions of high-ranking military personnel. The second officer in command appears as an intelligent, friendly, experienced, and differentiated man (12, 16, 22, 48–49, 61). The commanding officer wins the narrator’s approval because of his sense of humor and self-reflexivity (10).

The German army is thus characterized by its human behavior: birthdays are acknowledged during morning roll call (18), mothers send greetings to their sons via the radio show (13), homesickness and phone calls home are mentioned (21), army barracks are adorned with posters of Neuschwanstein (41), a canteen woman named Gertrud provides a friendly place to hang out (12, 50, 56, 59), and the narrator enjoys the “the peaceful tumult of evening leisure” (15). Even “the first German officers who will be part of a UN staff” are “excited like children on their way to summer camp” (30–31).

Acknowledging the humanity of the German soldiers and the carnivalesque and exotic aspect of the mission to Somalia, the narrator’s portrayals remain superficial; they do not take into consideration issues of power within the army and with regard to the relationship between Germans and Somalis. The reader is not informed about the average German soldier's thoughts about Africans, his status in Somalia, how he understands the role he plays in this mission, why this mission is actually occurring, how well the soldiers are informed about the reasons leading up to the intervention, or the ultimate goal of the operation. In contrast to the average soldier, the high-ranking officials are presented as well-informed, identifying with the mission, believing in the humanist goals, and differentiated in assessing the complex situation. Yet the narrator does not offer a single questionable or contradictory character in his account.

This generalizing attitude toward the German army is not convincing. In July 1997 the discovery of a video, produced by seven German soldiers who were stationed in Bosnia, provoked a public outcry. The video, filmed during lunch breaks in the spring of 1996, simulates scenes of torture, rape, and crucifixion and was circulated among comrades, none of whom found anything objectionable in the brutal mimicry of civil war violence. The ensuing public debate produced additional uncomfortable stories and an acknowledgment that even the army of a democratic country is still trained to kill.[39] The incident became a lightning rod for further debates; articles in the popular press criticized the way the Bundeswehr handled the incident and unearthed even more disquieting information.

Earlier accusations in conjunction with alleged human rights violations committed by Belgian, Canadian, and Italian soldiers in Somalia had also emerged against the German soldiers.[40] These charges of torture, rape, and other abuses of Somalis at the hands of UN soldiers proved to be unfounded with regard to the Germans; the creation of the Bosnian video, however, with other incidents publicized in the wake of the debate, revealed elements of brutality present in the German army that are entirely glossed over in Kirchhoff's account, which reads like a promotional piece for the German military.

The validity of the narrator's portrayal of German soldiers becomes doubtful particularly in comparison to his presentation of other troops, especially the Americans, the Italians, and the Nigerians, whose camps flank that of the Germans, to protect the Germans and the area as a whole (11). In contrast to the more humane and disciplined German army, we see the Italians with "shaved bald skulls and hand grenades on the blouse" (24); they are "in every respect different from the German soldiers, in every respect picturesque. . . . cursing, flirting, photographing, weapon present, a child at their hand—in camouflaged battle suit, with a fragmentation vest looking like it was designed by Armani" (37), self-confident in "their manliness" (47). The Nigerians are exclusively characterized through their nightly activities: using binoculars, German soldiers observe from a watchtower how the Nigerian soldiers frequent the same hut every night (20, 55). Such passages reduce the respective soldiers to clichés, namely, the image of the semi-fascist gigolo and that of the sexualized African, and thus replicate familiar stereotypes.

The Americans are characterized by figures such as General Montgomery, "a man with a tough boy's face who forced the Germans . . . into Belet Huen because they would not be included under the UN mandate in the area in the North originally determined" (24–25); and the American marines: "People who look as if they were genetically engineered, sweeping gestures, bald, unattainable, and even in shorts still as if armed" (41). In particular, the Americans are criticized for their approach to the preeminent Somali warlord Mohammed Farah Aideed (39–40) and an attack on allies of Aideed on July 12, which ends fatally for the German reporter Hansjörg Krauss (41–42, 64).

These portrayals of U.S. soldiers are diametrically opposed to those offered by Mark Bowden in his documentary account *Black Hawk Down: A Story of Modern War* (1999), on which Ridley Scott's film version, *Black Hawk Down* (2001), is based. Bowden's account of the intervention in Somalia is designed as "a reminder that the seemingly inhuman machine of the American military is made up of individual men and women, often serving at great personal sacrifice even when not thrust into war. . . . They deserve to be honored and remembered."[41] Both the book and the film adhere to this premise, and, as a result, the portrayal of the conflict is limited by a one-dimensional perspective. Bowden holds Somalis solely responsible for the famine in Somalia and does not provide background information on the larger genesis of the problems.[42] In a similar vein the film makes no attempt to include a Somali perspective of the events. In contrast to Kirchhoff's narrator, the U.S. soldiers in Bowden's and Scott's versions of the conflict emerge as differentiated individuals who—for the most part—are inspired by a genuine desire to help.

Kirchhoff's narrator, on the other hand, ascribes to the American soldiers a particularly thoughtless, cold-blooded way of killing. The July 12 attack had resulted in the deaths of a number of civilians, among them women and children. It had produced "a bloodbath close to the building that the pilots bombarded so thoughtlessly, with this kind of lightness, which, I think, exists only in America—which all of us who are thoroughly appalled by Major Swieckowski's [the American spokesman] world love fully with this same heart in Hollywood films" (42). Even if the narrator offers a self-critical look at German ambivalence toward American culture, the upshot of this account of Americanness is a thoroughly negative image of the American troops. They appear exceptional in their relationship to killing ("as it only exists in America"), and their martial nature is emphasized by the contrasting representations of the Germans. Interestingly, this feature—to set off Germans traveling abroad favorably against Americans, who generally come across as imperialist, insensitive, and self-centered—is a standard trope in German literature, from novels by Karl May to contemporary texts by Hans Christoph Buch.

The fundamental differences between national armies come to the fore in a scene at Gertrud's canteen, where the soldiers gather after the Supreme Court ruling that allowed the German mission in Somalia to continue: "Almost uncanny rationality, even later, at Gertrud's: no free beer, no singing—only in the media coverage about these hours; Americans and Italians, congratulators that evening, they marvel: such a sober, unpretentious army, is that at all conceivable?" (29) In these passages the national armies are reduced to types, types that quite obviously reproduce clichés and prejudices about each nation. Most important, however, these portraits of other troops result in evoking a generally positive image of the Bundeswehr, which, as opposed to the other troops, is not characterized by sex (Nigerians, Italians), violence, and vanity (Americans, Italians) but by the singing of lullabies and the distribution of gummy bears and whose officers are only driven by honorable motivations.

The narrator's views on the media coverage of UNOSOM, his account of the ambitions of journalists from different nations, emerge as the most convincing part of *Herrenmenschlichkeit.* The text presents the various news agencies with their scores of journalists and photographers as the true warring factions, the actual soldiers of this intervention, hunting for war scenes, for blood, famine, and despair. While the UN troops have come to Somalia to bring an end to war, the journalists, in their search for sensationalist moments, capitalize on the continuation of strife. The anagrams of television stations stand for the contending factions: "CNN, ABC, CBS, ARD, NTV, WTN, ZDF, RTL, AFP, AP, etc., the military badges of the era" (32). Photographers keep "the camera ready to shoot" (33); the photographer Hansjörg "Hansi" Krauss "could also be a soldier, pilot" (32; also 34). A television crew asks soldiers, who have peacefully settled on top of a tank, to pose and display bellicose determination for the cameras (11). Kirchhoff's narrator thus impressively captures aspects of sensationalist coverage whose exploitation of the shock effect of war and human suffering has led critics to examine the motives behind media coverage, its relation to power and politics, to profit and status.[43] Remarking on the nexus of profit and media coverage, the photojournalist Perry Kraetz is quoted in Kirchhoff's account: "Today, journalists are adventurers rather than professionals. And: A network like CNN would need its four wars in the world in order to work profitably" (42).

This critical view of journalists and photographers motivates the reader to reflect upon the impact of this kind of coverage: obviously distorted, staged for the blood- and tragedy-hungry audiences of the world, the footage on Somalia becomes questionable as a result of the factors influencing the coverage. This distortion in turn leads to a questioning of the motives for the intervention: How are the ambitions of the media and those of the German state, for example, related? Do the media turn the mission in Somalia into something other than a humanitarian intervention, into something different from what Germany wants to accomplish? Or are the sensationalism and related questions of power and status significant factors that also determined the German decision to participate in UNOSOM? Kirchhoff's narrator does indeed make this connection in his final conclusion; ultimately, however, his valuable critique of sensationalism and power games falls short of an in-depth analysis and, as we will see, remains trapped in ahistorical speculation.

The perceived differences between journalists from various nations add a layer of prejudice to Kirchhoff's otherwise thought-provoking and incisive observations. Whereas German journalists are described more intimately and remain positive individuals throughout (cf. portrayals of Hansi and Karsten), the presentation of an American journalist picks up the biased tone observed in the representation of the American soldiers: "The journalists divided by nationalities. At the next table a woman, the first non-indigenous woman in a week, tanned like an American Indian, in a kind of karate outfit, black, next to her, ready to be picked up, a fragmentation vest, blue, as well as the steel helmet of the marines; in her hand a radio set, on her arms countless silver bracelets, around her dark hair a reflective headband, on the headband: CNN. She doesn't talk to anyone, eats rations from American stocks, barely touches the bread, at the same time listens to her radio set, seems to see nothing and nobody, at least not me" (34).

This "CNN Indian," as she is then called by the narrator (34, 45, 46), is the first to run out of the room once two explosions are heard, and she is the first to arrive on top of the roof. On the one hand, this passage succeeds in conveying the journalist's cold-blooded hunger for terrifying news, and the description of this martial figure suggests a link between the hunt for horror, a sports workout, and a military exercise. Yet this depiction of the American reporter is set against a portrayal that follows immediately and shows two German reporters who do not seem to share these belligerent features: "Across from me Karsten and Hansi, Karsten without appetite, indigestion, Hansi, with cameras around the neck, as if armed" (34). Even though Hansi is also likened to a soldier, he and Karsten, as representative German journalists, appear as more humane and accessible throughout the text. As opposed to the CNN Indian, they are referred to by their first names; they eat chocolate pudding and read (32, 41, 46); Karsten seems vulnerable because of his indigestion (34); Hansi misses his fiancée and escorts the narrator to the airplane that will take him from Mogadishu back to the German camp in Belet Huen (40, 46–47). A friendly handshake before boarding the airplane concludes the encounter, and the reader, who was informed about Hansi's death on the second page of the account (8), knows what will happen to the journalist: Hansi will die at the hands of Somalis, stoned by an angry mob (64), after the Americans have attacked an area inhabited by civilians and killed dozens of innocent Somalis.[44] Kirchhoff dedicated this account to the journalist, and heartfelt descriptions of Hansi pervade the text. In fact, he is the only individual who dies and whose name is mentioned; he clearly functions as an identification figure. In his portrayals of Hansi the narrator expresses his own feelings of guilt and shame for having survived Somalia: "Why especially him and not somebody else, me for example . . . and in the midst [of these fantasies] a shame-faced triumph: that of the survivor" (64).

In spite of the narrator's success in denouncing the sensationalist nature of media coverage, the reader is brought to empathize with the German journalists. In this regard the narrator succeeds in conveying the complexity of the situation: generalizations are challenged in the face of individual life stories. Oddly, however, the scores of Somali victims are not lamented in any way comparable to the personalized portrayal of the German journalist. Only later, in his essay "Dem Schmerz eine Welt geben," does Kirchhoff express his horror at the fate and death of a Somali boy, Abdul Ismail.[45] In *Herrrenmenschlichkeit* just the passages about the Somali woman Dawarkir and her children, which will be discussed later, convey the tragedy of Somali suffering. The fate of the German journalist emerges as more accessible and, ultimately, more important than the lives of individual Somalis.

Apart from his views about the troops or the reporters and photographers, Kirchhoff's narrator bases his evaluation of the meaningfulness of UNOSOM on a perception of Somali difference. The Somali way of life, claims the eyewitness, is completely different from our (implicitly German) way of life. The Somali way is one of death and suffering; it has always been so, and it therefore should not be changed according to our Western notions. The narrator emphasizes the radical difference of Somalis, and he stresses the impossibility (for the Westerner) of understanding Somali ways. How does the narrator arrive at such a judgment?

The text begins with a brief introduction to "the Somalis," who are presented in juxtaposition to an equally unambiguous "we": "The Somalis, as far as I was able to observe—and I was able to observe twenty or thirty out of the seven or eight million Somalis—are predominantly nomads, in a country twice as big as ours." After this initial division into "us" and "them," the introductory paragraph of the diary ends with an attempt to identify with the Somalis. The narrator himself, writing on his laptop, claims to be a nomad: the computer enables him to move "freely . . . like a nomad through the pages." In another example the narrator again compares the Somali way of moving across space to that of the writing process (7–8). But the comparison is a questionable one: the narrator is modern, a very different kind of nomad, one who confuses social paradigms and equates traditional nomadism with modern physical and ontological mobility.

Except for this awkward comparison, which can be interpreted as an attempt to build bridges between the German way of life and that of the Somalis, Somali people and culture are rendered as utterly incomprehensible: "People walk a little, squat down, seem to notice something and again cover a certain distance, thirty, forty meters, without it becoming evident (to me) what advantage the place where they . . . squat now has over the previous one" (39). The disclaimer "to me" again indicates Kirchhoff's reflexivity, his awareness of his own perspective as a German. Yet his initial attempts at identifying with the nomads have failed; he now reinforces the impossibility of understanding what the Somalis are doing, what moves them, how they function.

This perception of "too much strangeness" becomes most evident in the narrator's claim that the Somalis have a different relationship to suffering (10; also 31).[46] In Somalia, he contends, "suffering is a way of living, just like contentment for us" (19). For the narrator the Somalis are inured to pain; they are numb. It seems to him as if they accept and do not question death and suffering. Observing scenes in a hospital he comments: "Nobody complains, nobody cries, as if death was as normal as the sun" (20).[47] Similarly, the narrator reports an encounter with a Somali woman, called Dawarkir, who has lost four of her eleven children: "How did her children die, I ask, and she says, children always die, as if it hadn't been her children who died" (26). Somali males appear apathetic and strange in descriptions of the bodyguards of the photographer Hansi (40, 43, 64), the nameless looters of Mogadishu (31, 44 67), the khat-chewing men and hardworking women.

The narrator, who came to Somalia "in order to find out whether this operation can be meaningful or not" (28), is appalled by the Sisyphus-like work of the German medical service. Witnessing how doctors, nurses, and soldiers, lacking sufficient supplies and personnel, have to select the neediest from a large group of desperate human beings, Kirchhoff's narrator grasps the uncomfortable position in which the helpers find themselves: "Humanism and selection, good intentions and the constraints of circumstances. Panic and perfectionism; maybe the beginning of another tragedy connected to the Germans: humanity of the masters" (53; also 62). Rather than decrying the inadequacy of supplies and the shortage of personnel, the narrator focuses on the role the German helpers play in Somalia. On what basis do they decide whom to save?

The strangeness and absurdity that the narrator detects in the lives of the Somalis, combined with the difficult role the Germans (and other UN troops) play in this mission, lead him to declare the humanitarian intervention futile (10). His verdict about Somalia rests on the perception of insurmountable differences: "We, coming from a culture of survival, carry our obsession with life into a country where death is a confidant, even an ally. Humanitism [Kirchhoff's neologism *Humanitismus* in the German text] means the idea of life at any cost" (28). Germans should thus stay out of Somalia, because Somalis have a different relationship to death and life and suffering is an essential part of their way of life. As a consequence, Germans should not oppress them with their "obsession for life." Yet the narrator ignores the fact that Somalis asked for help and that not all of the participants in UNOSOM came from Western "cultures of survival." It is safe to say, however, that those asking for help did not envision the kind of intervention that followed in the wake of the appeal for help, which at least in part explains the resistance that UN troops encountered at the hands of scores of Somalis.[48]

The narrator's essentializing of the Somali way of life leads him to call for withdrawal from Somalia: "What I see here is a new kind of crusade. A crusade fought under the banner not of humanism, but humanitism—like catholicism, capitalism, socialism" (28). This call for withdrawal from Somalia is based on the assumption of a radical difference between African and European culture. Sameness becomes a precondition for help from the West.

Certainly, there are cultural differences between Germans and Somalis. But the result of the narrator's assessment of Somali difference is worth questioning. How does the narrator arrive at the conclusion that the Somalis have a different relationship to death, suffering, life, and pain? How can he claim that the war in Somalia is an "age-old, African war . . . a completely unchristian war" (45)? These judgments are not based on his two-week stay in Somalia; rather, they reflect widespread cultural beliefs about Africa. Just as Kirchhoff reveals his indebtedness to clichés about the dishonesty, greediness, perverse sexuality, and indifference of Africans in his report about Ethiopia from the early 1980s, the narrator of *Herrenmenschlichkeit* reproduces stereotypes that have been the standard tropes of racist literature about Africa for centuries. The numbness to pain, in particular, is a central topos of theories of biological racism, from Christoph Meiners and Nietzsche to today's sports coverage. Nietzsche, for example, writes: "It may be that—to comfort the tender-hearted—pain did not hurt as much as it does today; at least a doctor might conclude this who treated negroes (taken as representative prehistoric humans) with serious inner inflammations; these drive even the most strong-willed European almost to desperation—in the case of negroes, they don't."[49]

These stereotypical views do not take into consideration that there is a difference between the experience of pain and, as John Hoberman points out, the "differing expectations about what constitutes pain and how it is to be resisted or endured."[50] Nancy Scheper-Hughes has shown that poor women in Brazil, whose children have a greatly reduced chance of survival, emotionally detach themselves from their children.[51] There is no indication in Kirchhoff's text that the narrator comprehends the observed numbness of Somalis as a defense mechanism. What needs to be understood as an emotional survival strategy is presented in Kirchhoff's diary as indicative of the radical difference of Somali women and men. His views regarding the alleged insensitivity of the Somalis toward pain becomes even more annoying in light of the ado Kirchhoff makes about his own role as a fighter against the pain in this world, one whose designated tool of resistance is writing (cf. "Dem Schmerz eine Welt geben").

Kirchhoff's account never reaches a level of complexity that could enable him to interpret the observed phenomena contextually, that would allow him, for example, to relate to expressions of pain that emanate from circumstances other than his personal background. Instead, the text reproduces clichés about cultural difference that are not only visible in the representations of the Somalis but also in those of soldiers and journalists from various nations. The narrator's account becomes a paradigmatic example for racializing discourse. In his presentation of the insurmountable gap between the German and the Somali worlds, Kirchhoff's narrator seems to apply Herder's theories on the ultimate incommensurability of cultures, presented in *Über den Ursprung der Sprache* (1772), *Auch eine Philosophie der Geschichte zur Bildung der Menschheit* (1774), and *Ideen zur Philosophie der Geschichte der Menschheit* (1784–91).[52] But, whereas Herder's writings—understood in their historical context—can be interpreted as an appeal for tolerance toward cultural difference, the notion of incommensurability resonates with nationalist or Germanocentric (such as Meiners's or de Gobineau's) theories. Kirchhoff's tolerance for cultural difference comes in liberal disguise but barely conceals his racist frame of mind; his views prove, as Samir Amin remarks, the anti-universalist nature of Eurocentrism.[53]

The narrator insists on a "neutral, unbiased" eyewitness perspective and consciously rejects background information. Repeatedly, he announces that it would be "useless" to try to "imitate . . . the secret language of clan names and abbreviations" (43); he is "determined to no longer jot down abbreviations and clan-names" (16), that is, information about Somalia that he experiences as impenetrable chaos. What kind of picture could have emerged if background materials had been included, if the eyewitness account had been supplemented? Presented by sources based in a historical understanding, the situation in Somalia appears to be complex yet not as inaccessible as Kirchhoff's narrator wants us to believe.

What Kirchhoff Leaves Out

The Somali-speaking people can trace their history to biblical times; trade relations are reported since the third millennium B.C.E. Egypt, for example, imported frankincense and myrrh from the northeastern region of Somalia, the region known as Punt. As mentioned by Arab geographers in the ninth century, Zeila and Mogadishu were important commercial centers, exporting "ivory, hides, aromatic gums, slaves, spices, and cattle from the hinterlands and imported and redistributed textiles, metal, pepper, tobacco, coffee, sugar, and manufactured goods."[54] The Somalis form one of the largest single ethnic blocs in Africa. The primary area inhabited by Somalis, who coexist with minority groups of

Bantu and Arabs (together constituting approximately 5 percent of the area's population), stretches from the periphery of the Ethiopian highlands along the Gulf of Aden and the Indian Ocean to the Tana River in northern Kenya. This accounts for the fact that, from the Djibouti Republic to Garissa on the Tana River in Kenya, the standard Somali language—apart from dialectal variations—"provides a single channel of communication."[55] On account of the language and with regard to definitions of social identities, Somali territory is thus relatively homogeneous. The culture, however, largely unwritten until the 1950s, is distinguished by a rich and culturally diverse heritage of oral traditions.[56] Sir Richard Burton, who traveled to Somalia in 1854–55, took notice of the vibrant oral culture: "It is strange that a dialect which has no written character should so abound in poetry and eloquence. . . . The country teems with poets, poetasters, poetitos, poetaccios."[57]

In addition to language, oral culture, and the identification with millennia of history connected to a large territory, Somalis derive their sense of national identity from shared features regarding the organization of social and political life, a significant Islamic heritage, and their predominantly pastoral lifestyle. The Somali people consist of two larger groups, the Samale and the Sab. Social relations are to some extent organized according to a system of clans or clan families. It is important to note, however, that contemporary forms of the clan system are not identical with those of the traditional society. Contemporary clanism represents a variation of the former system and is a result of the confrontation with the colonial state, the nation-state, and the patriarchal, capitalist social and economic order.[58]

In addition, the draconian measures taken by President Siad Barre since the 1970s, which were geared toward abolishing the clan system and represent the attempt (quite common in those days in many African and Asian countries) to implement a national and new social identity in its place, achieved the opposite and led to an increased valorization of clan identity.[59] Therefore, clanism in its current form has to be understood as a modern phenomenon. Catherine Besteman argues that the Somali society was transformed over the last 150 years, "produc[ing] a deeply stratified and fragmented society," an image quite at odds with the notion of homogeneity suggested by earlier scholars.[60]

The colonial period in Somalia began in the nineteenth century; England, France, and Italy were the occupying powers in different parts of Somalia. Somalia became independent in 1960; its initial democratic government came to an end in 1969, when the military under Siad Barre took over. War against Ethiopia, failed economic reforms, and internal conflicts between the various clan families all led to a civil war, which began in full force in 1988, reached the capital Mogadishu in 1990, and led to the flight of Siad Barre and his government. At that point the oppositional groups that had been unified in their struggle to depose Barre turned on one another. Political anarchy in connection with ecological crises threatened the lives of the six to seven million Somalis. In 1992 the crisis reached unprecedented dimensions, and the United Nations decided to intervene.[61]

According to historians and social scientists, the nation's current situation is largely a result of the repercussions of colonialism, Cold War politics, and failed attempts at modernization.

1. As an effect of the European division of Africa, Somalis live in different states. This accounts for the war in the Ogaden area of Ethiopia in 1977–78, which was a Somali attempt to annex territory populated by Somali people. Peace with Ethiopia followed in 1988; at this point, 800,000 refugees from Ethiopia had moved into Somalia. The imposition of a centralized nation-state also accounts for the animosities between the different segments of the society, because it imposes a political hierarchy alien to the previously existing mechanisms of power.[62]

2. Both Somalia and Ethiopia became pawns in Cold War politics. After the 1969 takeover, Somalia was first supported by the USSR. It expelled the Soviet advisors in 1977 in response to the USSR's decision in 1976 to supply Ethiopia with weapons as well and its eventual termination of aid to Somalia. Since 1977 the United States has assisted Somalia economically and politically.[63] Somalia's cooperation in the German attempt to capture a hijacked airplane at the Mogadishu airport in 1977 is regarded as the beginning of pro-Western Somali politics.

3. Over the last few decades it has been difficult for the nomadic population to fight the repercussions of repeated and extensive droughts because of political friction within Somalia and because the nomadism that would allow migration to less arid areas is stifled by international borders. While nomads traditionally counter ecological crises through migration into more advantageous areas, modern nomads become pris-

oners of the nation-state. Nomadism is also economically weakened by the commercialization of the economy and the mechanism of modern state politics. In Somalia programs aimed at sedentarization and modernization further worsened conditions for nomads. The logic of the traditional nomadic economy was thus destroyed, and a viable alternative mode of subsistence has not been established in its place.[64] In addition, conflicts arose between the newly modernized elite and those segments of the population that continued to pursue a traditional lifestyle. According to Abdalla Omar Mansur, "international aid worsened the political, economic, and social situation of the country for the following reasons. First, the aid given fostered the dictatorial regime, endowing it with a new life. Secondly, it created a dependency on imported foodstuff, discouraging local food production. Last, but not least, aid made thieves of nearly all the state employees, whose salaries were not enough to support their families even for a week."[65]

In sum, the ability of Somali society to deal with large-scale ecological crises has been diminished due to the legacy of colonial structures, the repercussions of Cold War interventions, aid politics, and the commercialization and modernization of traditional economies.

The reasons for the Somali crisis are, according to these scholars, identifiable, even if individual aspects might be open to controversy. Kirchhoff's *Herrenmenschlichkeit,* however, mystifies the circumstances. The comments Kirchhoff's narrator makes about clans in Somalia reveal that he is not informed about the genesis of clanism. Rather, he presents the violence and disorder he observes as essential African features (45), thereby reinforcing notions about African social lawlessness (40). This gesture, to interpret contemporary African (or, for example, Asian or Latin American) conditions as proof of the inherent backwardness of African cultures, brings to mind once more Claude Lévi-Strauss's comments on photographs depicting South American Indians: as mentioned in the analysis of Schweitzer in Gabon, Lévi-Strauss insists that the Indians he presents to a (mostly Western) audience are "remnants . . . of more advanced and more populous civilizations" who were destroyed by European colonizers.[66] Explaining contemporary "regressiveness" among the Indians as indicative of essential features would erase the impact of European colonial history. Similarly, Kirchhoff's narrator ascribes the label "traditional" or "African" to those societal phenomena (like lawlessness and chaos) that are emanations of modernity's unsettling influences on traditional societies, thereby eliminating European colonialism, modernization, and the failing of the local elite as culpable factors.

As much as the neologism *humanitism* describes an ideology that rightly deserves to be criticized, Kirchhoff does not go far enough. He does not discuss the motives behind actions that use the language of humanism for other purposes, and he does not attempt to understand the Somali situation in depth. Kirchhoff's report does not enable readers to understand that the United Nations did not entirely act out of altruistic reasons (although many supported the intervention out of a genuine will to help). As Jasmin Touati, Mohamed Sahnoun, and others have demonstrated, the original UNOSOM mission was also an attempt to improve the image of the United Nations, especially vis-à-vis Islamic nations, in the aftermath of the disastrous first Gulf War. Moreover, for President George H. W. Bush initiating "Operation Restore Hope" was a welcome way to leave office and an attempt to create situations for Bill Clinton that would hamper cuts in the U.S. military budget.[67] In addition, Kirchhoff's approach masks the geopolitical reality that the Horn of Africa is of considerable strategic importance because it provides access to oil fields in Saudi Arabia, Iraq, and Iran and determines free access to two of the world's most important shipping routes, through the Suez Canal and the Cape route. From the humanitarian perspective that Kirchhoff's narrator mocks, Somalia in crisis means the unacceptable loss of human life. Yet a politically stable Somalia also means continued Western access to other potential areas of crisis and to other resources in the area.[68]

UNOSOM was initiated for some good reasons, out of some questionable motives, and partially or largely failed because of other, largely identifiable reasons. Sahnoun's account points to alternative strategies that in his view would have allowed the world community to fight the crisis in Somalia by enabling Somalis to solve the crisis themselves; Robert Oakley and John Hirsch, on the other hand, representing the official view of the United States government, consider the operation largely a success. German public opinion differs substantially from this assessment; that only 2.3 million marks of the 500 million spent by the Germans on their operation in Belet Huen were used for humanitarian purposes is an aspect of the intervention that certainly deserves questioning. In addition, the fact that 1.3 million marks were spent on disposable dishes and flatware aroused German ecological concerns, compounded by the revelation that five dishwashers, costing 36,000 marks, remained unused in the Somali desert. Especially in reports of the popular press, the widespread perception in Germany is that UNOSOM, and the German participation in it, failed.[69]

Generally, the analysis of UNOSOM reveals that the role of the United Nations needs to be rethought in the post–Cold War world. Calls for a reform of the United Nations indicate that the current structure of the organization has become obsolete in the face of changing realities. Yet Kirchhoff's text does not enable the reader to come to a clearer assessment of the situation in Somalia; using the language of cultural relativism, he seemingly voices justified criticism of the intervention, along the lines of widely accepted criticism emerging from discussions of both development aid and military interventions. But his critique contains untenable judgments on Somalia and the Somalis that perpetuate prejudices about Africa and its inhabitants. Rejecting humanitarian intervention on the grounds of perceived cultural differences amounts to intellectual laziness; the political, economic, and social reasons behind the crisis in Somalia defy culturalist explanations.

Invocation of the Tragic

The human rights advocate Rakiyah Omaar, in her analysis of the presence of foreign troops in Somalia, points to the absurdity of interventions that do not take into consideration local conditions.[70] Likewise, an eyewitness account, a subjective report based solely on a fortnight in a country that up to that point was entirely foreign to the witness, cannot take into consideration the dimensions presented here. A subjective view has its place if the observations are relativized and identified as reflecting a limited, one-dimensional perspective. The problem arises, however, when Kirchhoff's narrator uses his experiences to come to far-reaching conclusions.

Kirchhoff's references to the religious songwriter Paul Gerhardt (1607–76), who wrote his pious lyrics in order to encourage Germans to endure and spiritually survive the horrors of the Thirty Years' War, underline this urge to mystify the circumstances by presenting suffering as predestined and unavoidable (30, 35). Kirchhoff's diary begins with an epigram, a quote by Guido Ceronetti (b. 1927), which likewise appeals to the tragedy of life: "Every individual relief from the burden of the tragic results in an increase of the tragic in the world, which burdens everybody." Does this mean that the amount of the tragic in the world remains constant? That the individual cannot be helped or the collective would otherwise suffer? This invocation of the tragic as a motto for the account of Somalia reveals how much the author is trapped in beliefs about the inevitable tragedy of life, and it explains why he abstains from attempting to identify the reasons for the civil war in Somalia *and* the problematic aspects of the UN operations. But, as we have seen, Kirchhoff's refuge in the metaphor of the tragic, in a premodern worldview that sees destiny as the moving force of history, is a result of inadequate information, cultural stereotypes about Africa, and a belief in the validity of eyewitness reports. Ultimately, the narrator's criticism, couched in the language of cultural relativism, calls for a denial of help to poorer and culturally different nations. Sameness—the same understanding of life, pain, death, and suffering—becomes the precondition for help from Germany.

The narrator closes his account with the image of a wounded bandit: "Later, when an injection against pain had set in, he began to mumble verses from the Koran (I believe), while his fingertips stroked the frame of his sunglasses; it was the simple black plastic glasses of the looters and police aides of Mogadishu, and he stroked the frame just as one of us would stroke a completed manuscript or others the rail of their snow-white yacht" (67). In this passage Kirchhoff's narrator picks up the basic division of "us" versus "them" from the beginning of the account, only to emphasize the radical differences. As a closing image, this passage reduces the situation in Somalia to an image of ultimate incomprehensibility. The seemingly unattainable essential nature of Somalis is evoked again in this image of the bandit, which once more provokes the question of whether it is worthwhile to save that kind of person.

Kirchhoff's views are representative of those voiced by other German intellectuals who advocate the abolition of aid to developing countries and who claim that Germany does not owe anything to the countries of Africa and Asia and has no moral or financial obligations whatsoever.[71]

Proponents of these views disregard the fact that Germany's wealth is to a large extent a result of centuries of disparities in wages and prices, of the mechanisms of international financial systems, the debts, which foil the economies of developing countries, or the currency rates, which secure economic and political domination by industrial countries. They also ignore or discount the critique of development aid that identifies factors of failure and that argues for a greater involvement of Africans in the conception and realization of development projects.[72]

In light of these discussions the value of Kirchhoff's account becomes more and more questionable. Did the author, much like Handke and other writers, believe that the eyewitness report alone would allow for substantial conclusions? (Imagine, for example, a report by an African who spends two weeks in a devastated Germany in the summer of 1945, without knowing anything about the history of the war, especially the Holocaust. A merely descriptive report might have had *some* benefit, but any larger judgment based on a subjective, uninformed encounter would have led to a very distorted perspective.)

The problem seems to be related to the question of genre. A reader has different expectations of a diary than of a fictional text. A realistically presented diary (with, for example, a dust jacket, advertisement, or lay-out) about a journey, which has already been partially published in *Der Spiegel,* will be received as an authentic text containing historical materials and personal opinions, as a contribution to a discussion. Even the passages about the hospital or the stay in Italy, although they imply reflexivity and add literary dimensions to the diary, do not alter the basic nature of this text, since the statements about Somalia are not affected by these expansions. Therefore, *Herrenmenschlichkeit* is not comparable to the fictional diary *Tagebuch über Čarnojević (Dnevik o Čarnojeviću,* Carnojevic Diary, 1921) by the Serbian author Miloš Crnjanski (1893–1977), which Kirchhoff's narrator reads while in Somalia and to which he refers repeatedly (9, 13). Although the composition of this text was likewise biographically motivated, the text documenting Crnjanski's traumatic experiences as a soldier during World War I, the author and the narrator are more clearly distinguishable than in this work by Kirchhoff. Choosing Crnjanski as a reference furthermore emphasizes the tragic aspects of war and catastrophe (much like the references to Gerhardt and Ceronetti), without identifying the uniqueness of the Somali situation. Moreover, the text of the Serbian author brings the reader to fundamentally different conclusions: while Crnjanski criticizes war, Kirchhoff's narrator wants the Somali war to take care of itself.

If Kirchhoff intended to provoke his readers into reflection about the Somali crisis, the image of Africa in German culture, and the relationship between richer and poorer nations through the construction of this narcissist and biased narrator, he fails because of his choice of genre. Rather, this diary contributes to support for anti-aid initiatives on account of culturalist reasoning. Had Kirchhoff simply related subjective impressions rather than making grand statements about the situation in Somalia, his account could persist as an important document about the Somali situation. Considering once again the dust jacket of the book, it becomes obvious that the way the text's title intrudes on the Somali body mirrors the relationship between the author's words and the Somali situation. While Kirchhoff's intended message might have been that "Herrenmenschlichkeit" is an ideology violating the bodies of the Somalis, this analysis has shown that the author's words obstruct the images, that Kirchhoff's words do not allow us to see the entire picture.

Kirchhoff's text highlights the tension between racist and culturalist views, on the one side, and the missionary stance toward Africa, on the other. While Kirchhoff's trajectory, to critique the West's questionable mandate to "better" situations in Africa, seems quite compatible with the line of thought pursued in this study, his critique is based on culturalist notions of African difference and ignores a complicated political and economic history. Kirchhoff's text does not enlighten the reader about the situation in Somalia or about the merit or meaninglessness of UNOSOM; read without additional commentary, *Herrenmenschlichkeit* gives such a one-dimensional view of the situation that it only obscures the circumstances. Kirchhoff does not achieve the level of analysis present in John Le Carré's novel *The Constant Gardener* (2001), set in Kenya, which succeeds in laying out the interplay between aid politics, corruption of the local government, and the schemes of international companies.

Kirchhoff's rhetoric, moreover, points uncomfortably to a continuation of German racist and ethnocentric politics that influences not only the discussion of development aid but also the ongoing debate over Germany's citizenship laws. Clichés about essential cultural differences (pain, death, and suffering as characteristic features of Africans; sexualized Nigerians; romanticized yet fascist Italians; serious, innocent, and genuine Germans) remain unchallenged. The self-reflexive critical potential that is a striking feature of Kirchhoff's fictional texts gets lost in this diary. The narrator who carefully sets up this position, and so reveals self-reflexivity, turns out to be a variant of the narcissistic characters of Kirchhoff's literary oeuvre whose egocentrism blinds him to other realities.

One wonders why Kirchhoff, rather than resorting to Gerhardt and Ceronetti, did not bother to read the novels of his Somali colleague Nurrudin Farah, one of the most eminent contemporary writers. Farah's texts would have provided him with differentiated insights about the Somali conflict. Whereas the Somalis in Kirchhoff's text are devoid of individuality, Farah's novels restore their humanity. Not shying away from harsh criticism of internecine Somali warfare, corrupt politics, and widespread abuse, Farah provides a critique from within that does not hold Western powers alone responsible for the crisis in his country. We cannot blame Kirchhoff for failing to arrive at a differentiated analysis of the Somali situation after his two-week stay, but, in light of the grand claims he is making, we can deplore the lack of an effort that should have involved a dialogue with Somalis and their history.

5

Tourism

Repeat Visitors Turned Aid Workers in Kenya

Then they talked at length of traders, Arab and European, wandering the African continent, propagating their faith, making gifts of their deities and beliefs (like present-day foreign aid), presents that the Africans accepted with little question. —Nuruddin Farah, *Gifts*

Hemingway's Kandinsky

The opening scene of Ernest Hemingway's *Green Hills of Africa* (1935), his autobiographical account of a safari in East Africa, pays tribute to a distinct kind of German, or, in this case, Austrian presence in Africa. Hemingway begins by describing how his attempt to track down a *kudu,* a large antelope, is suddenly thwarted by the loud noise of a truck passing the hideout of the hunters. Later, as he drives through the night, he spots first a fire and then the same disruptive truck nearby. He asks his driver to stop the car and witnesses the following scene: "There was a short, bandy-legged man with a Tyroler hat, leather shorts, and an open shirt standing before an unhooded engine in a crowd of natives."[1]

Hemingway offers his help to the man, whose truck has died. The Austrian introduces himself as "Kandinsky" and, upon hearing Hemingway's name, asks him whether he knows Hemingway, the *Dichter.* This question starts off an extended conversation in which the two men discuss writers, such as Joyce, Sinclair Lewis, Heinrich Mann, Rilke, Ringelnatz, and Valéry, and also the issue of game hunting. The Austrian, evidently more a lover of literature than of killing animals, is opposed to the practice and insists that it is nonsense to hunt a particular animal. After Hemingway's departure into the night, the writer wonders about the curious man and regrets not having asked the Austrian "why he had twenty up-country natives with him, nor where he was going" (9). Later he again meets the Austrian, who continues to be highly critical of Hemingway's passion for hunting and even suggests that the American should interest himself more in concern for African people: "'I kill nothing, you understand,' Kandinsky told us. 'Why are you not more interested in the natives?'" (14).

Hemingway's humanist Austrian, surrounded by Africans, might serve as a leitmotif for this exploration of contemporary German tourists' fascination with Kenya. Hemingway sketches the image of one type of traveler to Africa, an image that raises a number of questions about the traveler's motivations for his journey to Africa, about his self-perception and his view of others, and about the position of the visitor among Africans. These questions will guide the following discussion, which explores the interaction between German repeat visitors and the local population on the coast south of Mombasa, in Kenya. Since this study as a whole revolves around the concept of mission, it might not seem fitting to include in it an analysis of tourists and their outlooks. Rather than bringing something to their holiday destination, tourists are usually thought to be eager only to take from the place they visit, usually for only a short period. This case study of German repeat visitors, however, brings to the fore another facet of the notion of mission, as it has survived in today's global culture from its earlier manifestations. In the analysis of tourism in Kenya, motivations and ideological factors that inspired the behavior of individuals discussed in the previous chapters emerge once more. Views about development and attitudes reflecting civilizationism and modernization crucially determine the interaction between Kenyans and Germans. On the other hand, and perhaps surprisingly, repeat visitors at times display qualities that were largely absent from the individuals investigated in the previous chapters.

Tourism has been a controversial topic for decades.[2] In both popular and academic discussions tourists often appear as prototypical representatives of the capitalist and colonial system, combining an unrelenting thirst for consumption with the ruthless invasion of foreign territories. In many studies the tourist is considered as an ideal vehicle to ponder the essential nature of modernity.[3] Anthropologists, in particular, tend to see tourists as embodying the antithesis to their own approach toward culture, as tourists seem to destroy what anthropologists want to preserve.[4] In this regard the issue of "authenticity" emerges as a central concept in discussions denouncing the superficial and market-driven attitude of the tourist toward other cultures. Here tourism is seen as being driven by the tourists' desire for the inauthentic, or it stages inauthentic events for the tourist, who is unable or unwilling to unmask the falseness of the experience.[5]

This assessment, however, has been challenged by analyses demonstrating that all cultures are constantly undergoing change, which makes the question of authenticity irrelevant.[6] As Maxine Feifer argues, tourists themselves (or "post-tourists," as she calls them) are aware that there is no authentic tourist experience.[7] In this approach tourists are also no longer seen as a coherent mass of people sharing similar goals but, rather, are regarded as a diverse lot of individuals who are driven by quite dissimilar desires in their tourist quests. Another set of studies is inspired by the work of Victor Turner. Drawing on Arnold Van Gennep's 1908 study *Rites of Passage,* Turner argues that in *rites-de-passage* and other transforming rituals individuals are torn out of the structural process of everyday life. He identifies three different stages of alienation from profane life—separation, liminality, and reintegration. Turner's model has proven quite useful to a number of researchers who study tourist situations.[8]

Among the more recent studies offering new insights into the various aspects of tourism are those that focus on tourism's nexus of economic, ecological, and social dynamics and explore the potential benefits as well as detriments to areas that have become preferred tourist destinations. The notion of sustainable development is crucial to these analyses and seen by some as a concept representing a realistic (if limited) option for tourism development. As John Pigram and Salah Wahab point out, "Tourism certainly can contribute to environmental degradation and be self-destructive; it also has potential to bring about significant enhancement of the environment."[9] Martin Mowforth and Ian Munt have a much more pessimistic outlook, however, about the notion of sustainability and new forms of tourism, such as ecotourism. The authors emphasize that notions of sustainability and environmentalism reflect First World interests and perpetuate a basically colonial system of hegemony and power.

The project I discuss in this chapter neglects these concerns. Rather, the case presented here is inspired by approaches that consider the social interaction occurring between tourists and their hosts. These studies are based on the premise that no culture is fixed in time and space, that cultural formations are always subject to transformation, and that interaction between representatives of different cultural spheres has and will bring about change for the individuals involved. Drawing on models presented in, for example, the anthology *Tourists and Tourism: Identifying with People and Places,* I consider "tourism as a process" and subscribe to the idea that "tourist encounters generate change for tourists as well."[10] The authors articulate a conceptual framework central to my project: "The present collection . . . observes the interplay between government interests, the tourism industry and the development of concepts of heritage, local identity and perceptions of belonging. We show how the power relation is more than mutual exploitation, giving examples of 'hosts' biting back, and blurring the distinctions between actors."[11]

Another insight useful for understanding German repeat visitors' actions in Kenya is Alma Gottlieb's idea of tourism as an inversion of the everyday, a notion inspired by the work of Victor Turner. She argues that, depending on the social class of the traveler, the social hierarchy is either dissolved or accentuated during the vacation.[12] Gottlieb's thesis helps to understand German tourists' behavior toward unfamiliar cultures. Reports appearing in the popular press regularly point out the offensive conduct of German tourists.[13] The behavior displayed by German repeat visitors in Kenya, however, seems at odds with this widespread image of Germans as culturally insensitive people, whether abroad or at home. Providing some contrasts with the general reputation of German tourists overseas, the example of German repeat visitors in Kenya raises questions concerning the discrepancies between people's behavior at home and abroad and between distinct groups of tourists who travel to different destinations.

My interest in Kenya began with six stays in the country in the early to mid-1980s, during which I assisted a doctor on the coast south of Mombasa. This physician treated tourists at the hotels situated on Diani Beach and in the adjacent villages, including Ukunda. In this context I first learned about repeat visitors who had developed friendships with

Kenyans and who supported them in various ways. One of these repeat visitors was Dorothea M., then in her sixties, who, in her own words, "held office hours on the beach," gathering requests from different people which she then tried to accommodate.[14] She would collect money for a surgery or a new boat for a fisherman, find a donor for a scholarship, figure out ways to gather the materials to fix a roof, or pay for school uniforms and sewing machines. She was even asked to bring back a husband who had eloped with another woman. Dorothea M. was also active in an organization in her hometown in Germany, where she raised large sums each year that supported various projects in Kenya.

The memory of this kind of interaction between tourists and Kenyans inspired the research project presented here. One of the initial goals of the study was to find out whether Dorothea M. was an exception. If she was not an exception, it would be interesting to know how Germans, most of whom had come to the country originally because of the climate, the beaches, and the animals, gradually established contacts with the local population and supported them materially. The goal was to understand who these people are, what social groups they belong to, what age they are, how they see themselves, and why they assisted Kenyans financially or in other ways. The data gathered in three research stays in the summers of 1998, 1999, and 2000 shed light on the diverse behavioral patterns and strategies these tourists develop in order to come to terms with the unfamiliar and challenging situations with which they are faced.

This study does not address the views Kenyans hold about Germans. The many conversations I had with Kenyans about the German repeat visitors indicate that, in spite of the extensive interaction, there are areas of miscommunication, differing expectations, and diverging analyses of the interaction. But the views and actions of Kenyans must be the subject of another study.

Before presenting the results of the research conducted in Kenya, let me place the encounter between Germans and Kenyans in the larger history of the German fascination with Kenya.

Kenya in the German Imagination

Apart from North African states such as Morocco, Tunisia, and Egypt, no other African country rivals Kenya's past and present appeal as a destination for European colonizers, adventurers, explorers, linguists, anthropologists, and, last but not least, tourists. Many areas in Africa were attractive to Europeans only as long as they were able to exploit the region's natural resources or as long as the European colonizers were still in charge of the country. Kenya never lost its attraction and charisma and is probably still the most popular site for Western novels and films staged in Africa. Best-sellers such as Ernest Hemingway's *Green Hills of Africa* (1935) and *The Snows of Kilimanjaro* (1936) and Karen Blixen's *Out of Africa* (1937) helped to promote the image of Kenya as a place where natural beauty mixes with the thrill of adventure. Like Hemingway's and Blixen's novels, other popular English-language films and books were also translated and widely distributed in European and non-European countries. Two popular cinematographic representations of East Africa were staged in Tanzania but largely employed the formula that is generally associated with Kenya, namely Howard Hawk's *Hatari* (1962) and the TV show "Daktari." *Hatari* is a safari and adventure film about a group of men catching animals for European and American zoos, starring John Wayne and Hardy Krüger, who plays a former race car driver called Kurt Müller. "Daktari" was highly popular in the 1960s and broadcast in many countries around the world; the series focused on the daily life of a veterinarian (*daktari* is a Swahili version of the English *doctor*) and his daughter.[15] After the 1960s Tanzania, by then a socialist country, hardly ever provides the backdrop to movies about East Africa.

The list of widely read novels staged in Kenya is substantial. James Fox's *White Mischief* (1982; turned into a film in 1987) takes a critical look at the British upper class in colonial Kenya. One of the most popular recent novels about Kenya is Barbara Wood's lengthy *Green City in the Sun* (1988). It tells the story of white settlers and black Kenyans from the times of the British colonial occupation to independence. The most successful motion picture staged in Kenya was undoubtedly *Out of Africa* (1985), based on Blixen's novel and starring Robert Redford and Meryl Streep. According to the manager of one of Kenya's most prestigious hotels, the movie did more to promote tourism in Kenya than years of advertising by travel agencies ever could have. More recently, Disney's *The Lion King* (1994) and Hugh Hudson's *I Dreamed of Africa* (2000; based on the autobiographical novel by Kuki Gallman) attest to the continuous inspiration Kenya's and, generally, East Africa's landscapes, animals, cultures, and languages provide to Western audiences.

The German enthusiasm for Kenya needs to be seen in the context of Germany's interest in East Africa, which can be traced back to the days of German colonialism. Chapter 3 discussed Ernst Udet's account from the 1930s as a document for the unceasing German focus on the area, beyond the existence of a colonial empire. This passion for East Africa, which Germans first associated primarily with their former possession, the Tanganyika area, was transferred onto Kenya beginning in the early 1960s.

After World War II, but before the founding of the nation-states Tanzania and Kenya, German publications still applied the term *Ostafrika* to address mostly the wider geographical area or the former German colonial territory. Deutsch-Ostafrika's last military commander, Paul von Lettow-Vorbeck, for example, lived long enough to continue to publish his only slightly altered views on East Africa. The fate of missionaries, hunters, and the legacy of colonialism, recounted in books by Oskar Koenig, Kurt Ronicke, and Karl Kurt Wolters, continued to capture the interest of German audiences far into the postwar era. After independence German scientific studies, political analyses, and ethnographic texts about East Africa began to focus on the newly founded nation-states of the region. *Ostafrika* was now generally used in historical accounts to refer to the former German colony, and it continues to appear in reference to the larger geographical area in the titles of travel guides, adventure novels, and monographs about missionaries, whose work often transcends national boundaries. While Tanzania chose to follow a socialist model after independence and only recently developed an infrastructure conducive to tourism, Kenya opened its doors to Western tourists soon after it gained independence. During the course of the 1960s Germans gradually shifted their literary fantasies about and their actual activities in East Africa from the area of former Deutsch-Ostafrika to Kenya.

Of particular relevance in this context are the films, writings, and activities of Bernhard Grzimek (1908–87). His book and film *Serengeti darf nicht sterben: 367,000 Tiere suchen einen Staat* (*Serengeti Shall Not Die: 367,000 Animals Are Looking for a State*) was tremendously successful in increasing the public's interest in the area. Grzimek's film was honored with an Oscar, which marked the first time that the prize was awarded to a German filmmaker. The publication and release date is significant: 1959 was only a few years away from Kenyan (1963) and Tanzanian (1964) independence. It is quite curious that the title avoids direct references to the decolonization process that was under way at the time and only implicitly evokes the political context. But even before Grzimek became famous with *Serengeti darf nicht sterben* and managed to turn the world's attention to East Africa, his highly popular TV show "Ein Platz für Tiere" was launched in the 1950s. Between 1956 and 1987, 175 episodes of the series were aired, contributing greatly to the raising of popular consciousness about wildlife protection and ecology as well as promoting the popularization of both Kenya and Tanzania. The combination of exotic appeal and humanitarian mission distinguishes Grzimek's approach, whose endeavors bore a painful personal dimension: his son Michael (1934–1959) died in an airplane accident during the shooting of *Serengeti darf nicht sterben.* Grzimek played a crucial role in keeping the interest in East Africa alive in Germany, was instrumental in turning the public's attention toward Kenya, and even contributed to the expansion of tourism, which he saw as one of the sources for the financing of wildlife preservation.[16]

Beginning in the late 1950s, German language publications on Kenya have explored almost every aspect of the country, and to this day Kenya continues to be the subject of popular novels and autobiographies that reach large audiences of readers. In the more recent period Evelyn Sanders's *Hühnerbus und Stoppelhopser* (1990), a fictional account of a family's vacation in Kenya, presents a humorist commentary on the pleasures and displeasures of tourism in the country. More prominently, Stephanie Zweig's novels, in which the author draws on her experiences as the child of Jewish emigrants in Kenya, have become best-sellers in Germany. Her novel *Nirgendwo in Afrika* (1995) is a particularly captivating narrative documenting a thus far virtually unknown chapter in the history of the relationship between Kenya and Germany. Caroline Link's 2001 film version of the novel won the Oscar for best foreign film in 2003.

In the context of this study, accounts reflecting the reality of the activities of development aid workers are especially noteworthy. Germans and other Europeans who served in development aid programs have been eager to write about their experiences, raising issues about the objectives of development aid and the role of aid workers.[17] Among the more recent texts is *On m'appelle Mama Daktari* (1994; German 1997) by Anne Spoerry, who was born in Alsace in 1918 and died in Nairobi in 1999. She was one of the founders of the African Medical and Research Foundation, which initiated the Flying Doctor Services. Her enterprises were documented as early as 1968, in a short film by Werner Herzog about the flying doctors of East Africa, in which he explores the limitations of development aid.

Another type of autobiography documents the personal experiences of German or Swiss tourists with the Kenyan population. Corinne Hofmann's highly popular *Die weiße Massai* (*The White Masai*) gives an account of a Swiss woman's relationship with and marriage to a Masai.[18] After the author had lived for four years in a Masai village and in other parts of Kenya, the marriage ended in divorce. The author returned to Switzerland, having taken along the daughter she bore in Kenya, without the knowledge of the father. The book, an evidently enticing mix of romance and adventure themes, was published in August 1998. Beginning in the spring of 1999, it held the first and second spot on German best-seller lists for several months.[19] By September 2001, 1.3 million copies of the book had been sold, including 700,000 paperback copies; by March 2003 the paperback sales had increased to more than a million copies. Assuming that most copies of the autobiography were read by more than one person, a large percentage of the German-speaking population showed interest in the book. *Die weiße Massai* has been translated into Danish, Dutch, Estonian, Finnish, French, Hebrew, Italian, Japanese, Norwegian, Polish, Spanish, and Swedish. Similar accounts originally appeared in other languages and are also highly popular, such as novels by Kuki Gallman, Francesca Marciano, Cheryl Mason, and Catherine Oddie.

A more self-reflective account is Miriam Kwalanda's *Die Farbe meines Gesichts: Lebensreise einer kenianischen Frau* (The color of my face: Life journey of a Kenyan woman), published in 1999 and cowritten with Birgit Theresa Koch. This autobiography also tells the story of a cross-cultural marriage and divorce, but this time the subject is approached from the perspective of a Kenyan woman. After working as a prostitute and sustaining a series of romantic relationships, Kwalanda married a

German man and moved to Germany. This marriage also ended in divorce, and the autobiography clearly represents an attempt by the author to come to terms with her life and the situation she and her three children are facing in the new country.[20]

The current interaction between Germans and Kenyans as well as German language representations of Kenya need to be seen in the context of this extensive textual and visual history that has formed the German image of Kenya for the last generation. The contemporary situation —and this is the argument presented here—is on a continuum that goes back to the nineteenth century, when German ideas about modernization, development, and colonization were first formulated and Germans descended on Africa with missionary zeal and modernizing fervor. Topoi that were already prominent in accounts about German East Africa made their way into writings about today's Kenya. Early writings of missionaries and doctors, of travelers and settlers, set the stage for the more recent writings and actions of development aid workers. Drastic changes have occurred, however, since decolonization. It is one of the foci of this chapter to evaluate in what ways the attitudes of contemporary German tourists vis-à-vis Kenyans compare to earlier paradigms.

Informal Development Aid?

Kenya gained independence from Britain on December 12, 1963, after more than a decade of militant resistance to British colonial rule. The insurgency that led to the final triumph over the British, known as the Mau Mau rebellion, was for the most part initiated by the Kikuyu people, one of the largest ethnic groups in Kenya.[21] It began around 1950, was fought brutally on both sides, and finally provoked the British to declare a state of emergency that lasted from October 1952 until early 1960. As a result of the growing resistance to colonial rule, a number of legislative reforms were expedited, and the participation of Africans in the government increased. By 1960 Africans became the majority in the Legislative Council, and in 1963 full independence was achieved.[22] Kenya has been one of the most consistently pro-Western African countries since the founding of the republic. Jomo Kenyatta, the first president of the republic and the most powerful leader during the Mau Mau rebellion, had been incarcerated from 1953 to 1959.[23] In death as prominent a figure as in life, he ruled until 1978. After Kenyatta's death in that year, Daniel arap Moi of the minority Kalenjin people held the office of president until 2002. Under President Moi's rule the government increasingly became the target of internal and external criticism due to widespread corruption and abuses of power.[24] In December 2002 a new government under the leadership of President Mwai Kibaki was voted into power, promising to reverse the decline the country had experienced over the previous twenty years.

Kenya has an area comparable to that of France, covering a territory of 224,961 square miles. Its quickly growing population was estimated at nearly thirty million people in 2003. Kenya's economy has a large traditional sector based on agriculture, which contributes about 30 percent of the gross national product, employs 75 to 80 percent of the population, and generates about 60 percent of the foreign exchange earnings.[25] Coffee and tea are the key foreign items for export, producing between 33 and 40 percent of foreign receipts. Kenya also exports petroleum, cotton, sisal, fruits, wattle bark, cashew nuts, and horticultural products. Fishing, mining, and manufacturing are other important sectors of the economy. Next to the United Kingdom, Germany is presently Kenya's most important trade partner.

Apart from the trade in coffee and tea, tourism is the main sector of the Kenyan economy, providing, according to publications by Kenyan tourist organizations, about 20 percent of the nation's jobs.[26] But these figures are somewhat inflated and probably include figures from employment in the feeder industry. Nevertheless, the tourism industry supports a very large number of people, given that every working Kenyan provides for five to ten family members. In the mid-1990s revenues from tourism reached up to five hundred million dollars per year.[27]

After Kenya gained independence, its leaders quickly understood that developing the tourism industry was a profitable endeavor. The country has a lot to offer: beautiful white beaches, adorned with palm trees and lush tropical bushes, trees, and flowers; the vast national parks that are home to lions, elephants, antelopes, and other rare species; mountains, such as Mount Kenya; spectacular highlands; and a rich cultural history. The coast has been populated by Africans and Arabs for well over one thousand years, and many of the historical sites are well preserved. The port town of Mombasa has an Arabic old town, Muslims mosques, Hindu temples, and a huge fort built by the Portuguese. Other settlements along the coast, such as Malindi and Lamu, are famous for their architecture and history. A variety of ethnic groups with diverse customs and heritage are further proof of the cultural richness of the country.

Beginning in the mid-1960s, cottages and larger tourist resorts were built on the coast, and new lodges were added to the existing ones in game parks. My study focuses on a beach to the south of Mombasa, Diani Beach, a strip of several kilometers of immaculate white sand. As opposed to the north coast, Diani Beach lies farther away from the main highway, allowing for a more private atmosphere. The first lodge on Diani Beach was built in the late 1930s and was run at the time by two Britons. This lodge was expanded into a hotel in the 1960s, and other hotels opened soon afterward. The hotels were built on land that was confiscated or bought from the local Digo people. By the mid-1970s a boom reflected the increase in tourism, and by 2000 Diani Beach had twenty-one hotels and a number of smaller lodges. The hotels can accommodate between two hundred and six hundred guests. With a couple of exceptions the architecture of the hotels heeds the various Kenyan traditions, in particular Arabic and African styles. Many hotels have palm leaf roofs, and often buildings feature Arabic design patterns.[28]

German tourists have been traveling to Kenya since the late 1960s, in ever-increasing numbers. Beginning in the early 1980s, visa requirements were lifted for Germans, which made travel to Kenya significantly easier. By the mid-1990s German tourists outnumbered British tourists, and on average they spent a longer period in Kenya than did their British counterparts. Of the 554,900 holiday visitors departing Kenya in 1996, Germans made up 18.9 percent (104,800) and British 17.6 percent (97,600).[29] Germans booked 25 percent of all overnight stays (1,275,600), whereas British visitors booked 18 percent of them (934,100). In comparison to Italians, French, and Americans, only a small number of Swiss travel to Kenya (4.2%); however, they stay much longer in the country, book more nights (301,900), and vacation almost three times longer than, for example, the average American tourist. All in all, German-speaking tourists represent the largest group of visitors to Kenya. Since they vacation mostly on the coast, they are also the most visible group in this area and book more than 30 percent of all overnight stays.[30]

In 1997 tourism in Kenya entered a major crisis. In August political unrest in conjunction with the upcoming elections led to violence on the south coast. Kenya was about to hold its second multiparty elections, and President Moi's rule was on the verge of being challenged. The violence on the south coast was aimed at upcountry people who were working at the coast and had been registered to vote in the coastal district, one of the districts traditionally loyal to Moi. The rioters sought out individuals who, it was feared, could tip the vote against Moi, forced them and their families to leave, and thereby prevented them from voting in the district in which they were registered. The riots, a case "of ethnicised violence, . . . left hundreds of people killed or maimed for life, thousands of others displaced and millions of dollars in property and revenue lost through arson and the resulting decline of the tourist industry."[31] Approximately seventy people were killed in residential areas not far from the tourist centers. The events were covered extensively in the German press, and, as a consequence, tourism dropped by 80 percent within a couple of weeks.

Not a single tourist was hurt or affected in significant ways, however, during the rioting. The rioters consciously stayed away from foreigners, a fact that is documented by an anecdote about an encounter between rioters and tourists that was told by many south coast residents after the events. When rioters arrived at the German Biergarten in Ukunda, the larger settlement adjacent to the hotels, a couple of Swiss guests were at the bar. The rioters asked the tourists to finish their beers and pay and then put them on a *matatu,* a minibus, which is the common means of transportation for locals and which brought the Swiss to their hotels. Only then did the rioters burn down the place. Nevertheless, the riots were covered extensively in the German language press. In addition, Kenya suffered very much from the repercussions of the worldwide climatic changes brought on by El Niño; many roads were left impassable, and higher cases of malaria and cholera during that time stirred fears of disease. Hotel reservations were canceled, and some airlines stopped service to Mombasa altogether.

Kenya has still not completely recovered from those events. Although tourism was picking up in 1999 and 2000, visitation rates are still far below those of previous years. It should be noted, however, that tourism had already dropped since the beginning of the 1990s. Other destinations, such as South Africa and the Dominican Republic, had gained in popularity. Also, Germans and other Europeans have less spending money now as compared with the 1980s. As a result, prices of lodging and travel have declined drastically; in 1998, 1999, and 2000 a two-week stay in Kenya was offered for as low as seven hundred dollars, which included a round-trip flight from Germany and half-board accommodation in a three- or four-star hotel.

These political, economic, and climate-related events brought a new group of visitors to Kenya. In fact, Germans continued to travel to Kenya in increasing numbers, most likely in response to the lower prices; in 1999, 152,589 Germans departed for Kenya, and in 2000 the figure was even higher (163,168).[32] This development is important with regard to the study presented here, which documents the interaction between the Kenyan population and German-speaking repeat visitors. The tourists documented in this study consists of both the old and the new repeaters; about 50 percent of the tourists interviewed had traveled to Kenya more than four times and could be considered as part of the earlier group of repeaters, but the other 50 percent were more recent Kenya aficionados. According to this analysis, it seems too early to draw conclusions regarding possible differences between the old "Stammpublikum" (repeat visitors) and the emerging new clientele, but the study possibly documents a transitional period and the emergence of new patterns.

Analyses of tourism in Kenya follow the range of different approaches to tourism research outlined earlier. Philipp Bachmann, for example, points out the negative effects of tourism, such as the "restriction of fishing rights because of beach development for tourism, the sale of land to tourism companies, the spread of prostitution and criminality, [and] the rise of living costs during the tourist season."[33] He comes to the conclusion that "the economic benefits of tourism are quite small for the Kenyan nation and virtually non-existent for the poor population majority, but important for some transnational firms and local businessmen."[34] Others draw a similar picture in their studies of tourism in Kenya.[35] A more recent discussion paper is inspired by the notion of sustainable tourism and offers solutions that could amend the current situation.[36]

How have Germans fared in studies on the contact between German tourists and the local population? Most analyses from the 1970s and early 1980s generally dismiss any sort of productive cross-cultural communication. The local population appears as victimized, while the tourists are not interested in learning about Kenyan realities.[37] While Eva Kurt grants locals the ability of demystify the visitors, in her opinion cross-cultural communication is not possible.[38] Christiane Schurian-Bremecker's study of different types of German tourists conveys a similar outlook: during the course of their visits tourists do not arrive at a more sophisticated understanding of the country and its people.[39]

Whereas studies on German tourism offer largely negative conclusions regarding cross-cultural contact between tourists and Kenyans, more recent investigations, mostly written at U.S. institutions, have asked different questions, in particular by focusing more on Kenyans than on tourists. David Jamison's study considers the impact of tourism on notions of ethnicity and national identity among the local population. He shows that ethnic antagonisms between Kenyans are to some degree suspended when it comes to interacting with tourists.[40] Johanna Schoss argues that local agency is present and needs to be considered in analyses discussing the impact of tourism.[41] In a similar vein a study conducted by Kenyan researcher S. E. Migot-Adholla and others demonstrates that Kenyans displayed a generally positive attitude toward the tourists and did not consider themselves victimized by the foreigners.[42] Other analyses discuss the romantic relationships between tourists and Kenyans, for example, by acknowledging the various types of relationships between female tourists and local men and suggesting investigations of the complexity of power relations engaged by such interactions.[43]

Encouraged by these recent approaches, the study presented here attempts to address questions of cross-cultural interaction not by investigating attitudes or views held but, rather, by focusing on social action. The documentation of material support extended to Kenyans by repeat visitors and the analysis of marriage patterns provide indicators for investigating the social action existing between tourists and locals. Although the question of motivation is not directly addressed through the acknowledgement of social practice, such an approach sheds light on the extent of the interaction between Kenyans and Germans.

Evidence for such interactions and the verbal account describing it need to be interpreted just as much as any textual evidence. The data presented here document previously unacknowledged dimensions of the relationship between Germans and Kenyans, dimensions that can be understood within the larger history of interaction between Germans and Africans.

Repeat tourism in Kenya is 5 to 10 percent higher than in other areas. Several hotel managers stated that 20 to 40 percent of their guests are repeat visitors, with some hotels drawing more repeat visitors than others. Over the years this repeat tourism in Kenya has generated a number of developments and has had a significant impact on the local infrastructure. Tourists venture beyond the traditional boundaries of the tourist ghetto and develop extensive relations with the local population. Along the Diani coast signs confirming the presence of Germans are everywhere. Language schools teach German to locals, while Swahili is offered to Germans at the pools of some of the hotels. The weekly newspaper the *Coast* features one page of its articles in German. German language signs announce special events, and bulletin boards at the supermarkets are filled with ads for yoga, massage, and used cars for sale. One advertisement put up by the German owner of a small restaurant catering especially to Germans read: "Wir kochen für Euch! We are cooking for you! Am Freitag, den 25.6. ab 19:00 / on Friday evening / Sauerbraten mit Rotkohl und verschiedenen Knödeln / Pudding mit Vanillesoße."

Some repeat visitors and individuals who work in the tourism industry have bought houses on the south coast and no longer live in the hotels. Real estate business involving Germans has been very lucrative since the early 1990s, when it became legal for foreigners to own land in Kenya. Landownership in turn also guarantees the right to become a Kenya resident. One company sold over 250 homes to Germans by 1999, a large part (possibly up to 60 percent) of which are owned by residents of the former East Germany. House ownership has brought many repeat visitors to spend even longer periods in Kenya. Some of the repeat visitors and others who came for reasons of work have become residents; in 1999 a German Residents Association of Kenya was formed, mostly by members of the large concentration of German residents living on the Diani coast, but the organization disbanded within a year.[44] An increasing number of tourists and residents marry Kenyans, an aspect that will be discussed in detail later in the chapter. In addition, a small group of

Germans, Swiss, and Austrians who came with the first wave of tourism to work in Kenya have lived on the south coast for many years. Often they are permanent residents of Kenya. They operate many of the stores along the Diani coast beach road, such as clothing boutiques, a telecommunications store, butcher store, general store, discotheque, and restaurants.

These developments are comparable to those observed by Jacqueline Waldren in her analysis of Majorca and those reported by Tamara Kohn, who studied a small Inner Hebridean island off the west coast of Scotland. Kohn's study demonstrates that "tourists over time may possibly become part of and thus create the host community."[45] Waldren's case shows that the high level of interaction between visitors and their hosts can enable a particular community "to gain full advantage from the economic opportunities opened up by foreigners without losing the fabric of social relations, the meanings and values of their culture."[46] Whether this last claim is applicable to the current situation at the Diani coast remains to be explored in future studies.

The research conducted for this study aimed at documenting the complexity of social interaction between German repeat visitors and the local host community. The statistical evaluation does not include the many repeat visitors who have become Kenyan residents or Germans who came to Kenya because of work, some of whom became residents, or the group of Germans who bought property, mostly during the last decade. Yet, in order to broaden the scope of the analysis, I have gathered information about intermarriage between Kenyans and German-speaking individuals, a few of whom were Kenyan residents or were working in the tourism industry. The primary target group was composed of the repeat visitors staying at hotels. I used a questionnaire and conducted interviews, some of which were taped. Altogether, 110 tourists filled out the questionnaires, and 28 Germans agreed to a taped interview. Additional information was gathered during conversations with managers, hotel employees, resident Germans, and others who worked in the tourism industry.

The objective of the questionnaires, which were distributed to travelers before they left for their vacation at the airports in Frankfurt and Düsseldorf and in six different hotels in Kenya, was to document the extent of the interaction. The taped interviews provide more specific information about the kind of interaction occurring. The data on intermarriage give further insight into the range and specificity of relations between Kenyans and Germans. The visitors included individuals who traveled alone, couples, and families with children.

The majority of German travelers to Kenya, roughly two-thirds (62.4%), were between forty-one and sixty years old; in comparison to the women, fewer men under thirty (6.9%; women 11.8%) and more men over sixty (19%; women 11.8%) visit Kenya.[47] The visitors' professions reflect the entire spectrum of German society. *Bootsbauer* (boat builder), *Einzelhandelskaufmann* (trained retail salesman), *Gartenlandschaftbauer* (gardener), *Malermeister* (painter), *Fliesenleger* (tiler), *Architekt* (architect), *Chemiefacharbeiter* (skilled chemical worker), *Beamter* (state employee), *Rentner* (retiree), *Sekretärin* (secretary), *Kinderkrankenschwester* (pediatric nurse), *Büroangestellte* (office worker), *Verkäuferin* (saleswoman), *Vertriebsassistentin* (sales manager), and *Hausfrau* (housewife) are some of the professions listed in the questionnaires. Most of the twenty-seven men and women who did not list a profession indicated that they were housewives or pensioners.

According to this data, the majority of travelers were of working-class and middle-class background; only about 20.6 percent of the individuals work in an area requiring an academic education (including non-university institutions, such as engineering colleges). These figures largely correspond to the educational background of German society in general. Today roughly 30 percent of the population acquires a diploma permitting access to the various institutions of higher education, although not everybody who is entitled to study will pursue or complete an academic degree.[48] These percentages, however, reflect the current situation; only twenty or thirty years ago the group of Germans with a background in higher education was much smaller, between 40 and 50 percent of today's levels. Therefore, the percentage of repeat visitors who work in professions requiring academic training, many of whom are between forty and sixty, is largely proportional to the German population in general.[49]

In order to travel to Kenya repeatedly, however, it can be assumed that these tourists from different social backgrounds are financially comfortable. On the other hand, the data on the level of education complicate earlier arguments that emphasize the high social status of travelers to

Kenya.[50] The widespread claim that only educated individuals are inclined to interact with other cultures is challenged by the data presented here; the analysis of the interviews that were conducted addresses this issue in more depth.

The questions put forth in the questionnaire avoided topics that would have solicited opinions or views about specific issues. The only instance that involved the subjective definition of a concept was contained in a question asking whether tourists considered one or more Kenyans to be their "friends." All other inquiries were geared toward the quantitative identification of social action.

First of all, most people (79.1%) claimed that they knew one or more Kenyans well (see appendix, table A1). Seventy percent indicated that they visited Kenyans in their homes, which might have included visits during organized tours. When asked whether they would consider one or more Kenyans as friends, 57.3 percent answered positively. This was further supported by over 49.1 percent stating that they had exchanged letters with Kenyans since their last visit. Of those Germans who claimed that they did not make friends with Kenyans, some still brought presents for acquaintances or for orphanages and schools. Altogether, the figure for people who brought presents was 70 percent. This is a clear indication of the interest tourists take in the lives of locals. Many had talked to people on their previous visits and responded to existing needs when deciding about what to bring for whom. Visitors bring a variety of items, from clothing and school supplies to electronic appliances. A lot of people also leave clothes, shoes, towels, watches, and other things behind. The results from the questionnaires thus document that there is a great deal of interaction between Germans and Kenyans.

This might be a good moment to add a few words about Kenya's image as a prime destination for "sex tourism." Most of the studies investigating personal contacts between tourists and Kenyans focus on romantic relationships or prostitution and do not appropriately explore other types of interactions. *Sex tourism* is a loaded term, one that is often used in thoughtless and moralizing ways to describe quite different situations. While the existence of prostitution aimed at tourists is a fact, not all encounters between tourists and Kenyans are sexual, and not all sexual encounters are connected to prostitution. The term *sex tourism,* the way it is currently used to describe encounters between Kenyans and tourists, implies a large-scale victimization of Kenyans by tourists that does not reflect the range of interactions existing in the country.

There is certainly established prostitution in Kenya, and economic need dominates many relationships. Generally, however, about half of all sex tourists are interested not in short-term sexual encounters but in long-term relationships.[51] In many cases the desire for a sexual encounter is coupled with other social and emotional needs.[52] Also, many sexual encounters between German-speaking tourists and Kenyans develop into longer relationships, even marriages.[53] In addition, significant differences exist between female and male sex tourists; the female sex tourist has often distinct expectations, is more vulnerable than her male counterpart, and is at times subject to exploitation.[54] For most female sex tourists sexuality is not at the center of the encounter, but, rather, they are motivated by a longing for a romantic relationship.[55] And, finally, economic need and dependency are factors in many relationships everywhere. Patterns existing in the home countries of the tourists need to be considered as well.

No reliable figures exist that detail how many tourists are engaged in either a romantic or purely sexual relationship with Kenyans. In comparison to Thailand, sex tourism evolves much more secretively in Kenya. The majority of people I interviewed did not travel alone. Many hotels register double occupancy for most of the rooms; in some hotels a high percentage of children accompany their parents.[56] Several managers stated that single occupancy does not exceed 20 percent. This indicates that many tourists travel as couples, families, or with friends, which reduces the chance that they travel in order to find a sexual partner. These figures suggest that the percentage of sex tourists amounts to a small group among tourists, even if the number may be higher among the repeat visitors. If one assumes, however, that 10 percent of the German-speaking tourists who travel to Kenya engage in sexual relationships, a large group of people emerges.[57]

The stigma associated with sex tourism influenced the behavior of some of the tourists interviewed. Several repeat visitors who were accompanied by their Kenyan lovers declined to fill out the questionnaire or to talk about their experiences. Others censored their answers; to some extent, however, that holds true for all interviewees and is part of the dilemma of the interview situation. One woman, for example, who had initially stated that she did not know any Kenyans well, turned out to have a relationship with one of the hotel animators and talked about it only after she had completed the questionnaire and felt more comfortable with the interview situation.

The existence of romantic relationships between Germans and Kenyans also explains the higher figures indicating more extensive interaction involving the travelers interviewed at the airports in Germany. These travelers included a larger group of Germans married to Kenyans and also other people who did not stay at hotels but, instead, with Kenyan friends or lovers. The slightly higher figures for visitors in 1998 might point toward a larger percentage of tourists belonging to the older group of repeat visitors. Generally, however, figures for men and women are very similar.

Most of the twenty-one taped interviews were conducted during the four o'clock tea time in hotels in Kenya. Five of the interviews were held in Germany. To a large extent the time and place of the interviews determined the kind of people interviewed. Had the interviews taken place at local bars in the vicinity of the hotels, a different group of tourists would have emerged (which, for reasons explained earlier, I do not consider representative of the majority of tourists). The four o'clock tea proved to be an ideal occasion to talk to an average group of people, including all different types of tourists present in Kenya. Altogether, conversations with twenty-eight Germans were taped. For the most part no appointments were made for the interviews, and conversations were recorded on the spot during the first encounter.[58] I was not selective in choosing interview partners but recorded everybody who was willing to sit down for an interview. The almost equal number of thirteen men and fifteen women was a coincidence. All but three individuals (one couple and one man) were repeat visitors; I included these conversations to get a sense of the reactions of people who had been to Kenya for the first time. While it is not possible to draw larger conclusions based on the views of these three tourists, the information is nevertheless relevant in that it resonates with the data gathered from the repeat visitors.

Eighteen individuals, or roughly two-thirds of the people interviewed, traveled with a partner and were (most likely) not romantically involved with Kenyans.[59] Of the remaining ten people (six women and four men) five women and two men had or are likely to have had sexual relationships with Kenyans, whereas one woman and two men probably did not engage in sexual encounters with Kenyans. Contrasting those who traveled alone to tourists who traveled as couples allowed me to tackle two questions: (1) are Germans who travel alone more or less likely to develop contacts with the local population? and (2) are Germans who travel alone more or less likely to extend support to the local population? While the statistical base here is rather small, it nevertheless indicates tendencies that gain a greater significance when compared to the results of the questionnaires.

An overview of the results from the interviews summarizes the nature of the relationship between repeat visitors and the local population (see appendix, tables A2 and A3). In all cases significant contact between the local population and the tourists existed. The majority of repeat visitors did support Kenyans materially in one way or another. Five of the six repeat visitor couples and all three of the individuals who traveled with a partner had extended some kind of support. The man who traveled with a group of friends, while not establishing relations with Kenyans, turned out to be substantially supportive of a Sri Lankan family he had gotten to know during one of his travels in that country. The couple, who had been to Kenya for the first time, asserted that they were planning to send gifts and would bring something the next time they visited. Of the individuals traveling alone, five women and two men supported Kenyans in some way. Altogether, 20 of the 25 repeat visitors (that is, 80 percent) thus extended some sort of support. This indicates that the group of people interviewed even surpassed the findings from the questionnaire-based survey conducted of 110 repeat visitors.

Again, the majority of travelers was between forty-one and sixty years old (57.1 percent, which is slightly lower than the 62.4 percent gathered from the questionnaires). It is interesting to note that ten of the twenty-eight informants worked in a field requiring an academic training, which is higher than the figures presented in the analysis of the questionnaires. Yet this might be explained by the fact that five of the six individuals with an academic background had been referred to me personally. Taken out of the statistics, the percentage of people interviewed in Kenya without a university education increases to 75 percent (17 out of 22 total) and is thus closer again to the figures reflected in the evaluation of the questionnaires. As mentioned before, this is quite contrary to the findings of earlier studies that emphasize the proportionally higher level of education and social status among travelers to Kenya—which brings us back to the question whether social status determines the attitudes that visitors hold toward other cultures. Four of the five people who had not developed friendly relations with Kenyans that included material support were academics. All four expressed the thought that they felt very differently from Kenyans and had experienced unease at one point or another as a result of those differences. One woman, who was in the process of writing a social science dissertation, stated that, even if one had conversations with Kenyans (and she was actually learning Swahili), the ability truly to understand one another was limited. Another woman with academic training emphasized that she had been able to develop friendships only with people from the hotel's management and that her experiences with members of the lower classes had been disappointing.

These statements suggest—and a larger database is certainly warranted to make any profound claims—that social status plays a more crucial role than cultural identity in determining the relationship between Kenyans and Germans. Even if educated Germans describe their experience with Kenyans in terms of cultural difference, they are most likely more irritated by the encounter of social differences, by the confrontation with poverty and a lack of access to education. Yet, due to conventions that often confuse social and cultural factors in the analysis of intercultural relations, these Germans ethnicize their experience of the social gap between the cultures. Two of the interviewees with an academic education also talked about gender differences, especially the different status of women in the respective societies.

On the other hand, those Germans without an academic education seemed to cross the cultural boundaries by identifying with the social situation of Kenyans. Even though the actual social difference between these Germans and Kenyans is substantial, middle- to lower-class Germans seemed to empathize with Kenyans more easily than did interviewees from higher-status social backgrounds. This conclusion is supported by the evidence from the questionnaires, the interviews, and additional conversations that were conducted. In a representative example a conversation developed with a young working-class couple after they had filled out the questionnaires; he was a worker in a chemical factory, she a saleswoman; both were in their twenties. It turned out that the husband made sandwiches every morning for hotel employees working on the compound. He had learned that gardeners are lowest on the pay scale in the hotels, and, even though it was strictly forbidden to pass on food to hotel employees (at first the wife did not want him to tell this story), the young man, visibly upset about the working conditions of these employees, was inspired to go out of his way to smuggle out sandwiches. While the actual deed might not seem to amount to much, the man's agitation while he related his thoughts and actions indicates a substantial reflective process.

In interesting ways this data suggesting that Germans communicate based on their ability to relate to the social situation of Kenyans is in line with the results of Migot-Adholla's study, a project conducted by Kenyan researchers. This study reports that more than one-third of Kenyans (38.5%) who work in the tourism industry see no difference between themselves and tourists. Only 13.8 percent identified wealth as the most important difference, while 36.6 percent named race (distinguished by skin color).[60] While this might seem odd in light of the obvious material differences between visitors and the local population, it can be taken as an indication that Kenyans are not primarily concerned about social differences, which might account for the atmosphere that allows Kenyans and Germans to develop contacts. This attitude might be fostered by the interaction with lower- and lower-middle-class Germans who feel empowered because they notice their own material wealth in comparison to Kenyans but who, for the same reasons, also seem to display signs of solidarity with them.

As evident from tables A2 and A3 in the appendix, the support extended by the tourists addresses different areas of need. Many tourists pay educational fees for different types of school, such as primary and secondary schools, language institutes, and driving schools; they buy school supplies and uniforms; they take care of hospital bills and pay for other medical needs; they bring clothes, household items, or electronic appliances; and they even help people build their own homes. The stories of these repeat visitors are often quite surprising.

Uwe and Bärbel G. come from a small town in northern Germany and, when interviewed for this study, were in Kenya for the third time.

Both were forty-nine years old; he worked as an official with the German railway; she was an office worker with an engineering company. The first two times they had traveled with their son Tobias. The couple related a number of stories involving Kenyans whom they got to know more closely, who had, for example, served as guides on tours through Mombasa. Although most of the encounters were positive, they also reported some negative experiences in which they felt used by Kenyans. The couple voiced a common complaint—namely, that people they met got "pesty" after an excursion undertaken together. In one case a guide had imposed a visit to his private home after the tour, which was interpreted by Uwe and Bärbel as an attempt to extract additional money from them. For the rest of the vacation the guide continued to stalk the couple, up to a point where they felt most uncomfortable.

This encounter, however, seems to have been their only truly negative experience. Uwe and Bärbel G. had learned about an orphanage in Ukunda, and on their second trip to Kenya they filled their suitcases with clothes and school supplies for the institution. After their return to Germany they also tried to organize a shipment from Germany. The couple collected items from friends and family, but, after months of dealing with a number of relief organizations, ultimately failed to get the clothes and other supplies to Kenya because of bureaucratic obstacles. On the visit during which I interviewed them, they again brought so many items for the orphanage that they had paid a DM 300 penalty for additional luggage. They also planned to leave clothing and other items behind, mostly for people they had befriended in the hotel. Both Uwe and Bärbel G. were well informed about political issues in Kenya, expressed repeatedly that they felt safe in the country, and generally demonstrated a great deal of affection for the country and its people.

Another repeat visitor who had developed extensive contact with locals was sixty-three-year-old Heinz S., who at the time of the first interview had just retired after having worked his entire career as a lower-ranking employee for GEMA, a German company protecting copyrights in the music industry. While he used to travel with a friend, he was now on his own, which, as he emphasized, enabled him to get to know people much better than before. The interviews took place in 1998 and 1999, during his thirteenth and fifteenth stay in Kenya. Heinz explained that since his retirement he traveled to Kenya twice a year. While being interviewed the first time, Heinz mentioned a piece of land he had bought together with a Kenyan named David, to enable this man to build a house for his family: "We even bought a piece of land together here. I mean, I don't really want it, I did it for the family, right, outside of Ukunda. . . . And I believe, I probably paid most of it. Was four and a half thousand Marks, what we paid for it." The following summer Heinz was a little disappointed with his friend; David had evidently married a British woman, left for England, and not done any work on the house. David's brother keeps asking him for money, but Heinz said he refuses to give more before he sees any progress on the house.

In light of this somewhat disappointing situation, the German retiree quickly found other ways to spend his money. For example, he paid the hospital bill for the birth of a child born to one of the employees in the hotel where he was staying. His contact with locals was extensive; Heinz often frequented bars in Ukunda and, in his absence, regularly exchanged letters with a number of people. Given the nature and extent of his contacts, it was surprising to hear that Heinz never ate at the homes of his friends. Heinz said that he could not get himself to eat from a pot that everybody had their hands in. But, because he did not want to offend his hosts, he told them that he has severe stomach problems and had to watch his diet. Heinz did not know much about the political situation in the country and entertained only vague notions about current affairs. At the same time, he was obviously significantly involved in the lives of a number of Kenyans, from whom he probably got more attention than from people in Germany, where, over the last few years, he had lost a number of friends and family members. It seems that, while Heinz has little social power and status in Germany, he feels needed and respected in Kenya, where the little money he has can make a substantial difference.

One of the most remarkable stories was told by a couple who were both fifty-seven-year-old residents of the Erzgebirge, a region in eastern Germany. Hilde M., a sales manager by training, used to sell baked goods in the market and had also worked as a truck driver; Walter M. was employed as a skilled worker in a chemical plant. Hilde M. claimed that she never had had much of a chance to travel during GDR times and that nobody from her village had ever been to Africa. This was the couple's third time in Kenya. After their first stay Hilde and Walter had departed with only the clothes they were wearing; among other items the husband, for example, had left twenty-three undershirts behind. This time around, they brought loads of clothing for people in the village, together approximately 110 pounds, among which were thirty bikinis, twenty sandals, and fifty pairs of socks. These items were bought; others had been collected from friends and coworkers. Hilde M. explained that they had come to Africa with the intention to help. For a long time they had donated money for relief efforts in Africa through church organizations but had realized that not much of the money ends up with African people themselves. She emphasized that one of their reasons to come to Africa was that they wanted to find out where and how they could help best.

Apart from bringing clothes and school supplies, the couple paid school fees and bought school uniforms for children, occasionally went shopping with friends, paid for groceries and household items, in one instance picked up the rent for a family, opened an account for another friend, and passed out smaller amounts of money. Hilde M. also reported some cases in which she felt betrayed. At some point, for example, she discovered that the school certificate for a child she wanted to support was falsified. Ever since then, she pays the money directly to the school, an option available and made use of by a number of repeat visitors.[61] The couple said that at times they felt asked to help too often and in unreasonable ways and were frequently confronted with stories that were obviously fabricated. Later in the conversation, however, both claimed that, generally, nobody asked them for money directly, which they greatly appreciated. In a curious comment that reveals how much Hilde M. had been shaped by the postwar experience and also the difficult economic living conditions in the GDR, she expressed her amazement at the villagers' unwillingness or inability to mend clothes: "On the other hand, it also amazed me that—since the poverty is so great—women do not mend clothes, as we do." In response to this situation, Hilde M. had brought plenty of yarn with her and set out on a mission to teach some of the villagers how to mend clothes.

Even though this was only their third stay in Kenya, Hilde and Walter knew many people and had learned much about their lives. They had visited several homes, and Hilde M. emphasized how impressed she was with the cleanliness she observed: "That's how I always used to imagine African women: dressed impeccably, impeccably." Both Hilde and Walter seemed very content with the extent and the nature of their contacts in Kenya: "The people in general, the mentality of the people, let's say—I can't, I can't really describe it, let's say—I like the people here very much. They are friendly, let's say, up to 90 percent. They are everywhere, in every country, you will find people, that are sulky, but you can't, you can't judge everybody based on that."

Interestingly, when Hilde M. talked about her life in Germany and her relationships with friends and family members, many of whom she also supported in various ways, she basically expressed similar concerns and revealed much of the same attitude toward others as she did when talking about Africans. It seems obvious that this woman is a person who wants to be needed and whose self-esteem is very much connected with being useful to others. Whether motivated by religious beliefs, the discourse about helping Africans, by some residual notion of socialist solidarity with the needy, or by a psychological longing to be needed, Hilde and Walter M. were thoroughly interested in the lives of Kenyans and in wanting to share what they had.[62] There was no newspaper to report about their actions, and no immediate payoff other than the acknowledgment that the couple could give to each other.

Horst P. is a dentist who first came to Kenya in 1986 as a tourist. Since then, he comes to Kenya once or twice a year, and has been involved in a number of local projects, some of them connected to missionary societies. For example, he helped set up three nurseries, two in the coastal region and one in the Nairobi area. Horst P. also supports the education of several individuals. He raises money in Germany, and the donors are friends, family members, and patients. To illustrate his fund-raising efforts, he mentioned the example of one of his patients, who gave him a check for over DM 3,000 to support a specific project. Only recently was Horst P. asked to help in his function as a dentist: he was appointed dean and asked to build up the dentistry department at a Kenyan university. What motivates him to dedicate so much of his life to Kenya? "That is somewhat connected to my love for the matter. I identify very much with this country and these people. Of course, I see also the predicaments and the problems, and I also see the weaknesses. But precisely because of all that we try to develop projects that enable people to help themselves. After all, giving only money doesn't work." It is significant that this insight—that giving is most fruitful when it enables people to help themselves—determines the actions of many German repeat visitors who support Kenyans.

Günther und Roswitha O. were visiting Kenya for the sixth time. He was, at the time of the interview, a fifty-seven-year-old teacher, she a fifty-four-year-old housewife. Their contacts with locals were quite extensive, as over the years they have supported a number of people. Günther O. enjoyed relating how at one point they had paid for the delivery of a friend's child. Afterward he and the father had been out drinking in honor of the newborn child, and he even bought a rooster that was then slaughtered to celebrate the occasion. The couple had also set up a bank account for this family. In addition, Günther and Roswitha O. were helping another family to build a house. They emphasized that they are monitoring the progress: "We do check on that. That is, they don't simply get a thousand marks blindly from us, in order to spend this somehow in other ways. We would really like the house to be built." In a nutshell this story, and many others like it, mirrors crucial problem areas familiar from discussions of development aid. The entire Pandora's box of questions regarding Western help to Africa—having to do with paternalism, dependency, and sustainable development—is contained in most of these anecdotes.

A larger project that is supported almost exclusively by funds obtained from tourists is the aforementioned orphanage, to which a number of tourists donate. The orphanage was founded in 1994 by the Dutch-born wife of a local hotel manager and housed twelve children in 1999. Each child has a sponsor, who pays roughly thirty-five dollars every month. The sponsors are Swiss, British, Dutch, German, and American nationals, most of them repeat visitors. In the summer of 2000 a new building was under construction, which, when complete, will be able to house thirty-six children. While the land was donated by a Kenyan, a local architect drew the plan free of charge, and a local doctor volunteers his medical services, most of the funds for the construction of the new orphanage and the maintenance of the current home are raised through bingo games played at the hotels, a fund-raiser bazaar, and fund-raiser concerts and through donations from repeat visitors and other sponsors abroad.

Another example of a charitable institution on the Diani coast that is supported largely by tourists is an eye care center that was founded in 1993 and which has a substantial impact on the local community. In 1999 alone the clinic saw 2,560 new patients and continued to monitor those registered in the previous year. In that same year 335 operations were performed at the clinic, 213 of them for removal of a cataract, the most common cause of blindness, and insertion of intraocular lenses. Of those operated on, 93 had been completely blind and were able to see after the surgery. Also in the area is the Clinic for the Welfare of Epileptics, which is connected to the Kenya Association for the Welfare of Epileptics. The local branch was founded in 1998, and the clinic is entirely run by volunteers. Both the eye center and the clinic for epileptics are supported by donations from tourists and by the proceeds of bingo games played at hotels. Similar projects exist on the coast north of Mombasa, such as the Bombolulu Workshops and the Culture Center for the Handicapped. Physically handicapped children are trained in workshops to fabricate clothing, carvings, jewelry, and leather items. Marketing targets primarily tourists, and many tour buses visit the shops. In addition to enabling the handicapped to earn a living, a clinic connected to the workshops treats more than 1,000 children annually and operates on approximately 150 children free of charge. The clinic is funded exclusively by donations.

The results from the questionnaires and the interviews document the extent and nature of the contact between Germans and Kenyans. Another relevant area that speaks to the cross-cultural encounter is the increasing rate of intermarriage between Germans and Kenyans.

Recent Marriage Patterns

Beginning in the mid-1990s, a growing number of German repeat visitors have married Kenyans. Even without the availability of statistical data, it seems that every larger family at the Diani coast has at least one member married to a German. Many of the Kenyan hotel managers are also married to Germans and other foreign nationals. The aforementioned books by Kwalanda and Hofmann and their great popularity with Germans speak to the extent of the attention given to this phenomenon. In order better to understand the nature of these developments, I compiled two sets of data that shed light on recent marriage patterns.

First, the German and Swiss embassies and federal agencies for statistics provided data regarding cross-national marriages that were recorded between 1994 and 2000. Second, an overview of records kept at the Registrar of Marriage in Mombasa documents the interaction at the coast and gives detailed information about the social profile of both Kenyans and Germans (and German-speaking tourists in general), in particular regarding their age and profession. Swiss and Austrians were included in this survey to get a better sense for the difference between members of the respective nationalities.

Since 1994 there has been a steady increase in the rates of marriage between Kenyans and Germans. In 1994, 97 couples were married; by 1997 this figure had doubled to 192 couples and increased again by 46.9 percent, to 282 couples, in 1999.[63] In evaluating this data, it is noteworthy that the increasing tendency to get married did not begin *after* the riots in late summer 1997 but was already prevalent in the years preceding those events. In comparison, a slower increase occurred regarding marriages between Swiss and Kenyan citizens. Uniting Swiss and Kenyans, 27 couples were married in 1994, a number that increased by 65.8 percent to 41 couples in 1999. In 2000, however, the number went down to 35; for the year 2001, 36 marriages were registered.[64] While these figures may seem low to begin with, we should not forget that most of the encounters occur on the Mombasa coast. The total number of 264 Swiss-Kenyan (1994–2001) and 1,161 German-Kenyan (1993–99) couples that got married in the course of a few years is certainly felt in the closely knit communities along the coast, where most of the Kenyan marriage partners stem from.

The information gathered at the Registrar of Marriage in Mombasa provides more detail on these figures and also differs in some areas.[65] Generally, not every marriage in Kenya is registered. It is very expensive for the average Kenyan to do so. At the office in Mombasa, the ceremony costs 6,250 KSh, outside of the office 10,150 KSh.[66] That is more than the average monthly salary of the average Kenyan who holds a job. These figures increased to the current amount on July 1, 1997; before this jump, they used to be lower, at 1,250 KSh and 2,100 KSh, respectively. One can only speculate why the fees were raised to such astronomical heights. Generally, Kenyans only register their marriages if the official documentation entails remuneration, such as allowing employee benefits for spouses. It is important to note that the data from the Registrar of Marriage in Mombasa reflect the tourism in the area. Data from Nairobi would probably show a larger percentage of British citizens marrying Kenyans; data from Malindi should document the high percentage of Italian tourists who frequent the area.

The marriage certificates have entries not for citizenship but for place of residence, profession, and age. American and British residents with Indian surnames were not included in the statistics, because they might be either former residents of Kenya or relatives of Kenyan citizens. The Kenyan marriage partners are predominantly black Kenyans, even though it cannot be stated with certainty what the percentage is, because many Arab, Indian, and black Kenyans have similar Muslim names. The data in appendix tables A4 and A5 reflect the categories used for the files kept at the office of the registrar.[67] According to this data, over the five-year period from 1994 to 1998, marriages between Kenyans and foreigners increased by 64.3 percent and between Kenyans and Germans by 56.4 percent (table A4). The percentage of German-speaking tourists (Germans, Swiss, and Austrians) ranged from 68.2 to 77.4 percent (1994: 65 of 84; 1995: 75 of 103; 1996: 88 of 129; 1997: 100 of 133; 1998: 105 of 138). Germans alone make up between 55 and 65.5 percent of all marriage partners (1994: 55 of 84; 1995: 58 of 103; 1996: 71 of 129; 1997: 81 of 133; 1998: 86 of 138).

The percentage of all foreign women and men who married Kenyans remained at approximately 60 percent for men and 40 percent for women. Only in 1995 was that ratio significantly different; in that year men made up 74.8 percent of the marriage partners. These data contradict the popular belief that mostly Kenyan women marry Western tourists. In the Swiss case, however, 32 men and 40 women married Kenyans. This figure also conflicts with the figures provided by the Swiss Bundesamt für Statistik, in which 198 men (86.8%) and 30 women (13.2%) were said to have married Kenyans between 1994 and 2000. This discrepancy might be an indication that marriages registered in Mombasa or at other locations in Kenya are not registered concurrently in Switzerland (and other countries). Kenyans will still benefit locally from registering the marriage and will, for example, be able to obtain a passport. The fact that Swiss and others do not register the marriages in their home countries suggests that they either deem this step unnecessary or that they are less inclined to make their marriages with Kenyans public.

These figures confirm findings from the questionnaires and interviews. First, the social makeup of the tourists is comparable to the other results. The detailed analysis of the data from 1998, based on the certificates of 138 couples, 105 of whom were German-speaking (table A5), shows that the occupations of 18 men and 9 German-speaking women (30.3 percent of those who worked) were based on an academic training.[68] Forty men and 22 women worked in areas that do not require an academic education, even though some might have studied at a university. According to these figures, 69.7 percent of the German-speaking tourists marrying Kenyans work in areas not requiring a higher education degree, which largely corresponds to the figures from the questionnaires and interviews and to the social makeup of German society in general. Although this does not provide a clear indication of the financial situation and economic status of the individuals, the significant number of tourists with a working-class or middle-class background, who work as electricians, secretaries, nurses, carpenters, tailors, drivers, and waitresses, is noteworthy. It is further indication of the fact that cross-cultural marriages are not necessarily predicated upon the social background of the individuals involved and that attitudes toward other cultures are not dependent on the social class of the German tourists. While the attitudes toward Kenyans might not correspond to the attitudes held by Germans within Germany or generally by Germans who do not travel to Africa, this data should inspire further research that compares the differences regarding the attitudes and behavior of Germans abroad to that of Germans at home. Also, the impact of frequent traveling in non-European countries on attitudes and behavior patterns vis-à-vis these other cultures deserves a closer look.

In addition, the statistics provide insights into the age patterns among tourists marrying Kenyans. The data show that most of the tourists or other foreign-born individuals are older than their Kenyan spouses; only 6 men and 6 women of all 138 couples were younger than the Kenyans they married (8.7%). The age gap between German-speaking tourists and Kenyans is slightly higher in comparison to the non-German-speaking individuals. Germans, Swiss, or Austrians who were younger, the same age or between one and ten years older made up 41 percent of the marriage partners (36.2% for men, 50% for women). Among non-German-speaking tourists that percentage was 57.5 percent (50% for men, 64.7% for women). Among the German-speaking tourists, Swiss and Austrians who marry Kenyans tend to be older than the German marriage partners; only 36.8 percent belonged to the younger age group. Germans who are older than their Kenyan partners by thirty-one years or more made up 12.8 percent. Among the Swiss and Austrians 21.1 percent are in that age group, while the percentage for non-German-speaking tourists is much lower (6.1%).

These data confirm widely held assumptions that the majority of Germans and other tourists or foreign-born individuals marrying Kenyans are older than their Kenyans spouses. The age gap by far exceeds the average age difference in Western societies, in which a larger percentage of men is older than the women they marry and the median age difference for different age groups stays mostly below ten years.[69] The cliché of the aging, rich Westerner, the "sugardaddy" or "sugarmommy," who marries a young Kenyan is challenged, however, by the significant number of marriages in which the age difference is less than ten years (45%). This corresponds to data from research on sex tourism that show that three-quarters of sex tourists are between eighteen and thirty-five years old.[70] Whether the relatively young age of many tourists who are interested in romance, marriage, or sex is a phenomenon of the last few years can only be answered by a long-term study.

Paternalism or Intercultural Encounter?

The study of the interaction between Kenyans and German tourists makes evident that a large group of German repeat visitors develop different types of relationships with Kenyans, challenging the widespread notion about sex tourism in Kenya as the dominant existing form of closer interaction between locals and visitors. Many German couples and individuals entertain close relationships and provide concrete support to families living on the Diani coast. Tourists traveling as couples or families are just as likely as visitors who travel alone to develop more in-depth relations with Kenyans. The primary areas of support they choose are education, clothing, medical needs, and housing. These areas of need are all widely acknowledged as basic human rights. That is, the tourists are guided by generally accepted notions of what makes for a humane life, corresponding, for example, to articles 25 and 26 of the Universal

Declaration of Human Rights. The visitors rarely pass out money, which might be spent on more immediate needs, such as eating and drinking. In a way the help they provide is geared toward creating humane living conditions and, in a number of cases, toward enabling Kenyans to help themselves, especially through education. That is, notions of sustainable development are also guiding the kind of support these repeat visitors provide. As this study of German tourists confirms, the spectrum of relations between visitors and locals is diverse, and the power relations do not evolve according to only one model.

The data on marriage patterns show that significantly more tourists and other foreign-born individuals marry Kenyans today than was the case before the mid-1990s. The age gap between the marriage partners is lower than common wisdom would have it. In addition, the social makeup reveals that Germans who are marrying Kenyans proportionally reflect the diversity of German social backgrounds and do not belong to the high society tourism with which Kenya was associated until recently. The most convincing explanation for the increasing marriage rates is the pressing economic situation in Kenya. There is no reason to believe that cultural attitudes have changed dramatically overnight. Most likely, the number of marriages is greater because Kenyans pursue marriage more vigorously, often with the goal of leaving the country, and Germans respond positively to the situation.

It will be worthwhile to explore whether the increasing tendency toward cross-cultural marriage also occurs in the countries of other popular tourist destinations, such as Tunisia.[71] Rosemary Breger shows that "marriages to non-Germans have increased slowly but steadily since the end of the Second World War. Mixed marriage comprised 7.7 percent of all marriages registered in Germany in 1980, and 9 percent in 1989."[72] While most of the spouses in these marriages come from the United States or Europe, a significant number of marriage partners are from Asia (men: 10%; women: 20%) and Africa (men: 9%; women: 4%).[73] Also, the lack of data on divorce rates, which are said to be high, does not allow for any predictions about the long-term effects of these relationships. In what ways the recent developments in marriage patterns will have an impact on German society is thus difficult to foresee.

It needs to be stressed once more that the issue of how Kenyans perceive the actions of the German repeat visitors and what they do with the support they are receiving are separate questions that could not be addressed in the framework of this study. Yet this question is central to a deeper understanding of the situation. Based on the insights gained in conversations during my research stays and previous visits, it is evident that tourists are received critically but are also appreciated. Conversation with Kenyans who worked in hotels as animators, pool guards, or waiters and with the so-called beach boys who peddle goods at the beach revealed a great understanding on the part of the Kenyans for the dilemmas existing on both sides. A detailed study exploring these perceptions would complement this investigation of German repeat visitors and generate a more complete picture of the situation. Such a study could also tackle the question of what happens if support to individuals is suddenly ended. Similar to issues related to development aid granted by nation-states or financial institutions, questions of continuity and dependency are crucial in this context.

The actions of German tourists in Kenya reveal the persistence of the German fascination with East Africa. The behavior the tourists display is clearly mobilized by humanitarian frameworks, be they primarily Christian or secular. Over the last century and a half, attitudes have developed that seem to make it mandatory for Germans to want to help in Africa. These attitudes are informed by traditions integral to German society, traditions that are defined by models such as Max Eyth, Albert Schweitzer, Ernst Udet, Bernhard Grzimek, and others, including the opera star Karl-Heinz Böhm, who initiated a relief operation, *Menschen für Menschen*, in 1981 to support people in Ethiopia. Regarding the more recent period, tourists are responding to images about Africa put forth in writings and films over many decades. Their actions are thus a reflection of the fact that helping needy Africans has been a central theme in German-speaking (and generally Western) media for many years. A humanitarian impetus, coupled with ideas about development and modernization, drives these individuals. Both consciously and unconsciously, the German visitors operate within and respond to a framework that conveys the moral imperative to help in Africa. On the other hand, one could also argue that the social background and the attitudes of the visitors toward Kenyans suggests that the urge to help might be at least partially based on an impetus to alleviate poverty generally, rather than African poverty in particular.

Even if the travelers' original motivations for their journeys to Kenya might have been primarily connected to the appeal of beaches and wild animals in their native habitats, their actions as repeat visitors depart quite drastically from the limited nature of the original inspiration. How these travelers see their role in Kenya is not easy to assess; some are conscious of their actions, many find themselves in more than one dilemma, and others operate without the slightest feeling of challenge regarding the legitimacy of their actions or the contested nature of their position among Africans. Most repeat visitors, however, have learned a great deal over the years and have become more aware of their actions. They have learned to anticipate the impact of specific behaviors. At times, but not always, the various visits to Kenya over an extended period resulted in a greater understanding of Kenyans and of the tourists themselves and even of the larger implications of their role in Kenya.

One of the remaining questions concerns the fact that more German-speaking tourists marry Kenyans than any other group of tourists. In comparison to the Germans, almost the same number of British tourists travels to Kenya, but their interaction with locals is very limited. One obvious explanation is the colonial legacy: the fact that the British colonized the country causes great reservations on both sides. Regarding the Germans, there are surely aspects of pity, empathy, and guilt inspiring the tourists' behavior. One tourist indicated that Africans knew how to exploit the feeling of guilt and shame Germans often harbor when it comes to questions of racism. To some extent Germans might be driven by a xenophilic desire to compensate or atone for the racist legacy resulting from German crimes committed during the period of National Socialism. On the other hand, as has been highlighted repeatedly in the course of this study, the tourists' actions reflect traditions of meddling with African affairs that go back to the time before World War II.

The power that Germans experience because of their economic superiority certainly plays a great role in these dynamics. With the expenditure of relatively small amounts of money, the visitors can set into motion profound developments in the lives of individual Kenyans. The satisfaction Germans potentially derive from this economic inequality is more than problematic and is one of the aspects of this cross-cultural interaction that is most difficult to assess. Nevertheless, one should also grant the possibility that some people are genuinely compassionate and feel inspired by a sense that they are needed and can help with relatively little means.

Finally, the example of German repeat visitors in Kenya also raises questions about the discrepancies between people's behavior at home and abroad. Although individual Germans might be friendly toward people from other cultures while abroad, their behavior can turn to hostility when confronted with immigrants from Africa and Asia at home, where the actions of the same German individuals are shaped to a greater extent by their relationship to a larger group, namely the German nation. Turner's understanding of rituals and *rites-de-passage* and Gottlieb's notion of the inversion of everyday life during tourist vacations might very well be models that best explain these conflicting behaviors. It would be worthwhile to study this phenomenon further in order to understand whether the discrepancy between behavior at home and abroad reveals a utopian desire for change or contains a compensatory function that will ultimately stifle substantial developments, at home or abroad.

Conclusion

One goal of this study was to acknowledge the complexity of the interaction between Germans and Africans. No single factor, whether civilizationism, biological racism, or attitudes based in a Christian religious worldview, determines the ways in which Germans relate to and act in Africa. In most cases a discrepancy exists between how Germans view their own role in Africa (as expressed in their writings and other documents) and the material repercussions of their presence. How can we summarize what has been observed in terms of this relationship between discourse, social action, and their repercussions? What are the criteria by which we evaluate this relationship?

Any tension between what is said or written and what has resulted from the presence of Germans in Africa is worth noting. When it comes to assessing the relationship of discourse to action and to the results of that action, the paradigmatic case studies of the first part of this inquiry and the examples taken from the contemporary context that constitute the second part share many structural similarities. In the case of Max Eyth his vision betrays an image of a modernizing world that differs substantially from what unfolded in Egypt in the latter part of the nineteenth century. While Eyth believed his actions were geared toward enabling Egyptians to modernize and benefit as a nation from the promises of technology, he did not foresee that the part he played in Egypt's modernization efforts contributed to making Egypt dependent on Europe and would result in Egypt's colonization. The case of Eyth in Egypt teaches a basic lesson of failed development, and the complexity of the situation defies explanations that relegate Egypt's economical and political defeat to a simple plot orchestrated by Europeans.

The analysis of Albert Schweitzer chronicles another facet of the relationship between discourse and action. While his work as a doctor relieved many Africans of physical pain, his symbolic status in Africa continues to legitimize Western dominance over Africans. Schweitzer's work through which he wanted to improve the life of Africans seems to contradict the views expressed in his writings, in which European superiority is not only unchallenged but also uncritically championed. In fundamental ways his actions and his paternalistic views complement each other. Without his actual work in Gabon, Schweitzer would not have become the public figure he was. And, without his writings and public performances, his work would not have been noticed. Words and actions combined to validate European rule in Africa, and these repercussions were concordant with Schweitzer's expressed intentions.

In Ernst Udet's case the link between representation and action is less obvious, because his interest in East Africa was limited to the production of images. He was not involved in an actual project that would allow concrete conclusions about the further repercussions of the encounter. The friendly interaction between Germans and Africans, however, can be linked to material circumstances: historical knowledge allows us to place the discursive conventions of the texts and images in the context of European economic and political involvement in Africa, with Germans (as representative Europeans) in the undoubtedly dominant position. The parameters of representation, especially in the realm of photography, reveal the larger perspective of the German visitors, who, as players in the framework of European expansionism, scout the land for development possibilities. While racist prejudice seems to be absent in Udet's work, this lack of a racist mind-set is no guarantee of an encounter on equal terms. The implications of these representational strategies propel us to probe them in light of current global economic and political developments.

Bodo Kirchhoff's final conclusion to his visit in Somalia is a call to put an end to humanitarian activities. What would the outcome be were Kirchhoff's vision actualized? Background information unmasked the writer's attitudes as culturalist and even racist notions of essential differences between societies. Rather than suggesting a reformed approach to aid and humanitarian intervention that would give local actors a greater say, Kirchhoff champions the complete withdrawal of European aid to

Africa. While his stance seems to be critical of interventionist belief systems questioned in this study, the unilateral action he calls for might have devastating consequences. His reasoning reveals that philosophies of intervention and philosophies of global segregation are based in beliefs about Western superiority. Neither mind-set is open to an engaged dialogue with Africans.

The case of the repeat visitors in Kenya focuses on social action; my analysis did not include a closer investigation of the discursive conventions employed by the tourists. Due to the nature of the interview situation, we do not know to what extent German tourists censored their language. We also do not know how Kenyans judged their actions or the behavior of the tourists. It is clear, however, that an extensive interaction exists, including intermarriage, which differs substantially from what occurs between Kenyans and other groups of tourists. German tourists who made return visits to Kenya exemplify the ways in which the larger discourse on helping Africans has become internalized to a degree that the tourists' actions are in fundamental ways inspired by decades of talking about and extending aid to Africa. As a result, the tourists' actions harbor the potential for creating long-term problems, as observed in the cases of Eyth and Schweitzer. The dilemmas created by the actions of individual tourists parallel the structural impediments of large-scale development and humanitarian aid. At the same time, the kind of help extended by the repeat visitors attempts to a large degree to create structures that enable Africans to help themselves, for example, by supporting education and the establishment of housing.

An aspect that has emerged in this study, somewhat indirectly, is that actions of Germans abroad and views held at home about Africa do not necessarily correspond. Colonial policy as it was drawn up in the fatherland often encountered resistance from settlers in the colonies; aid programs developed in the offices of the metropole did not address the concerns of aid workers and locals; military interventions, mostly designed in headquarters abroad, were primarily a response to crises that did not take local players into account.

In addition to the discrepancies between political, cultural, military, and economic policy concocted in Germany and the reality in Africa, the discourse on Africa also needs to be understood in terms of the specific environments of its reception. Today, as much as in the past, images of Africans that are absorbed by Germans in Germany serve different functions with regard to domestic and foreign affairs. Furthermore, the function of such images in the African context, for different kind of settlers, aid workers, tourists, or Germans who have come to Africa to do business, is also distinct, as they are evaluated against a background of experience that differs fundamentally from that of Germans who never traveled to Africa. While there might be considerable overlap in some areas, we again need to ask questions about the relation between actions and discourse and account for regional and historical differences.

We might also attempt to formulate a thesis about the distinctness of German colonialism in comparison to that of other European powers. During and after the colonial period Germans did not seem to have attempted to "Germanize" Africans explicitly; their attempts to "civilize" Africans did not include turning Africans culturally into Germans. For Germans the focus was economic modernization and Christianization. Can we detect, as Russell Berman argues, an acceptance of cultural difference in this attitude?[1] That might very well be, but the flip side of this seemingly tolerant attitude is cultural incommensurability. Just as Germans did not enforce specific German customs or the German language upon colonial subjects, they also did not grant citizenship to Africans in ways comparable to French and British policies. This particular aspect of German policy and behavior toward Africans corresponds to the racism practiced at home in Germany, in particular the resistance toward immigration and the changing of citizenship laws, long after the colonial period. According to these views, Africans are to be developed and modernized but cannot be incorporated into the nation. In Africa, outside of the German national context, however, these norms and attitudes were often subverted through extensive contacts between Africans and Germans.

It is possible to identify, in hindsight, the reasons for Eyth's ultimate failure or to unmask Schweitzer's approaches toward Africans. In light of current global developments we do not even know whether the lessons of the past will enable us to make better decisions for the future. One element that surfaces in the evaluation of every case discussed here, however, is that intimate knowledge of local circumstances is crucial to a meaningful relationship with local lives. In this regard my study corroborates the findings presented by recent analysts of development policies. The outcome of aid politics; political, humanitarian, and military interventions; and economic development is dependent on this local knowledge and the role played by local actors in the decision-making process.

APPENDIX

Statistics on German Tourism in Kenya

Results from Questionnaires Distributed to Travelers, 1998 and 1999

TABLE A.1. German-speaking Repeat Visitors in Kenya: Interactions with Kenyans

	Total responses	By year		By sex		By location	
	110	1998 (55)	1999 (55)	Male (59)	Female (51)	Airports (40)	Hotels (70)
How often have you been to Kenya (including present stay)?							
2 times	31 (28.2%)	14 (25.5%)	17 (30.1%)	17 (28.8%)	14 (27.5%)	8 (20%)	23 (32.85%)
3–4 times	24 (21.8%)	13 (23.6%)	11 (20%)	13 (22%)	11 (21.5%)	7 (17.5%)	17 (24.3%)
> 4 times	55 (50%)	28 (50.9%)	27 (49.1%)	29 (49.2%)	26 (51%)	25 (62.5%)	30 (42.85%)
Did you get to know some Kenyans well?							
Yes	87 (79.1%)	45 (81.8%)	42 (76.4%)	47 (79.7%)	40 (78.4%)	33 (82.5%)	54 (77.1%)
No	23 (20.9%)	10 (18.2%)	13 (23.6%)	12 (20.3%)	11 (21.6%)	7 (17.5%)	16 (22.9%)
Did you visit Kenyans in their home?							
Yes	77 (70%)	39 (70.9%)	38 (69.1%)	41 (69.5%)	36 (70.6%)	32 (80%)	45 (64.3%)
No	33 (30%)	16 (29.1%)	17 (30.9%)	18 (30.5%)	15 (29.4%)	8 (20%)	25 (35.7%)
Would you consider one or more Kenyans your friends?							
Yes	63 (57.3%)	32 (58.2%)	31 (56.4%)	34 (57.6%)	29 (56.9%)	32 (80%)	31 (44.3%)
No	45 (40.9%)	21 (38.2%)	24 (43.6%)	24 (40.7%)	21 (41.2%)	8 (20%)	37 (52.9%)
Have you exchanged letters with Kenyans since your last visit?							
Yes	54 (49.1%)	29 (52.7%)	25 (45.5%)	28 (47.5%)	26 (51%)	25 (62.5%)	29 (41.5%)
No	52 (47.3%)	24 (43.6%)	28 (50.9%)	29 (49.2%)	23 (45.1%)	14 (35%)	38 (54.3%)
Do you bring presents for Kenyans?							
Yes	77 (70%)	42 (76.4%)	35 (63.6%)	40 (67.8%)	37 (72.5%)	28 (70%)	49 (70%)
No	30 (27.3%)	12 (21.8%)	18 (32.7%)	18 (30.5%)	12 (23.5%)	12 (30%)	18 (25.7%)

Note: Due to participants not answering all questions and rounding of figures, percentage values do not add up to 100.

TABLE A.2. Contact and Kind of Support Extended: Couples and Individuals Traveling with Partners or Friends (18 total)

Profile: Dentist (m), 40s
**Interviewed:* June 28, 1999, Ukunda Beach Resort
Times in Kenya: More than 15
Contact with population: Very extensive
Support extended: Worked as volunteer for missionary society; raises money in Germany for projects (three nurseries); pays for education of individuals; works now at Moi University

Profile: Social worker (f), 46; (husband is engineer [m], 52)
**Interviewed:* June 16, 1998, Darmstadt
Times in Kenya: Ca. 15
Contact with population: Close friends with (former) hotel managers; daughter lived with them during her medical internship in Nairobi; considers contacts with lower classes difficult
Support extended: Brought presents for friends and others; brought other items for which they were reimbursed

Profile: Former secretary at university (retired) (f), 60
**Interviewed:* June 26, 1998, Ukunda Beach Resort
Times in Kenya: 7
Contact with population: Visited private homes in village; knows lots of people
Support extended: Brought money, clothes, shoes, cosmetics, chocolate

Profile: Teacher (m) 57; housewife (f), 54
Interviewed: June 30, 1998, Matatu Hill Lodge
Times in Kenya: 6
Contact with population: Visited people in their homes; took many self-organized tours; well-informed
Support extended: Paid hospital bill for delivery; set up bank account; gave money to someone who was building house; brought clothes, shoes, jewelry, money

Profile: Worker in chemical plant (m), 57; market woman, truckdriver (f), 57
Interviewed: June 27, 1998, Serengeti Beach Hotel
Times in Kenya: 3
Contact with population: Visited people in their homes; extensive contact
Support extended: Paid school fees; bought school uniforms; opened an account for friends; brought 50 kg of clothes (e.g., 30 bikinis, 20 pairs of shoes, 50 pairs of socks); went shopping and paid bills; paid rent

Profile: Employee with German railway (m), 49; secretary with engineering company (f), 49

TABLE A.2. Continued

Interviewed: June 25, 1998, Ukunda Beach Resort
Times in Kenya: 3
Contact with population: Took self-organized tours through Mombasa; visited waiter at home; visited wealthy Kenyan at home; learned Swahili at community college; showed great interest in country
Support extended: Brought items for orphanage; tried to send large shipment from Germany (failed); left things behind for employees

Profile: Former restaurant owners; now cook (m), 53; and housewife (f) 60
Interviewed: June 26, 1998, Ukunda Beach Resort
Times in Kenya: 3
Contact with population: Took self-organized tour through village
Support extended: Brought clothes

Profile: High school teacher (m), ca. 60
**Interviewed:* July 10, 1998, Kassel
Times in Kenya: 3
Contact with population: Very limited
Support extended: Not in Kenya but supports family he met during vacation in Sri Lanka with regular substantial payments

Profile: High school teacher (retired) (m), 67; school principal (f), 65
Interviewed: July 11, 1998, Kassel
Times in Kenya: 2
Contact with population: Very limited; visited hotel employee at his home; she felt very uncomfortable; he went by himself to Mombasa
Support extended: —

Profile: Landscape architect (m), 29; computer programmer (f), 28; their two small children
Interviewed: July 3, 1999, on the beach; family was living in village
Times in Kenya: 1 time for him, 2 times for her
Contact with population: Lived in the village with a local whom they had hosted for three months in Germany
Support extended: Brought radio, jewelry, bags

Profile: Worker in sanitary sector (m), late 20s; medical assistant (f), late 20s
Interviewed: July 2, 1998, Coconut Lodge
Times in Kenya: 1
Contact with population: Met a number of people; knew many details about lives of people selling items on beach
Support extended: Were planning to send parcel; want to return

*Interviewed without presence of partner or spouse

TABLE A.3. Contact and Kind of Support Extended: Individuals Traveling Alone (10 total)

Profile: Tiler (m), 72; (Travels sometimes with male friend)
Interviewed: July 12, 1999, Maziwa Lala Hotel
Times in Kenya: 31
Contact with population: Extensive; well-known figure in village
Support extended: Paid fees for language schools several times; clothes

Profile: Nurse (f), 51
Interviewed: June 25, 1998, Ukunda Beach Resort
Times in Kenya: More than 20
Contact with population: Yes
Support extended: Brought presents, clothes; other kinds of support

Profile: Employee in supermarket (f), ca. 50
Interviewed: June 25, 1998, Ukunda Beach Resort
Times in Kenya: Ca. 20
Contact with population: Yes
Support extended: Brought presents; potentially other kinds of support

Profile: retired (m), 63, used to work for GEMA (Used to travel with male friend)
Interviewed: June 26, 1998, Coconut Lodge
Times in Kenya: 13
Contact with population: Several friendships; visits many people in their homes
Support extended: Bought property with Kenyan; paid hospital bill for childbirth; gave money; brought presents

Profile: Psychologist (f), 39
Interviewed: June 19, 1998, Darmstadt
Times in Kenya: 9
Contact with population: Extensive contacts; relationships with Africans; tried to get lover out of jail
Support extended: Brought tools for workshop, clothes, medicine, cosmetics

Profile: Self-employed (f), 39
Interviewed: June 26, 1998, Ukunda Beach Resort
Times in Kenya: 7
Contact with population: Yes
Support extended: Brought presents (e.g., shoes); potentially other kinds of support

Profile: Janitor (m), 39
Interviewed: June 18, 1998, Darmstadt

TABLE A.3. Continued

Times in Kenya: 3
Contact with population: Visited uncle; very limited contact with Kenyans; met a few Indians
Support extended: None to Kenyans; brought presents for uncle

Profile: Secretary (f), ca. 45
Interviewed: July 9, 1999, Matatu Hill Lodge
Times in Kenya: 2
Contact with population: Romantically involved with Kenyan
Support extended: Brought CD player, CDs, money

Profile: Ph.D. candidate in sociology (f), 47
Interviewed: July 2, 1998, Ukunda Beach Resort
Times in Kenya: 2
Contact with population: Met people at hotel and in village; was pessimistic about true communication
Support extended: —

Profile: Lawyer (m), 35
Interviewed: July 4, 1998, train Frankfurt-Kassel
Times in Kenya: 1
Contact with population: Met a number of people and visited them in their homes
Support extended: —

Recent Marriage Patterns

TABLE A.4. Marriages between Kenyans and Foreign Nationals, as Registered at the Office of the Registrar of Marriage in Mombasa, 1994–1998

	German		Swiss		Austrian		British		French		Italian		U.S.		Other		
	m	f	m	f	m	f	m	f	m	f	m	f	m	f	m	f	Total
1994	36	19	4	6	—	—	4	5	1	—	3	—	2	—	2	2	84
1995	50	8	7	9	1	—	9	4	—	2	1	—	1	1	8	2	103
1996	49	22	5	9	2	1	9	7	2	4	1	—	3	—	7	8	129
1997	56	25	8	10	—	1	5	6	2	6	1	—	2	—	8	3	133
1998	60	26	8	6	1	4	4	6	3	3	2	1	2	1	5	6	138
Total	251	100	32	40	4	6	31	28	8	15	8	1	10	2	30	21	587
	59.8%		12.3%		1.7%		10.1%		3.9%		1.5%		2%		8.7%		100%

TABLE A.5. Data from 138 Couples Registered with Registrar of Marriage in Mombasa in 1998: Age, Occupation, and Country of Residence

Men			Women		
Age	Occupation	Residence	Age	Occupation	Residence
January to March					
26	Security supervisor	Kenya	27	Optician	Austria
40	Nurse	Germany	21	Hairdresser	Mombasa
25	Businessman	Mombasa	33	Airline staff	England
77	Retired	Germany	46	Clerk	Mombasa
49	Florist	France	29	Business lady	Kenya
29	Acrobat	Kenya	51	Driver	Germany
49	Electrician	Germany	32	Dressmaker	Mombasa
24	Personal manager	Kenya	54	Hotelier	Germany
19	Student	Mombasa	66	Retired	Switzerland
32	Businessman	Kenya	45	Civil student	Switzerland
27	Acrobat	Mombasa	24	Saleslady	Altbach (Germany)
61	Retired	Germany	28	Tailor	Kenya
38	Motorcar assembler	Germany	33	Supervisor	Kenya
37	Printer	Germany	36	Housewife	Mombasa
37	Unemployed	Kenya	62	Doctor	Germany
42	Carpenter	Germany	21	Guest relations	Mombasa
53	Retired	Switzerland	22	Secretary	Mombasa
47	Company car inspector	Germany	32	Housekeeper	Mombasa

TABLE A.5. Continued

Men			Women		
Age	Occupation	Residence	Age	Occupation	Residence
January to March					
30	Driver	Kenya	36	Saleslady	Switzerland
26	Boat operator	Kenya	33	Teacher	Italy
46	Electrical supervisor	USA	27	Self-employed	Mombasa
65	Pensioner	Germany	27	Housewife	Mombasa
58	Driver	Germany	31	Clerk	Mombasa
63	Pensioner	Germany	42	Tailor	Mombasa
55	Clerk	Germany	25	Artiste	Mombasa
26	Unemployed	Kikambala (Kenya)	41	Veterinary engineer	Germany
25	Waiter	Germany	28	Hairdresser	Mombasa
51	Industrialist	Switzerland	26	Hotelier	Mombasa
26	Masaai dancer	Ukunda	30	Electrician	Germany
42	Pharmacist	Germany	23	Housewife	Mtwapa (Kenya)
62	Retired	Germany	21	Secretary	Mombasa
56	Lawyer	Germany	27	Housewife	Germany (Kenyan)
April to September					
26	Social worker	Ukunda	62	Pensioner	Germany
42	Driver	Germany	30	Housekeeper	Mombasa
20	Businessman	Mombasa	24	Clerk	Germany

23	Tourleader	Mombasa	25	Postal officer	Germany
24	Tourguide	Vipingo, Kenya	69	Retired	Finland
29	Food and beverages manager	Mombasa	38	Hotelier	Portugal
43	Pilot	United States	26	Sales executive	Mombasa
57	Businessman	Mombasa (Italian)	33	Housewife	Mombasa
28	Hotelier	Mombasa	28	Nurse	France
24	Acrobat	Vipingo, Kenya	42	Nurse	England
41	Taxi driver	Mombasa	57	Housewife	France
34	Barman	Mombasa	34	Nil	Mombasa (Swiss)
26	Engineer	Germany	22	—	Nairobi
41	Engineer	Ukunda (German)	21	Hairdresser	Ukunda
26	Student	Mombasa	33	Secretary	Germany
27	Electrician	France	20	Hairdresser	Ukunda
43	Storekeeper	Mombasa	57	Musician	Mombasa (German)
27	Clerk	Mombasa	33	Receptionist	Scotland (German)
59	Employee	Germany	36	Hairdresser	Mombasa
37	Tool's maker	Germany	23	Housewife	Mombasa
24	Boat man	Kwale (Kenya)	19	Hotelier	Germany
29	Demontage expert	Germany	26	Hairdresser	Mombasa
44	Tailor	Germany	39	Hairdresser	Mombasa
32	Shopping centre worker	Germany	36	Hairdresser	Mombasa
25	Driver	Mombasa	44	Photographer	Boston (USA)
30	Cook	Belgium	30	Unemployed	Mombasa
50	Dental technician	Vienna (Austria)	24	Unemployed	Mombasa
28	Seaman	Mtwapa (Kenya)	28	Social worker	Germany

TABLE A.5. Continued

Men			Women		
Age	Occupation	Residence	Age	Occupation	Residence
April to September					
54	Hairdresser	Switzerland	31	Hairdresser	Mombasa
45	Merchant	Germany	30	Business woman	Mombasa
27	Evangelist	Nyali (Kenya)	40	Secretary	Switzerland
26	Animator	Mombasa	30	Florist	Germany
46	Driver	Germany	42	Housewife	Mombasa
26	Room steward	Ukunda	29	Sales lady	Germany
51	Engineer	Germany	28	Hairdresser	Mombasa
35	Artist (creative design)	Germany	25	Waitress	Mombasa
25	Mason	Mombasa	22	Waitress	Germany
48	Technician	Germany	36	Designer	Mombasa
40	Barman	Germany	24	Housewife	Mombasa
33	Water sports	Mombasa	39	Bingo operative	England
26	Fashion designer	Nairobi	19	Waitress	Germany
32	Self-employed	Switzerland	26	Secretary	Mombasa
32	Musician	Mombasa	46	Shopkeeper	Germany
52	Painter	Switzerland	30	Hairdresser	Mombasa
28	Electrician	Germany	24	Hairdresser	Kajiado (Kenya)
33	Salesman	Mombasa	46	Nurse	Germany
46	Executive chef	Germany	25	Sales lady	Nairobi

30	Electrician	Belgium	20	Hairdresser	Mombasa
63	Retired	Germany	30	Business lady	Mombasa
37	Hotelier	Mombasa	51	Nurse	Mombasa (German)
53	Businessman	Germany	21	Businessman (sic)	Mombasa
29	Ex-policeman	Lodwav, Kenya	32	Psychiatrist	Denmark
63	Plumber	Germany	32	Housewife	Mombasa
36	Software engineer	Germany	20	Nil	Mombasa
28	Businessman	Mombasa	36	Police officer	Germany
33	Employee	Germany	31	Hotelier	Mombasa
37	Economist	Mombasa (German)	24	Sales assistant	Mombasa
29	Software worker	France	22	Waitress	Ukunda
34	Building contractor	Switzerland	33	Hairdresser	Mtwapa (Kenya)
22	Student	Kilifi (Kenya)	20	Student	Austria
71	Pensioner	Napoli (Italian)	35	Businesslady	Nanyuki (Kenya)
23	Turner	Germany	28	Tailor	Kilifi (Kenya)
29	Water sports attendant	Mombasa	34	Bank clerk	England
25	Supervisor	Mombasa	35	House keeper	England
23	Mechanic	Germany	20	Secretary	Mombasa
34	Dancer	Ukunda	47	Business woman	Germany
23	Tour guide	Ukunda	47	Nil	Belgium
36	Mill manager	Mombasa	45	Social worker	Ireland
31	Mason	Germany	23	Artist	Busia, Kenya
23	Businessman	Ukunda	35	Retired	Austria
28	Businessman	Ukunda	79	Retired	Austria

TABLE A.5. Continued

Men			Women		
Age	Occupation	Residence	Age	Occupation	Residence
October to December					
43	Factory worker	Germany	25	Hairdresser	Mombasa
48	Engineer	Germany	45	Housewife	Ukunda
41	Businessman	Germany	21	Hairdresser	Mombasa
58	Retired	Germany	27	Business woman	Mombasa
28	Driver	Mombasa	45	Nurse	England
60	Retired	Berlin (Germany)	33	Housewife	Mombasa
31	Chemical technician	Germany	31	Tailor	Tiwi (Kenya)
36	Businessman	Mombasa	40	Social worker	Mombasa (German)
35	Mailer	Germany	28	Housewife	Mombasa
55	Manager	Germany	35	Businesslady	Mombasa
40	Engineer	Germany	34	Civil servant	Mombasa
30	Municipal council worker	Germany	30	Nil	Mombasa
33	Sales marketing manager	Mombasa	33	Tour consultant	Denmark
29	Technician	Germany	30	Tour consultant	Mombasa
27	Waiter	Mtwapa (Kenya)	57	Banker	Germany
30	Salesman	Mtwapa (Kenya)	29	Restaurant manager	France
39	Postal worker	Germany	22	Hairdresser	Mombasa
64	Retired	Switzerland	21	Housewife	Kilifi (Kenya)
59	Storeman	England	29	Hairdresser	Mombasa

23	Artist	Mombasa	52	Employee	Germany
31	Accountant	Germany	24	Housewife	Mombasa
32	Factory worker	Belgium	28	Secretary	Mombasa
46	Businessman	Germany	23	Businesslady	Mombasa
31	Public relations officer	Holland	33	Hairdresser	Diani (Kenya)
38	Production worker	United Kingdom	34	Businesslady	Mombasa
42	Engineer	Germany	27	Secretary	Ukunda
28	Mechanic	Germany	22	Hairdresser	Ukunda
63	Engineer	Germany	29	Landlady	Mombasa
35	Artist	Ukunda	46	Postal employee	Switzerland
43	Electronic engineer	England	36	Dress maker	Mombasa
62	Businessman	Germany	22	Nil	Ukunda
52	Hairdresser	Belgium	36	Hairdresser	Mombasa
34	Carpenter	Switzerland	35	Secretary	Mombasa
40	Production engineer	England	25	Postal assistant	Mombasa
36	Employee	Germany	21	Nil	Nairobi

Note: I retained the spelling and terminology, including occupational descriptions, used on the certificates.

Seven marriage partners had German language names but listed Mombasa or Ukunda as place of residence; most likely, these individuals worked in the tourism business. I divided them proportionally among the Swiss and the Germans.

I recorded the place names of residences as listed on the certificate. In parentheses I added the country name when lesser-known Kenyan cities were recorded (apart from Mombasa, Nairobi, and Ukunda, which is adjacent to the hotels at the south coast).

NOTES

INTRODUCTION

1. See Horst Gründer, *Christliche Mission und deutscher Imperialismus* (Paderborn: Schöningh, 1982). On the extent of Christianity's role in the postcolonial society, see Achille Mbembe, *Afriques indociles: Christianisme, pouvoir et état en société postcoloniale* (Paris: Éditions Karthala, 1988).

2. Samir Amin, *Eurocentrism*, trans. Russell Moore (New York: Monthly Review, 1989), 82.

3. Ali A. Mazrui argues that "Judeo-Christian universalism did indeed illicitly mate with Western ethnocentrism in history—and gave the world a bastard called 'progress.'" "'Progress': Illegitimate Child of Judeo-Christian Universalism and Western Ethnocentrism—A Third World Critique," in *Progress: Fact or Illusion*, ed. Leo Marx and Bruce Mazlish (Ann Arbor: University of Michigan Press, 1996), 174.

4. See Johannes Fabian, *Time and the Other: How Anthropology Makes Its Object* (New York: Columbia University Press, 1983).

5. Ann Laura Stoler, "Rethinking Colonial Categories: European Communities and the Boundaries of Rule," *Comparative Studies in Society and History* 31.1 (1989): 138.

6. The questions I refer to are discussed in different disciplines under keywords such as *dependency theory, modernization theory, imperialism, development aid, development studies, sustainable development, humanitarian aid, debt politics,* and *global capitalism.*

7. Michael Adas, *Machines as the Measure of Men: Science, Technology, and Ideologies of Western Dominance* (Ithaca: Cornell University Press, 1989), 4.

8. Adas, *Machines as the Measure of Men*, 12. For another exploration of the role played by science in the "civilizing mission," see Lewis Pyenson, *Civilizing Mission: Exact Sciences and French Overseas Expansion, 1830–1940* (Baltimore: Johns Hopkins University Press, 1993); Kavita Sara Philip, "The Role of Science in Colonial Discourses and Practices of Modernity: Anthropology, Forestry, and the Construction of Nature's Resources in Madras Forests, 1858–1930" (Ph.D. diss., Cornell University, 1996).

9. Nicholas Thomas, among others, also argues against the "assumption that colonialism is primarily a social form of the past." *Colonialism's Culture: Anthropology, Travel and Government* (Princeton: Princeton University Press, 1994), 16.

10. An excellent overview of the different approaches to colonialism is given by Ann Laura Stoler and Frederick Cooper in "Between Metropole and Colony: Re-

thinking a Research Agenda," *Tensions of Empire: Colonial Cultures in a Bourgeois World* (Berkeley: University of California Press, 1997), 1–56.

11. Bill Ashcroft et al., eds., *The Post-Colonial Studies Reader* (London: Routledge, 1995); Patrick Williams and Laura Chrisman, eds., *Colonial Discourse and Post-Colonial Theory: A Reader* (New York: Columbia University Press, 1994).

12. The concerns of African Americans, for example, are not necessarily the same as those of Africans. See the debate between Ali A. Mazrui and Henry Louis Gates Jr. over Gates's documentary *Wonders of the African World,* November 10, 2001, http://www.africana.com/DailyArticles/index_19991117.htm.

13. Pierre Bourdieu and Loïc Wacquant, "On the Cunning of Imperialist Reason," *Theory, Culture, and Society* 16.1 (1999): 41. See also Timothy Brennan's analysis of Said's *Orientalism* as "a profoundly American book," *Critical Inquiry* 26.3 (2000): 560.

14. Arif Dirlik "The Postcolonial Aura: Third World Criticism in the Age of Global Capitalism," *Critical Inquiry* 20 (1994): 347. Dirlik contends that postcolonial discourse is an expression of the development of global capitalism.

15. Fabian, *Time and the Other,* 143.

16. Seminal studies are V. Y. Mudimbe's *The Invention of Africa: Gnosis, Philosophy, and the Order of Knowledge* (Bloomington: Indiana University Press, 1988); and *The Idea of Africa* (Bloomington: Indiana University Press, 1994).

17. Bill Ashcroft et al., *The Empire Writes Back: Theory and Practice in Post-Colonial Literatures* (London: Routledge, 1989), 2.

18. Aijaz Ahmad asks these questions in "The Politics of Literary Postcoloniality," *Race and Class* 36.3 (1995): 1–20.

19. Achille Mbembe, "Introduction," *Ways of Seeing: Beyond the New Nativism,* special issue of *African Studies Review* 44.2 (2001): 2–3.

20. Achille Mbembe, "African Modes of Self-Writing," trans. Steven Rendall, *Public Culture* 14.1 (2002): 272.

21. F. Abiola Irele, *The African Imagination: Literature in Africa and the Black Diaspora* (New York: Oxford University Press, 2001); Kwame Anthony Appiah, *In My Father's House: Africa in the Philosophy of Culture* (London: Methuen, 1992); see responses to Mbembe in the section "African Modes of Self-Writing Revisited" in *Public Culture* 14.3 (2002): 585–641.

22. The most vocal representative of this school of thought is George B. N. Ayittey. See his book *Africa in Chaos* (New York: St. Martin's Griffin, 1998).

23. A conference on the topic was organized by the Society of Research on African Cultures and brought together representatives of both schools in November 7–9, 2002, at Montclair State University, New Jersey.

24. See, for example, contributions to the special issue *Alter/Native Modernities* of *Public Culture* 11.1 (1999).

25. Achille Mbembe, *On the Postcolony* (Berkeley: University of California Press, 2001), 5.

26. "It should be noted, as far as fieldwork is concerned, that there is less and less. Knowledge of local languages, vital to any theoretical and philosophical understanding, is deemed unnecessary." Mbembe, *On the Postcolony,* 7.

27. An excellent analysis is given by Lora Wildenthal in "The Places of Colonialism in the Writing and Teaching of Modern German History," *German Colonialism: Another "Sonderweg"?* special issue of *European Studies Journal* 16.2 (1999): 9–23. See also Susanne Zantop, *Colonial Fantasies: Conquest, Family, and Nation in Precolonial Germany, 1770–1870* (Durham: Duke University Press, 1997), 3.

28. See, for example, Wolfgang Wippermann, *Der "deutsche Drang nach Osten": Ideologie und Wirklichkeit eines politischen Schlagwortes* (Darmstadt: Wissenschaftliche Buchgesellschaft, 1981). Lora Wildenthal argues that "German colonialism cannot be subsumed into Nazism, but neither can the two be treated in complete isolation." *German Women for Empire, 1884–1945* (Durham: Duke University Press, 2001), 8.

29. "The German Invention of Race," a conference hosted by Harvard's German Department in May 2001, focused on the Enlightenment period. Hardly any of the papers that were presented mentioned the issue of slavery or colonialism (which, however, was also due to the absence or cancellations of scholars such as Susanne Zantop and Pascal Grosse). The last event of the conference, a screening of a film on euthanasia, revealed the subliminal trajectory of the conference.

30. See Tina Marie Campt, "Afro-German": The Convergence of Race, Sexuality and Gender in the Formation of a German Ethnic Identity, 1919–1960" (Ph.D. diss., Cornell University, 1996); Pascal Grosse, *Kolonialismus, Eugenik und bürgerliche Gesellschaft in Deutschland, 1850–1918* (Frankfurt am Main: Campus, 2000); Fatima El-Tayeb, *Schwarze Deutsche: Der Diskurs um "Rasse" und nationale Identität, 1890–1933* (Frankfurt am Main: Campus, 2001); Beth Lilach, "From Africa to Auschwitz: The Herero Genocide and the Origins of the Holocaust" (paper presented at the 2001 meeting of the African Studies Association, Houston).

31. Susan Buck-Morss, "Hegel and Haiti," *Critical Inquiry* 26:4 (2000): 821–65. Zantop also demonstrates that the Haitian revolution was discussed widely in German fiction and nonfiction at the time. "Betrothal and Divorce; or Revolution in the House," *Colonial Fantasies,* 141–61.

32. Scholars from Africa who have gained increasing visibility are David Simo, who wrote *Interkulturalität und ästhetische Erfahrung: Untersuchungen zum Werk Hubert Fichtes* (Stuttgart: Metzler, 1993); Alain Patrice Nganang, the author of *Interkulturalität und Bearbeitung: Untersuchung zu Soyinka and Brecht* (München: Iudicium, 1998); and Adjaï Paulin Oloukpona-Yinnon, who published work on colonial literature and the presence of colonial Germans in Africa.

33. See my article "Multiculturalism, Reintegration, and Beyond: The Afrikan-

isch-Asiatische Studentenförderung in Göttingen" for a discussion of African and Asian intellectuals in Germany. *South Central Review* 16.2–3 (1999): 34–53.

34. See, for example, publications by Tina Campt, Ülker Gökberk, Deniz Göktürk, Pascal Grosse, Peggy Piesche, Azade Seyhan, and Fatima El-Tayeb. See also contributions to the anthology *Crosscurrents: African Americans, Africa, and Germany in the Modern World,* ed. David McBride et al. (Columbia: Camden House, 1998).

35. For a discussion of the notion of "escapism" in German literary criticism, see my discussion in *Orientalismus, Kolonialismus und Moderne* (Stuttgart: Metzler, 1997), 46–50.

36. Joachim Warmbold, *"Ein Stückchen neudeutsche Erd . . ." — Deutsche Kolonial-Literatur: Aspekte ihrer Geschichte, Eigenart und Wirkung, dargestellt am Beispiel Afrikas* (Frankfurt am Main: HAAG+ HERCHEN, 1982); *Germania in Africa: Germany's Colonial Literature* (New York: Lang, 1989) (both volumes by Warmbold contain extensive bibliographies on primary sources); Sibylle Benninghoff-Lühl, *Deutsche Kolonialromane, 1884–1914, in ihrem Entstehungs — und Wirkungszusammenhang* (Bremen: Im Selbstverlag, Übersee-Museum Bremen, 1983); Wolfgang Bader and Janos Riesz, eds., *Literatur und Kolonialismus I,* Bayreuther Beiträge zur Literaturwissenschaft 4 (Frankfurt: Lang, 1983).

37. Sander L. Gilman, *On Blackness without Blacks: Essays on the Image of the Black in Germany* (Boston: Hall, 1982); see also Peter Martin, *Schwarze Teufel, edle Mohren: Afrikaner in Bewußtsein und Geschichte der Deutschen* (Hamburg: Junius, 1993).

38. John K. Noyes, *Colonial Space: Spatiality in the Discourse of German South West Africa, 1884–1915* (Chur: Harwood, 1992).

39. Russell A. Berman, "German Colonialism: Another *Sonderweg?*" *German Colonialism: Another "Sonderweg?"* special issue of *European Studies Journal* 16.2 (1999): 27.

40. Zantop, *Colonial Fantasies,* 8.

41. Russell A. Berman, *Enlightenment or Empire: Colonial Discourse in German Culture* (Lincoln: University of Nebraska Press, 1998), 3.

42. Berman, *Enlightenment or Empire,* 18, also 235.

43. Katrin Sieg, *Ethnic Drag: Performing Race, Nation, Sexuality in West Germany* (Ann Arbor: University of Michigan Press, 2002).

44. See Michelle Moyd's study of language policy, "Language and Power: Africans, Europeans, and Language Policy in German Colonial Tanganyika" (Master's thesis, University of Florida, 1996).

45. Berman, *Enlightenment or Empire,* 8.

46. On the contradictions of universalism, see Immanuel Wallerstein, "Liberalism in the Modern World-System," *Nations, Identities, Cultures,* ed. V. Y. Mudimbe, special issue of *South Atlantic Quarterly* 94.4 (1995): 1161–78.

47. Marica Klotz, "Global Visions: From the Colonial to the National Socialist World," *German Colonialism: Another "Sonderweg?"* esp. 50–53.

48. For a French critique of the dark side of the Enlightenment, see Louis Sala-Molins, *Les Misères des lumières* (Paris: Robert Laffont, 1992).

49. Andrew Zimmermann, *Anthropology and Antihumanism in Imperial Germany* (Chicago: University of Chicago Press, 2001), 62.

50. Zimmermann, *Anthropology and Antihumanism,* 4.

51. Zimmermann, *Anthropology and Antihumanism,* 241. Manfred Gothsch's study *Die deutsche Völkerkunde und ihr Verhältnis zum Kolonialismus: Ein Beitrag zur kolonialideologischen und kolonialpraktischen Bedeutung der deutschen Völkerkunde in der Zeit von 1870 bis 1975* (Baden-Baden: Nomos, 1983) also addresses the effect of anthropological theory on colonial policy. Gothsch denies the significance of the evidence his own research provides by categorically rejecting the relevance of anthropological theory for the making of colonial policy.

52. Sara Pugach explores in what ways African language studies produced colonial knowledge. "Afrikanistik and Colonial Knowledge: Carl Meinhof, the Missionary Impulse, and African Language and Culture Studies in Germany, 1887–1919" (Ph.D. diss., University of Chicago, 2001).

53. Zantop, *Colonial Fantasies,* 9.

54. Berman, *Enlightenment or Empire,* 8.

55. Sara Friedrichsmeyer et al., eds., *The Imperialist Imagination: German Colonialism and Its Legacy* (Ann Arbor: University of Michigan Press, 1998).

56. Marcia Klotz also extends her exploration of colonial discourse in "White Women and the Dark Continent: Gender and Sexuality in German Colonial Discourse from the Sentimental Novel to the Fascist Film" (Ph.D. diss., Stanford University, 1994).

57. See also Alexander Honold and Oliver Simons, eds., *Kolonialismus als Kultur: Literatur, Medien, Wissenschaft in der deutschen Gründerzeit des Fremden* (Tübingen: A. Francke, 2002).

58. Arlene A. Teraoka, *East, West, and Others: The Third World in Postwar German Literature* (Lincoln: University of Nebraska Press, 1996), 5.

59. Paul Michael Lützeler, ed., *Schriftsteller und "Dritte Welt": Studien zum postkolonialen Blick* (Tübingen: Stauffenburg, 1998). Sara Lennox, in her review of the anthology, rightly questions the use of the term *postcolonial* to describe the writings of the German authors. *German Quarterly* 74.3 (2001): 315–16. See also Lützeler's response in *German Quarterly* 75.2 (2002): 200.

60. Valentina Glajar, *German Legacy in East Central Europe as Reflected in Contemporary German-Language Literature* (Rochester: Camden House, 2004).

61. Kristin Kopp, "Contesting Borders: German Colonial Discourse and the Polish Eastern Territories" (Ph.D. diss., University of California at Berkeley, 2001).

62. John K. Noyes, "National Identity, Nomadism, and Narration in Gustav

Frenssen's *Peter Moor's Journey to Southwest Africa*," *Imperialist Imagination*, 87–105.

63. Lisa Gates, "Of Seeing and Otherness: Leni Riefenstahl's African Photographs," *Imperialist Imagination*, 246.

64. My study *Orientalismus, Kolonialismus und Moderne* explores Germany's relationship to the Middle East during the colonial period, in the context of political and economic relations and modernization.

65. Daniel Joseph Walther, *Creating Germans Abroad: Cultural Polities and National Identity in Namibia* (Athens: Ohio University Press, 2002).

66. Christopher J. Brummer, "Blood and Iron in the Sand: Colonialism, Politics and Culture in German Southwest Africa" (Ph.D. diss., University of Chicago, 2001), 9.

67. The two-part division of *Imperialismus und Kolonialmission: Kaiserliches Deutschland und koloniales Imperium* (Wiesbaden: Steiner, 1982), addressing discussions of the subject in Germany and the question of policy in the colonies separately, acknowledges the multiple tensions between motherland and colony. The volume was edited by Klaus J. Bade.

68. "We need to be able systematically to take account of the fact that the very culture of European colonialism—even the colonialism of a single nation such as Germany—was heterogeneous and complex." Woodruff D. Smith, "Contexts of German Colonialism in Africa: British Imperialism, German Politics, and the German Administrative Tradition," in *European Impact and Pacific Influence: British and German Colonial Policy in the Pacific Islands and the Indigenous Response*, ed. Hermann J. Hiery and John M. MacKenzie (London: Tauris, 1997), 10.

69. For recent publications on Namibia, see Jan-Bart Gewald, *Herero Heroes: A Socio-Political History of the Herero of Namibia, 1890 and 1923* (Oxford UK: James Currey, 1999). Andrew Zimmermann discussed educational policies in Togo in "Development and the Problem of Free Labor in German Africa: Booker T. Washington's Cotton Expedition in Togo, 1901–1909," at the meeting of the African Studies Association, Houston, November 2001. See also Benjamin Nicholas Lawrance, "Most Obedient Servants: The Politics of Language in German Colonial Togo," *Cahiers d'Études Africaines* 159.40.3 (2000): 489–524.

70. Thaddeus R. Sunseri highlights the specificity of the situation in Tanzania under German rule in *Vilimani: Labor Migration and Rural Change in Early Colonial Tanzania* (Portsmouth NH: Heinemann, 2002).

71. See Konstanze Streese, who provides this connection between contemporary literature and German political and economic pursuits, in *"Cric?"—Crac!" Vier literarische Versuche, mit dem Kolonialismus umzugehen* (Frankfurt am Main: Lang, 1991), 189–95.

72. See also Teresa Hayter, *The Creation of World Poverty* (London: Pluto, in association with Third World First, 1981); Graham Hancock, *Lords of Poverty: The*

Power, Prestige, and Corruption of the International Aid Business (New York: Atlantic Monthly, 1989); Horand Knaup, *Hilfe, die Helfer kommen: Karitative Organisationen im Wettbewerb um Spenden und Katastrophen* (München: Beck, 1996); Hans Magnus Enzensberger, ed., *Krieger ohne Waffen: Das Internationale Komitee vom Roten Kreuz* (Frankfurt am Main: Eichborn, 2001).

73. Ali A. Mazrui and Robert L. Ostergard Jr., "From Pax Europa to Pax Africana," in *The Causes of War and the Consequences of Peacekeeping in Africa*, ed. Ricardo René Laremont (Portsmouth NH: Heinemann, 2002), 33.

74. Carol Lancaster, *Aid to Africa: So Much to Do, So Little Done* (Chicago: University of Chicago Press, 1999), 4.

75. Lancaster, *Aid to Africa*, 234–38.

76. Jürgen Osterhammel argues that the focus on national colonial empires is tenable only to a limited extent. *Colonialism: A Theoretical Overview*, trans. from German by Shelley L. Frisch (Princeton: Markus Wiener, 1997), 25–27.

1. THE MODERNIZING MISSION

1. Thomas Nipperdey, *Germany from Napoleon to Bismarck, 1800–1866*, trans. Daniel Nolan (Princeton: Princeton University Press, 1996), 113.

2. Klaus Tenfelde and Helmuth Trischler, eds., *Bis vor die Stufen des Throns: Bittschriften und Beschwerden von Bergleuten im Zeitalter der Industrialisierung* (München: Beck, 1986).

3. For material documenting the realities of work in the factories, see Wolfgang Ruppert, *Die Fabrik: Geschichte von Arbeit und Industrialisierung in Deutschland* (München: Beck, 1983); Hermann-Josef Rupieper, *Arbeiter und Angestellte im Zeitalter der Industrialisierung: Eine sozialgeschichtliche Studie am Beispiel der Maschinenfabriken Augsburg und Nürnberg (MAN), 1837–1914* (Frankfurt am Main: Campus, 1982).

4. Nipperdey, *Germany from Napoleon to Bismarck*, 121.

5. See Volker R. Berghahn, "Economy," *Imperial Germany, 1871–1914: Economy, Society, Culture, and Politics* (Providence: Berghahn, 1994), 1–42.

6. Klaus-Peter Sonntag, *Die soziale Rolle des Ingenieurs im Wandel der deutschen Gesellschaft: Eine sozialgeschichtliche Studie* (Würzburg: Creator-Verlag, 1988), 17. Others, such as Lewis Mumford in *Technics and Civilization* (1934), have argued that the invention of the mechanical clock in Europe during the late Middle Ages was an event most crucial to the development of industrial civilization.

7. Kees Gispen, *New Profession, Old Order: Engineers and German Society, 1815–1914* (Cambridge: Cambridge University Press, 1989), 3–4.

8. See Gispen's statistics on the employment situation of engineers (*New Profession, Old Order*, 57–59, 68).

9. See Gispen's statistics on the enrollment at different types of engineering schools between 1871 and 1914 (*New Profession, Old Order,* 337–40).

10. On the founding and early history of the VDI, see Sonntag, *Die soziale Rolle,* 28–44.

11. Helmut Klages and Gerd Hortleder, "Gesellschaftsbild und soziales Selbstverständis des Ingenieurs im 19. und 20. Jahrhundert," esp. 269–84, in *Ingenieure in Deutschland, 1770–1990,* ed. Peter Lundgreen and André Grelon (Frankfurt am Main: Campus, 1994); see also Lars Ulrich Scholl *Ingenieure in der Frühindustrialisierung: Staatliche und private Techniker im Königreich Hannover und an der Ruhr (1815–1873)* (Göttingen: Vandenhoeck & Ruprecht, 1978).

12. Gispen, *New Profession, Old Order,* 1.

13. Sonntag, *Die soziale Rolle,* 40.

14. See contributions in Hans Lenk and Günter Ropohl, eds., *Technik und Ethik* (Stuttgart: Reclam, 1987).

15. Sigrid Lange, "Ingenieure ohne Eigenschaften und die Philosophie der Technik in der Literatur der Moderne," *Der Optimismus der Ingenieure: Triumph der Technik in der Krise der Moderne um 1900* (Stuttgart: Steiner, 1998), 129–51; Harro Segeberg, ed., *Technik in der Literatur: Ein Forschungsüberblick und 12 Aufsätze* (Frankfurt am Main: Suhrkamp, 1987); Deniz Göktürk, "Fortschrittsmythen im 'Land der Zukunft,'" in *Künstler, Cowboys, Ingenieure . . . : Kultur—und mediengeschichtliche Studien zu deutschen Amerika-Texten 1912–1920* (München: Fink, 1998), 80–127.

16. See Wolfgang Hädecke, *Poeten und Maschinen: Deutsche Dichter als Zeugen der Industrialisierung* (München: Hanser, 1993); Keith Bullivant and Hugh Ridley, eds., *Industrie und deutsche Literatur, 1830–1914: Eine Anthologie* (München: Deutscher Taschenbuch Verlag, 1976).

17. Franz Anselm Schmitt, ed., *Beruf und Arbeit in deutscher Erzählung: Ein literarisches Lexikon* (Stuttgart: Hiersemann, 1952).

18. For a discussion of writing engineers, see Katja Schwiglewski, *Erzählte Technik: Die literarische Selbstdarstellung des Ingenieurs seit dem 19. Jahrhundert* (Köln: Böhlau, 1995).

19. Oliver Simons, "Dichter am Kanal: Deutsche Ingenieure in Ägypten," *Kolonialismus als Kultur,* in Honold and Simons, *Kolonialismus als Kultur,* 243–62.

20. My rendition of Eyth's life is based on Richard Hennig, "Max von Eyth, der Dichter-Ingenieur (1836–1906)," *Buch berühmter Ingenieure: Große Männer der Technik, ihr Lebensgang und ihr Lebenswerk* (Leipzig: Otto Spamer, 1911), 272–94; Carl Weihe, *Max Eyth: Ein kurzgefaßtes Lebensbild mit Auszügen aus seinen Schriften* (Berlin: Verlag des Vereines deutscher Ingenieure, 1922); G. Kittel, *Max Eyth und seine Sippe* (Hameln: Fritz Seifert, 1937); Conrad Matschoß, "Max Eyth," *Grosse Ingenieure: Lebensbeschreibungen aus der Geschichte der Technik* (München: J. F. Lehmanns, 1954 [1937]), 255–65; Theodor Heuss, "Max Eyth," *Deutsche Gestal-*

ten: Studien zum 19. Jahrhundert (Tübingen: Rainer Wunderlich Verlag Herman Leins, 1951), 305–14; Adolf Reitz, *Max Eyth: Ein Ingenieur reist durch die Welt. Pioniertaten eines Landtechnikers* (Heidelberg: Energie-Verlag, 1956); Klaus Herrmann, "Das Leben von Max Eyth," in *Max Eyth, 1836–1906: "Mein Leben in Skizzen,"* ed. Viktor Pröstler and Erwin Treu (Ulm: Süddeutsche Verlagsgesellschaft, 1986), 11–30. In addition, I draw on Eyth's own accounts.

21. Max Eyth, *Im Strom unserer Zeit: Aus Briefen eines Ingenieurs.* Vol. 1: *Lehrjahre* (Heidelberg: Winter, 1903), 4. References to this text are given in parentheses. All translations from German are mine, unless otherwise indicated.

22. E. J. Hobsbawm, *Industry and Empire: An Economic History of Britain since 1750* (London: Weidenfeld and Nicolson, 1968), 1.

23. See Heuss, "Max Eyth," 311–12.

24. According to Kittel, his collection contained over a thousand drawings and watercolors (21).

25. Max Eyth's claim in the foreword to *Im Strom unserer Zeit* (1903), that the *Wanderbuch* was first published in 1869, could not be verified. The last of the six *Wanderbuch* volumes, which also include narrative fiction and lyrical works by Eyth, appeared in 1884.

26. The earliest edition I found of volume 1 does not contain a date of publication; Eyth's foreword, however, is dated 1903, and the volume is generally cataloged as having been published in 1903. Editions from 1904 contain the publication date, and, while text and illustrations did not change, use a different page numbering system. In the following I quote from the 1903 edition.

27. An extensive bibliography is included in Reitz, *Max Eyth,* 309–14.

28. His first shorter literary publications date from the 1850s, and, while still in England, he awaited the publication of his first larger fictional work, *Volkmar.*

29. Anthony Giddens, *The Consequences of Modernity* (Stanford: Stanford University Press, 1990), esp. 17–21.

30. In another passage Eyth compares English "external" activism and "internal" contemplation to German external contemplation and internal activism (104).

31. In September 1869 he organized the competition in Halberstadt, in order to "push the noses of sluggish compatriots into history." See Herrmann, "Das Leben von Max Eyth," 21.

32. See, for example, Arnim Kössler, *Aktionsfeld Osmanisches Reich: Die Wirtschaftsinteressen des Deutschen Kaiserreiches in der Türkei 1871–1908* (New York: Arno, 1981); Jehuda L. Wallach, *Anatomie einer Militärhilfe: Die preußisch-deutschen Militärmissionen in der Türkei 1835–1919* (Düsseldorf: Droste, 1976); Lothar Rathmann, *Berlin-Bagdad: Die imperialistische Nahostpolitik des kaiserlichen Deutschlands* (Berlin: Dietz, 1962).

33. See Daniel Crecelius, *The Roots of Modern Egypt: A Study of the Regimes of*

'Ali Bey al-Kabir and Muhammad Bey Abu al-Dhahab, 1760–1775 (Minneapolis: Bibliotheca Islamica, 1981).

34. For an excellent account of the expansion of trade and the structural changes the Egyptian economy and society underwent in premodern times, see Nelly Hanna, *Making Big Money in 1600: The Life and Times of Ismaiʿil Abu Taqiyya, Egyptian Merchant* (Syracuse: Syracuse University Press, 1998).

35. Timothy Mitchell, *Colonising Egypt* (Cambridge UK: Cambridge University Press, 1988).

36. On agricultural reforms, see Afaf Lutfi Al-Sayyid Marsot, *Egypt in the Reign of Muhammad Ali* (Cambridge UK: Cambridge University Press, 1984), 137–61.

37. Khaled Fahmy challenges the success of the reforms and argues against Mitchell. *All the Pasha's Men: Mehmed Ali, His Army and the Making of Modern Egypt* (Cambridge UK: Cambridge University Press, 1997), 316–17.

38. Ehud R. Toledano argues against other historians that 'Abbas I was not the demented and cruel character many of his biographers and contemporaries claim he had been. Toledano suggests that while 'Abbas I withdrew from large-scale modernization efforts, the period of his reign was a time during which a new dynastic order emerged and significant changes in the social make-up of Egyptian society occurred (249). *State and Society in Mid-Nineteenth-Century Egypt* (Cambridge UK: Cambridge University Press, 1990).

39. Roger Owen, *The Middle East in the World Economy, 1800–1914* (London: Methuen, 1981), 122; see also 123–26.

40. Ira Lapidus, *A History of Islamic Societies* (Cambridge: Cambridge University Press, 1988), 616.

41. Trevor Mostyn, *Egypt's Belle Epoque: Cairo, 1869–1952* (London: Quartet Books, 1989), 43.

42. Mostyn, *Egypt's Belle Epoque*, 44.

43. Toledano, *State and Society*, 51.

44. Owen, *Middle East in the World Economy*, 127. On the buildup of the debt, see F. Robert Hunter, *Egypt under the Khedives, 1805–1879* (Pittsburgh: University of Pittsburgh Press, 1984), 38–40. See also Abdel-Maksud Hamza, *The Public Debt of Egypt, 1854–1876* (Cairo: Government Press, 1944).

45. Amira El-Azhary Sonbol, *The New Mamluks: Egyptian Society and Modern Feudalism* (Syracuse: Syracuse University Press, 2000), 216–17.

46. Owen, *Middle East in the World Economy*, 122.

47. See E. R. J. Owen's conclusion to *Cotton and the Egyptian Economy, 1820–1914: A Study in Trade and Development* (Oxford: Clarendon, 1969), in which he reviews the development of the Egyptian economy and attempts to explain the lack of sustained modernization (352–75).

48. For analyses of the cotton boom of the 1860s, see Owen, *Cotton and the Egyptian Economy*, 89–121; Andreas Budde, *Ägyptens Landwirtschaft im Entwicklungs-*

prozeß: Eine kritische Analyse (Aachen: Edition Herodot, 1988), 73–100; Owen, *Middle East in the World Economy,* 135–48.

49. For other detailed and appreciative portrayals of the Egyptian landscape, see Eyth, *Im Strom unserer Zeit,* 120, 135, 140, 167, 183. Descriptions of the desert take on a different tone at times, which reflects the engineer's struggle with the hostile environment (131). See also the account of a night in the countryside in which he is plagued by insects (138); a hike in an adverse environment (183–89); his visit to the pyramids (198–202).

50. For a selections of drawings, see Peter Lahnstein, ed., *Max Eyth: Das Schönste aus dem zeichnerischen Werk eines welterfahrenen Ingenieurs* (Stuttgart: Kohlhammer, 1987).

51. Arthur Goldschmidt Jr., "'Abd al-Halim, Muhammad," *Biographical Dictionary of Modern Egypt* (Cairo: American University in Cairo Press, 2000), 5.

52. For a comparative analysis of differing notions of work, see Auma Obama, "Arbeitsauffassungen in Deutschland und ihre literarische Kritik in ausgewählten Texten der deutschen Gegenwartsliteratur zwischen 1953 und 1983: Ein Beitrag zum Kulturvergleich Deutschland-Kenia" (Ph.D. diss., Bayreuth University, 1996); see also Reimer Gronemeyer, ed., *Der faule Neger: Vom weißen Kreuzzug gegen den schwarzen Müßiggang* (Reinbek bei Hamburg: Rowohlt, 1991).

53. El-Azhary Sonbol, *New Mamluks,* 60.

54. For a list of Eyth's twenty-six inventions and constructions, see Reitz, *Max Eyth,* 318. Eyth received patents for most of his inventions in England, and for some of them worldwide.

55. Adas, *Machines as the Measure of Men,* 4.

2. THE CIVILIZING MISSION

1. See Erich Brock, "Albert Schweitzer: *Verfall und Wiederaufbau der Kultur,*" *Logos* 12.2 (1923–24): 415–18; *Kultur und Ethik, Logos* 13 (1924–25): 264–69. One of the most recent critiques was presented by the Cameroonian director Bassek Ba Kobhio with his film *Le Grand Blanc de Lambaréné* (1994).

2. See Alice L. Conklin, *A Mission to Civilize: The Republican Idea of Empire in France and West Africa, 1895–1930* (Stanford: Stanford University Press, 1997); Pyenson, *Civilizing Mission.*

3. Mongo Beti, *The Poor Christ of Bomba,* trans. Gerald Moore (London: Heinemann, 1971), 153.

4. Alfred Boegner, "Henry Chapuis et les besoins de la Mission du Congo," *Journal des Missions Évangéliques* 79 (1904): 389–93.

5. "Du aber folge mir nach!" in Albert Schweitzer, *Geschichte der Leben-Jesu-Forschung, Gesammelte Werke in fünf Bänden,* ed. Rudolf Grabs (München: Beck, 1973), 3:887. This German edition of Schweitzer's works, which I will quote in the

following (GW 1, GW 2, etc.), was first published by the East German Union-Verlag in 1971.

6. Albert Schweitzer, "Brief an Alfred Boegner (Direktor der Pariser Missionsgesellschaft) vom 09. Juli 1905." Copy of original letter at the Centre International Albert Schweitzer, Günsbach, Alsace.

7. Johannes Scholl points out that passages of the letters contradict instances of Schweitzer's self-representation in which he claims that he had planned to go as a doctor from the beginning, which were deleted from editions of Schweitzer's letters. "Albert Schweitzers Motive für den Entschluss, Urwaldarzt zu werden," *Albert Schweitzer: Von der Ehrfurcht vor dem Leben zur transkulturellen Solidarität. Ein alternatives Entwicklungshilfekonzept in der ersten Hälfte des 20. Jahrhunderts* (Weinheim: Beltz Athenäum, 1994), 8–26.

8. "Der Entschluss, Urwaldarzt zu werden," *Aus meinem Leben und Denken,* GW 1, 111.

9. Gustav Woytt, "Albert Schweitzer und die Pariser Mission," *Albert-Schweitzer-Studien,* ed. R. Brüllmann (Bern: Paul Haupt, 1989), 120, 136–37.

10. A letter to Anna Schäffer from October 1905 explicitly states that his decision to study medicine came as a reaction to the rejection by the Paris Mission Society. Original letter in archives at Günsbach.

11. Scholl, "Albert Schweitzers Motive," 23–24; Woytt, "Albert Schweitzer," 211–12.

12. Woytt asserts that Schweitzer downplayed the hardships suffered during the internment ("Albert Schweitzer," 219). See Schweitzer's account, "Garaison und St-Rémy," GW 1, 175–86.

13. Woytt, "Albert Schweitzer," 187–88.

14. See letters by Jean Bianquis (e.g., April 14, 1923) in archives at Günsbach.

15. In the aftermath of World War I, Helene's father, Harry Bresslau, was forced to leave Strasbourg on account of his participation in a research project on German history. Ironically, the remains of Bresslau, who died in 1926, were unearthed by the National Socialists, who reburied "the Jew Harry Bresslau" in a grave for non-Aryans. See Jean Pierhal (pseudonym for Robert Jungk), *Albert Schweitzer: Das Leben eines guten Menschen* (München: Kindler, 1955), 253–54.

16. See Schweitzer's comments on local missionaries, for example, in "Das erste Wirken in Afrika, 1913–1917," GW 1, 154–56. See also Hermann-Adolf Stempel, "Die Predigttätigkeit Albert Schweitzers," in *Albert Schweitzer heute: Brennpunkte seines Denkens,* ed. Claus Günzler et al. (Tübingen: Katzmann, 1990), 279–93.

17. See, for example, his antinationalist statements in *Kultur und Ethik,* GW 2, 419.

18. See my article "K.u.K. Colonialism: Hofmannsthal in North Africa," *New German Critique* 75 (Fall 1998): 3–27.

19. See, for instance, "Paris und Berlin, 1898–1899," GW 1, 36–43.

20. "Das französische und das deutsche Buch über Bach," GW 1, 79.

21. See Claus Günzler, "Aus elsässischer Wurzel zur Weltphilosophie: Albert Schweitzer als interkultureller Denker," *karlsruher pädagogische beiträge* 40 (1996): 13–27; Sonja Poteau and Gérard Leser, *Albert Schweitzer: Homme de Gunsbach et citoyen du monde* (Mulhouse: Éditions du Rhin, 1994).

22. See, for example, Erica Anderson's photographs of Günsbach and Schweitzer's friends and the accompanying texts in *The Schweitzer Album: A Portrait in Words and Pictures* (New York: Harper & Row, 1965), 13–22, 129.

23. *Aus meiner Kindheit und Jugendzeit,* GW 1, 256.

24. See also Schweitzer's comment about the influence of Casalis in "Der Entschluss, Urwaldarzt zu werden," *Aus meinem Leben und Denken,* GW 1, 101–2.

25. "They knew he was somewhat short-tempered when things did not go just right; but they knew something, too, about the pressures under which he worked." Norman Cousins, *Albert Schweitzer's Mission: Healing and Peace* (New York: Norton, 1985), 54; see also Edgar Berman, *In Africa with Schweitzer* (Far Hills NJ: New Horizon, 1986), 140.

26. "Gelegentlich fällt auch mal ein schroffes Wort in Lambarene, denn immer wieder muß man die Schwarzen antreiben, sonst wäre längst der Urwald über Lambarene gewachsen." Rolf Italiaander, *Im Lande Albert Schweitzers: Meine Besuche in Lambarene* (Hamburg: Broschek, 1958), 54. "Und so hört man denn auch an diesem Tag mißmutige Äußerungen des Alten, verpackt in Ungeduld. *Stoß ihm in die Rippen,* ermuntert er einen weißen Helfer, weil der Schwarze nicht tut, was er soll." Harald Steffahn, *Albert Schweitzer, in Selbstzeugnissen und Bilddokumenten* (Reinbek bei Hamburg: Rowohlt, 1994), 9.

27. Volker R. Berghahn, *Imperial Germany, 1871–1914: Economy, Society, Culture, and Politics* (Providence: Berghahn Books, 1994), 21.

28. Berghahn, *Imperial Germany,* 6.

29. Berghahn, *Imperial Germany,* 7.

30. Berghahn, *Imperial Germany,* 9.

31. Wolfgang J. Mommsen, *Imperial Germany, 1867–1918: Politics, Culture, and Society in an Authoritarian State* (London: Arnold, 1995), 147.

32. Critics argue over the translation of this term: "It is generally translated 'thoroughgoing eschatology,' but this hardly does justice to the phrase. '*Konsequente*' means coherent, logical, consistent." James Brabazon, *Albert Schweitzer: A Biography* (New York: G. P. Putnam's Sons, 1975), 132.

33. See Oskar Kraus, "Albert Schweitzer: Zur Charakterologie der ethischen Persönlichkeit und der philosophischen Mystik," *Jahrbuch für Charakterologie,* vols. 2–3, ed. Emil Ututz (Berlin: Rolf Heise, 1926), 287–332; J. Middleton Murry, *The Challenge of Schweitzer* (London: Jason Press, 1948); Helmut Groos, *Albert Schweitzer: Größe und Grenzen* (Basel: Ernst Reinhardt, 1974); Werner Picht, *Albert Schweitzer: Wesen und Bedeutung* (Hamburg: Meiner, 1960).

34. See Claus Günzler, "Ehrfurchtsprinzip und Wertrangordnung: Albert Schweitzers Ethik und ihre Kritiker," in Günzler et al., *Albert Schweitzer heute,* 82–100. Other critics defending Schweitzer are, for example, George Seaver, *Albert Schweitzer—A Vindication, Being a Reply to "The Challenge of Schweitzer" by John Middleton Murry* (Boston: Beacon, 1951); Hermann Baur, "Für oder gegen Albert Schweitzer, *Hippokrates* 23 (1962): 982–86.

35. Gotthard M. Teutsch, "Ehrfurchtsethik und Humanitätsidee: Albert Schweitzer beharrt auf der Gleichwertigkeit alles Lebens," in Günzler et al., *Albert Schweitzer heute,* 101–9.

36. James F. Barnes, *Gabon: Beyond the Colonial Legacy* (Boulder: Westview, 1992), 26.

37. Cf. Schweitzer, "Der Entschluß, Urwaldarzt zu werden," GW 1, 99–101.

38. Gerald McKnight describes the extreme loyalty and devotion he observed in women who worked with Schweitzer. "Women and the Lure," in *Verdict on Schweitzer: The Man behind the Legend of Lambaréné* (New York: John Day, 1964), 86–97.

39. Barnes, *Gabon,* 12.

40. See Paul E. Lovejoy, *Transformations in Slavery: A History of Slavery in Africa,* 2d ed. (Cambridge UK: Cambridge University Press, 2000), 15–18, 24–45, 191–225.

41. Christopher J. Gray, *Colonial Rule and Crisis in Equatorial Africa: Southern Gabon, ca. 1850–1940* (Rochester: University of Rochester Press, 2002), 27.

42. Gray, *Colonial Rule,* 28.

43. Barnes, *Gabon,* 13.

44. For case studies on the impact of the slave trade on local communities, see G. Ugo Nwokeji, "The Biafran Frontier: Trade, Slaves, and Aro Society, c. 1750–1905" (Ph.D. diss., University of Toronto, 1999); Anne C. Bailey, "The Impact of the Atlantic Slave Trade on the Anlo Ewe of Southeastern Ghana" (Ph.D. diss., University of Pennsylvania, 1998).

45. For an analysis of the French slave trade, see Robert Louis Stein, *The French Slave Trade in the Eighteenth Century: An Old Regime Business* (Madison: University of Wisconsin Press, 1979).

46. Barnes, *Gabon,* 17.

47. K. David Patterson, *The Northern Gabon Coast to 1875* (London: Oxford University Press, 1975), 126.

48. Patterson, *Northern Gabon Coast,* 131–43.

49. See Theodor Bohner, *Die Woermanns: Vom Werden deutscher Größe* (Berlin: Die Brücke zur Heimat, 1935).

50. Hans-Otto Neuhoff, *Gabun* (Bonn: Schroeder, 1967), 7.

51. Douglas A. Yates, *The Rentier State in Africa: Oil Rent Dependency and Neocolonialism in the Republic of Gabon* (Trenton: Africa World Press, 1996), 90.

52. See Nicolas Métégué N'Nah, *Domination coloniale au Gabon: La Résistance d'un peuple, 1839–1960* (Paris: L'Harmattan, 1981).

53. See Barnes, *Gabon,* 109–12.

54. François Ngolet argues that Bongo's political longevity is not only due to economic and military factors but is also a result of his successful control of the symbolic sphere of Gabonese society. "Ideological Manipulations and Political Longevity: The Power of Omar Bongo in Gabon since 1967," *African Studies Review* 43.2 (2000): 55–71.

55. Yates, *Rentier State in Africa,* 65.

56. Yates, *Rentier State in Africa,* 70–73.

57. Barnes, *Gabon,* 72–73.

58. Barnes, *Gabon,* 115.

59. Claude Lévi-Strauss, "Saudades do Brasil," trans. Sylvia Modelski, *New York Review of Books,* December 21, 1995, 19–26.

60. Rolf Italiaander, *Im Lande Albert Schweitzers: Meine Besuche in Lambarene* (Hamburg: Broschek, 1958), 56.

61. Italiaander, *Im Lande Albert Schweitzers,* 56.

62. *Zwischen Wasser und Urwald,* GW 1, 344; 350; 363–65; 377; 405.

63. See Claus Günzler and Hans Lenk, "Ethik und Weltanschauung: Zum Neuigkeitsgehalt von Albert Schweitzers *Kulturphilosophie III,*" in Günzler et al., *Albert Schweitzer heute,* 20.

64. For a discussion of German racialist theories, see Zantop, "Racializing the Colonies," 66–80.

65. See May Opitz, "Rassismus, Sexismus und vorkoloniales Afrikabild in Deutschland," in *Farbe bekennen: Afro-deutsche Frauen auf den Spuren ihrer Geschichte,* ed. Katharina Oguntoye et al. (Frankfurt am Main: Fischer, 1992), 16–18; see also Gilman, who discusses the relationship of negrophilia in eighteenth-century drama to slavery (34–48).

66. Teutsch, "Ehrfurchtsethik und Humanitätsidee," 106.

67. "The Relations of the White and Coloured Races," *Contemporary Review* 133 (1928): 67. German original of the text in archives at Günsbach ("Die Beziehungen zwischen den weissen und farbigen Rassen," 1927).

68. W. E. B. Du Bois "The Black Man and Albert Schweitzer," in *The Albert Schweitzer Jubilee Book,* ed. A. A. Roback (Westport: Greenwood, 1945), 126.

69. "We have, I hold, the right to colonise if we have the moral authority to exercise this influence." "Relations of the White and Coloured Races," 5.

70. See *Zwischen Wasser und Urwald,* GW 1, 459–60; "Our Task in Colonial Africa" [in the table of contents "Our Task in Equatorial Africa"], *The Africa of Albert Schweitzer* (New York: Harper & Brothers, 1948), ed. Charles R. Joy and Melvin Arnold, n.p.; *Briefe,* GW 1, 610; 668; "Relations of the White and Coloured Races."

71. Notes taken during Chinua Achebe's lecture, "Images of Africa," twenty-fourth annual conference of the African Literature Association, March 26, 1998, Austin TX.

72. Schweitzer, "Our Task in Colonial Africa," n.p.

73. Cousins explains Schweitzer's letter, which was subsequently published by the French against Schweitzer's explicit wish, as a strategic move aimed at appeasing French government officials (*Albert Schweitzer's Mission,* 146–57).

74. Hanns Jürgen Küsters, ed., *Adenauer: Teegespräche 1959–1961* (Berlin: Siedler, 1988), 452.

75. I discuss biographies from the postwar period in detail in "Albert Schweitzer: Germany's Exculpation and Confirmation," *European Studies Journal* 16.2 (1999): 69–94.

76. Pierhal, *Albert Schweitzer,* 286.

77. Du Bois, "Black Man and Albert Schweitzer," 126.

3. THE GLOBALIZING MISSION

1. Robert Wohl, *A Passion for Wings: Aviation and the Western Imagination, 1908–1918* (New Haven: Yale University Press, 1994), 1.

2. Peter Fritzsche, *A Nation of Fliers: German Aviation and the Popular Imagination* (Cambridge: Harvard University Press, 1992), 2.

3. Fritzsche, *Nation of Fliers,* 64.

4. See, for example, Eckhard G. Franz and Peter Geissler, eds., *Das Deutsch-Ostafrika-Archiv: Inventar der Abteilung "German Records" im Nationalarchiv der Vereinigten Republik Tansania, Dar-es-Salaam* (Marburg GER: Archivschule Marburg, 1973).

5. Horst Gründer, ed., *"... da und dort ein junges Deutschland gründen": Rassismus, Kolonien und kolonialer Gedanke vom 16. bis zum 20. Jahrhundert* (München: Deutscher Taschenbuchverlag, 1999), 13.

6. John Iliffe, *A Modern History of Tanganyika* (Cambridge UK: Cambridge University Press, 1979), 72.

7. Ernst Hieke, *Zur Geschichte des deutschen Handels mit Ostafrika: Das hamburgische Handelshaus Wm. O'Swald & Co.,* vol. 1: 1831–1870 (Hamburg: Hans Christians, 1939), 221.

8. Hieke, *Zur Geschichte des deutschen Handels mit Ostafrika,* 230–33.

9. W. O. Henderson, *The German Colonial Empire, 1884–1919* (London: Frank Cass, 1993), 28.

10. Karl Evers, "Das Hamburger Zanzibarhandelshaus Wm. O'Swald & Co. 1847–1890: Zur Geschichte des hamburger Handels mit Ostafrika" (Ph.D. diss., University Hamburg, 1986), 206–32, 363.

11. See Thomas Pakenham, "Why Bismarck Changed His Mind," in *The Scramble for Africa: The White Man's Conquest of the Dark Continent from 1876 to 1912* (New York: Random House, 1991), 201–17.

12. See Bismarck's speech held in the Reichstag on June 26, 1884, reprinted in Gründer, *Rassismus, Kolonien und kolonialer Gedanke,* 90–92.

13. Evers, "Das Hamburger Zanzibarhandelshaus," 289–347, 365–66; Gründer, *Rassismus, Kolonien und kolonialer Gedanke,* 95.

14. See Thaddeus Sunseri, "Peasants and the Struggle for Labor in Cotton Regimes of the Rufiji Basin, Tanzania, 1885–1918," in *Cotton, Colonialism, and Social History in Sub-Saharan Africa,* ed. Allen Isaacman and Richard Roberts (Portsmouth NH: Heinemann, 1995), 180–99.

15. Thaddeus Sunseri, "Statist Narratives and Maji Maji Ellipses," *International Journal of African Historical Studies* 33.3 (2000): 573.

16. Iliffe, *History,* 200; G. C. K. Gwassa, "The Outbreak and Development of the Maji Maji War 1905–7" (Ph.D. diss., University Dar es Salaam, 1973), 389.

17. Iliffe, *History,* 200, quoted from *Deutsches Kolonialblatt,* April 15, 1907.

18. For an account of the reforms of Dernburg and Rechenberg, see Woodruff D. Smith, *The German Colonial Empire* (Chapel Hill: University of North Carolina Press, 1978), 183–212. For documents regarding the debate over reforms in colonial policies, see Gründer, *Rassismus, Kolonien und kolonialer Gedanke,* 233–51.

19. G. C. K. Gwassa and John Iliffe, eds., *Records of the Maji Maji Rising* (Nairobi: East African Publishing House, 1968), 1:3.

20. See Karl-Martin Seeberg, *Der Maji-Maji-Krieg gegen die deutsche Kolonialherrschaft: Historische Ursprünge nationaler Identität in Tansania* (Berlin: Dietrich Reimer, 1989), esp. 12–18 and 95–107.

21. Sunseri, "Statist Narratives."

22. Karim F. Hirji, "Colonial Ideological Apparatuses in Tanganyika under the Germans," in *Tanzania under Colonial Rule,* ed. M. H. Y. Kaniki (London: Longman, 1980), 207.

23. See the section on "Missionary Periodicals," in John William East, "The German Administration in East Africa: A Select Annotated Bibliography of the German Colonial Administration in Tanganyika, Rwanda and Burundi, from 1884 to 1918" (Master's thesis, London, Fellowship of the Library Association, 1987), 7–13.

24. In *Language and Power* Michelle Moyd argues that Germans officials were conflicted about their language policy because of the potential empowerment a knowledge of German would entail.

25. After his return from East Africa, Lettow-Vorbeck was subsequently accepted into the Reichswehr yet dismissed in 1920 because of his participation in the Kapp Putsch. Later he became a member of the Reichstag (1928–30,) as a representative for the DNVP.

26. Gründer, *Rassismus, Kolonien und kolonialer Gedanke,* 301.

27. See Gründer, *Rassismus, Kolonien und kolonialer Gedanke,* 327–31.

28. My overview is based on biographies by Heinz J. Nowarra, *Udet: Vom Fliegen besessen* (Friedberg: Podzun-Pallas, 1982); Ernst Friedrich Eichler's biography

Kreuz wider Kokarde: Jagdflüge des Leutnants Ernst Udet (Berlin: Gustav Braunbeck, 1918); Hans Herlin, *Der Teufelsflieger: Ernst Udet und die Geschichte seiner Zeit* (München: Wilhelm Heyne, 1974); Hans Waldhausen, *Ernst Udet: Vom Zauber seiner Persönlichkeit* (Neckargemünd: Kurt Vowinckel, 1972).

29. Udet's own account in *Mein Fliegerleben* (Berlin: Deutscher Verlag, 1935) seems to confirm these views on the relationship between him and Göring (114–16).

30. Fritzsche, *Nation of Fliers*, 82.

31. Udet, *Mein Fliegerleben*, 73–75.

32. Udet, *Mein Fliegerleben*, 105.

33. Fritzsche, *Nation of Fliers*, 135.

34. He also stared in Fanck's *SOS Eisberg* (1932–33), which featured Riefenstahl as well; Heinz Paul's *Wunder des Fliegens* (1935); and Carl Junghans's documentary of the Fourth Olympic Winter Games in Garmisch-Partenkirchen (1936).

35. *Fremde Vögel über Afrika* (Velhagen und Klasing: Bielefeld, 1932), 3. This was probably production manager Karl Buchholz.

36. Other relevant collaborators on the film were Fritz Wenneis (music), Hans Bittmann, Paul Rohnstein, Erich Palme, Arthus Kamps (sound), and Gösta Nordhaus (editing).

37. Reel no. 2 is 301 m, no. 3 is 297 m, and no. 4 is 292 m long.

38. See Thomas Brandlmeier, "ET EGO FUI IN ARCADIA: Die exotischen Spielfilme der 20er Jahre," *Triviale Tropen: Exotische Reise- und Abenteuerfilme aus Deutschland, 1919–1939*, ed. Jörg Schöning (München: edition text+kritik, 1997), 34–46.

39. See the critical reviews by P. A. O., "'Fliehende Schatten' Im Ufa-Pavillion," *Berliner Tageblatt*, evening edition, April 13, 1932; schffr., "Udets Afrika-Film: Fliehende Schatten im Ufa-Pavillion," *Vossische Zeitung*, morning edition, April 13, 1932.

40. Ludwig, "Im Ufa-Pavillion: 'Fliehende Schatten,'" *Der Film* April 16, 1932; n.a., "Im Ufa-Pavillion: Fliehende Schatten," *Berliner Börsen-Courier*, evening edition, April 13, 1932.

41. Schomburgk is credited with a series of film revolving around this topic. Gerlinde Waz, "Auf der Suche nach dem letzten Paradies: Der Afrikaforscher und Regisseur Hans Schomburgk," in Schöning *Triviale Tropen*, 95–109.

42. Walther Victor, "Persiflage des Afrikafilms," *8 Uhr Abendblatt*, April 13, 1932. Another critic had considered the comical aspects to be "unfreiwillig." See E. A. S., "Fliegende Schatten [*sic*]," *Germania: Zeitung für das deutsche Volk*, April 14, 1932.

43. L. H. Eisner, "Fliehende Schatten—Ufa-Pavillion," *Film-Kurier*, April 13, 1932.

44. For an overview of early German films made about Africa, see the filmography by Jörg Schöning, "Rund um den Erdball: Exotische Reise- und Abenteuerfilme 1919–1945," in Schöning, *Triviale Tropen*, 197–200.

45. On ethnographic and fictional elements in Schomburgk's films, see Assenka Oksiloff, *Picturing the Primitive: Visual Culture, Ethnography, and Early German Cinema* (New York: Palgrave, 2001), 79–84.

46. Carl Junghans, "Afrikanischer Expeditionsbericht im Telegrammstil," 3, *Beiblatt zum Film-Kurier* 79, April 4, 1931.

47. Udet, *Fremde Vögel über Afrika,* 3.

48. Susanne Zantop, "*Kolonie* and *Heimat:* Race, Gender, and Postcolonial Amnesia in Veit Harlan's *Opfergang* (1944)," *Women in German Yearbook* 17 (2001), 11.

49. See Mathias Mulumbar Rwankote, "Ostafrika in den Zielvorstellungen der Reichspolitik und der verschiedenen Interessengruppen im Rahmen der kolonialen politischen Aktivitäten in der Zeit der Weimarer Republik" (Ph.D. diss., University Köln, 1985), 174–208, 290–302.

50. Simon Schama, *Landscape and Memory* (New York: Vintage Books, 1996), 14.

51. Two photographs on p. 4 show the cameras attached to the planes. The pagination of the photographs begins again with p. 1.

52. Edward Said, *Orientalism* (New York: Random House, 1978), 7.

53. Noyes, *Colonial Space,* 166.

54. See Thomas Theye, "Anmerkungen zur Kolonialfotographie in Schwarzafrika," *Der geraubte Schatten: Die Photographie als ethnographisches Dokument,* ed. Thomas Theye (München: C. J. Bucher, 1989), 244–45; Ricabeth Steiger and Martin Taureg, "Quellentexte zur ethnographischen Fotografie aus Schwarzafrika," *Der geraubte Schatten,* 246–63.

55. Barbara Wolbert points out this fact in "The Anthropologist as Photographer: The Visual Construction of Ethnographic Authority," *Visual Anthropology* 13 (2000): 323.

56. Derrick Price, "Surveyors and Surveyed," in *Photography: A Critical Introduction,* ed. Liz Wells (London: Routledge, 2000), 68.

57. Noyes, *Colonial Space,* 188–214. See also Uwe Moeller, who argues that many German writers excluded or diminished the presence of African men from their texts and, instead, focused on eroticized African women. "A Place in the Sun: The Image of the Black in German Realism and the Colonial Novel" (Ph.D. diss., University of Texas at Austin, 1997).

58. Frantz Fanon, *Black Skin, White Masks* (New York: Grove, 1986), 109–40; Anne McClintock, "Soft-Soaping Empire: Commodity Racism and Imperial Advertizing," in *The Visual Culture Reader,* ed. Nicholas Mirzoeff (London: Routledge, 1998), 305–16; Malek Alloula, *The Colonial Harem,* trans. Myrna and Wlad Godzich (Minneapolis: University of Minnesota Press, 1986).

59. See Alloula, *Colonial Harem,* esp. 17–26, 67–124.

60. James C. Faris, "Photography, Power and the Southern Nuba," in Edwards, *Anthropology and Photography,* 214–16; "Polluted Vision," *Sudanow* 5.5 (May 1980): 38.

61. James C. Faris, "Fascism and Photography," *Newsweek,* December 13, 1976, 4.

62. Suleiman Musa Rahhal, *The Right to Be Nuba: The Story of a Sudanese People's Struggle for Survival* (Lawrenceville NJ: Red Sea Press, 2001).

63. The most famous of these Africans who were brought to Germany during the Enlightenment period was Anton Wilhelm Amo (ca. 1700–after 1753) who taught as a professor of philosophy in Halle and Jena. Cf. n. 65 in chap. 2.

64. Helmut Regel, "Der Schwarze und sein 'Bwana': Das Afrika-Bild im deutschen Film," *Triviale Tropen,* 62.

65. See, for example, the films *Die Reiter von Deutsch-Ostafrika* (1934) by Herbert Selpin; *Das Sonnenland Südwest-Afrika* (1926) by Hans Dietrich von Trotha; *Sehnsucht nach Afrika* (1939) by Georg Zoch; *Deutsches Land in Afrika* (1939) by Walter Scheunemann and Karl Mohri. Alain Patrice Nganang, "Koloniale Sehnsuchtsfilme: Vom lieben Afrikaner deutscher Filme der NS-Zeit," *Welfengarten* 11 (2001): 111–28.

66. For a critique of the term *globalization,* see Victor Li, who argues that the term masks the crass inequalities of the global economy. "What's in a Name? Questioning 'Globalization,'" *Cultural Critique* 45 (Spring 2000): 1–39.

67. Udet, *Mein Fliegerleben,* 140. Subsequent references to this text appear in parentheses.

68. The 1955 film version of Zuckmayer's play by Helmut Käutner, with Curd Jürgens as General Harras, played a crucial role in Germany's attempts at coming to terms with its National Socialist past.

4. HUMANITARIAN INTERVENTIONS

1. The texts of UN Security Council resolutions on Somalia between January 23 and December 3, 1992, are included in Mohamed Sahnoun, *Somalia: The Missed Opportunities* (Washington DC: United States Institute of Peace Press, 1994), app. B, 59–80.

2. Sahnoun, *Somalia,* 15.

3. See Christopher Greenwood, "Gibt es ein Recht auf humanitäre Intervention?" *Europa-Archiv* 48.4 (1993): 101.

4. Sahnoun, *Somalia,* 78.

5. Resolution 733 (Sahnoun, *Somalia,* 59). This phrase is also used in resolutions 746, 751, 767, 775, and 794 (Sahnoun, *Somalia,* 62, 65, 68, 72, 75).

6. Reflecting the official stance of the U.S. government, see John L. Hirsch and Robert B. Oakley, *Somalia and Operation Restore Hope: Reflections on Peacemaking and Peacekeeping* (Washington DC: United States Institute of Peace Press, 1995), esp. 49, 109, 110.

7. Resolution 814, adopted by the Security Council on March 26, 1993, called for the replacement of UNITAF forces with a UN peacekeeping force.

8. See "Der Golf-Krieg als Katalysator einer neuen deutschen Normalität?" *Vergangenheit als Zukunft,* ed. Michael Haller (Zürich: pendo, 1991), 10–44; Werner Ruf, "Allemagne: au péril du pacifisme," *Matériaux pour l'Histoire de Notre Temps* 48 (1997): 26–34. Ruf points out that the discussion centered on the legacy of German antisemitism and Germany's contemporary relationship to Israel rather than the specific issues of the Gulf War.

9. Michael Stürmer, "Wohin die Bundeswehr? Über Diplomatie, Strategie und Bündnistreue," *Internationale Politik* 50.4 (1995): 33. See also Peter Goebel, *Von Kambodscha bis Kosovo: Auslandseinsätze der Bundeswehr seit Ende des Kalten Krieges* (Frankfurt am Main: Report, 2000).

10. In the following review of the legal debate I draw primarily on Wolfgang März, *Bundeswehr in Somalia: Verfassungsrechtliche und verfassungspolitische Überlegungen zur Verwendung deutscher Streitkräfte in* VN-*Operationen* (Berlin: Duncker & Humblot, 1993).

11. März, *Bundeswehr in Somalia,* 44.

12. Regarding different views expressed in the discussion, see Ole Diehl, "Außenpolitische Handlungszwänge und innenpolitischer Konsensbedarf," *Europa-Archiv* 48.8 (1993): 219–27; Ernst Benda, "Deutsche Außenpolitk vor Gericht: Bundesverfassungsgericht und auswärtige Gewalt," *Internationale Politik* 50.12 (1995): 39–46; Rudolf Scharping, "Deutsche Außenpolitik muß berechenbar sein," *Internationale Politik* 50.8 (1995): 38–44.

13. See *Der Spiegel* 20 (1993): 36–37; and 32 (1993): 16. Cf. also Bodo Kirchhoff, *Herrenmenschlichkeit* (Frankfurt am Main: Suhrkamp, 1994), 25.

14. *Der Spiegel* 26 (1993): 230.

15. *Der Spiegel* 26 (1993): 230.

16. Paul Klein et al., *Die Bundeswehr an der Schwelle zum 21. Jahrhundert* (Baden-Baden: Nomos, 2000); Ulrich Kremer and Dieter S. Lutz, eds., *Die Bundeswehr in der neuen Weltordnung* (Hamburg: VSA, 2000); Peter Rzeczewski, "The Bundeswehr in Military Peace Operations: Have Conditions for Participation Improved?" (Carlisle Barracks PA: U.S. Army War College, 1999); Arthur Hoffmann, "Germany and the Role of the Bundeswehr: A New Consensus?" (Birmingham: University of Birmingham, Institute for German Studies, 1998).

17. Teraoka, *East, West, and Others,* 5.

18. In contrast, Uwe Timm's novels *Morenga, Der Schlangenbaum,* and *Kopfjäger* stand out for the high degree of historical research that went into their writing and the self-reflexivity displayed by the author.

19. Regarding differences between the German and the Anglo-American legal system, see Christoph Mueller, "Toward Trial Reform," *American German Review* 32.3 (1966): 2–7.

20. See Peter Handke, *Eine winterliche Reise zu den Flüssen Donau, Save, Morawa und Drina, oder: Gerechtigkeit für Serbien* (Frankfurt am Main: Suhrkamp, 1996);

and *Sommerlicher Nachtrag zu einer winterlichen Reise* (Frankfurt am Main: Suhrkamp, 1996). Regarding the controversy that arose over these texts, see *Die Angst des Dichters vor der Wirklichkeit. 16 Antworten auf Peter Handkes Winterreise nach Serbien,* ed. Tilman Zülch (Göttingen: Steidl, 1996).

21. Another German response to the Somali crisis is the film *United Trash* (1995) by Christoph Schlingensief. Here UN involvement in Africa is staged as a farcical encounter. Africans, Americans, and Europeans are portrayed as irrational freaks, driven by their greed for sex, power, money, and blood. The film is nauseating to watch, with blood and human excrement in almost every scene, and actors, naked or in grotesque attire, run screaming and cussing through an African landscape. The discrepancy between the film's intellectual aspiration and its artistic realization resulted in a largely negative reception.

22. Excerpts from *Herrenmenschlichkeit* are translated into English by Otto Tetzlaff and Christine Tetzlaff-McFarland. See "Humanity of the Masters—Excerpt," *Dimension*^{2} 2.3 (September 1995): 362–73.

23. The list of publications on the topic is extensive; see, for example, Connie Peck, *Sustainable Peace: The Role of the* UN *and Regional Organizations* (Lanham: Rowman & Littlefield, 1997); Werner Ruf, *Die neue Welt-*UN*-Ordnung: Vom Umgang des Sicherheitsrates mit der Souveränität der "Dritten Welt"* (Münster: agenda, 1994).

24. *TransAtlantik* 8 (1981): 30–39.

25. *TransAtlantik* 5 (1982): 40–49.

26. *TransAtlantik* 10 (1982): 52–64.

27. *Kursbuch* 68 (1982): 119–25.

28. *Errungenschaften. Eine Kasuistik,* ed. Michael Rutschky (Frankfurt am Main: Suhrkamp, 1982), 185–94.

29. *Legenden um den eigenen Körper: Frankfurter Vorlesungen* (Frankfurt am Main: Suhrkamp, 1995), 133–72.

30. Benjamin Henrichs, "Die Reise von Frankfurt nach Sodom," *Die Zeit,* December 10, 1979: Feuilleton.

31. "Der Mittelpunkt des Universums," *Body-Building* (Frankfurt am Main: Suhrkamp, 1980), 27.

32. Compare the reviews and reactions to performances of the monologue in the popular press, especially between February 1994 and April 1997.

33. "Unterm Strich," *die tageszeitung,* July 7, 1997, 16.

34. *Der Spiegel* 26 (1993): 27.

35. "Staub in allen Briefen: Deutsche Soldaten in Belet Huen; Aus dem Tagebuch des Schriftstellers Bodo Kirchhoff," *Der Spiegel* 30 (1993): 160–65.

36. This spider (*Kamelspinne*) seems to have made an impression; it was also mentioned in *Der Spiegel* 25 (1993): 118.

37. Cf. *Tageszeitung* 30 (1993), quoted in *Der Spiegel* 31 (1993): 182.

38. See pp. 7, 19, 27, 39, 42, 45, 59, 66, 67.

39. See, for example, Matthias Geis, "Prima amüsiert," *Die Zeit* 29, July 18, 1997, 4.

40. Werner Raith, "Was geschah in Somalia?" *Die Tageszeitung*, June 16, 1997, 8.

41. Mark Bowden, "Afterword," in *Black Hawk Down: A Story of Modern War* (New York: Signet, 2001), 429–30. The book is based on a newspaper series that first ran in the *Philadelphia Inquirer* in 1997.

42. Bowden, "Afterword," 426.

43. See, for example, Doug Kellner's excellent study of the media coverage of the Gulf War: *The Persian Gulf* TV *War* (Boulder: Westview, 1992).

44. *Der Spiegel* 29 (1993): 17; Hirsch and Oakley, *Somalia*, 121.

45. "Dem Schmerz eine Welt geben," 138–42.

46. Kirchhoff's struggle with the "absolute other" (185), the "uncanny other" (187), in a "terribly strange country of the Third World" (186), can also be observed in "Zeichen und Wunder: Ein Reisebericht."

47. See also Clemens Höges, "Der Tod gehört hier zum Leben," *Der Spiegel* 33 (1993): 24.

48. According to Sahnoun, the United Nations were encouraged to intervene by "the elders in all regions" (25, 16–17). For other interpretations, see Ruf, *Die neue Welt-*UN*-Ordnung*, 134–42, 151; Hirsch and Oakley, *Somalia;* and Mohammed Farah Aidid and Satya Pal Ruhela, *Somalia: From the Dawn of Civilization to the Modern Times* (New Delhi: Viaks, 1994).

49. Friedrich Nietzsche, *Jenseits von Gut und Böse; Zur Genealogie der Moral* (Berlin: de Gruyter, 1988), 303.

50. John Hoberman, "Black 'Hardiness' and the Origins of Medical Racism," *Darwin's Athletes: How Sport has Damaged Black America and Preserved the Myth of Race* (Boston: Houghton Mifflin, 1997), 176.

51. Nancy Scheper-Hughes, *Death without Weeping: The Violence of Everyday Life in Brazil* (Berkeley: University of California Press, 1992).

52. A discussion contrasting Diderot's anticolonial notions of universal brotherhood to the idea of the incommensurability of cultures in Herder is presented by Anthony Pagden in his analysis of works by Diderot and Herder. See "The Effacement of Difference: Colonialism and the Origins of Nationalism in Diderot and Herder," in *After Colonialism: Imperial Histories and Postcolonial Displacements*, ed. Gyan Prakash (Princeton: Princeton University Press, 1995), 129–52.

53. Amin, *Eurocentrism*, vii.

54. Mary Jo Arnoldi, "The Artistic Heritage of Somalia," in *Somalia in Word and Image*, ed. Katheryne S. Loughran et al. (Washington DC: Foundation for Cross Cultural Understanding, 1986), 17.

55. I. M. Lewis, *A Modern History of Somalia: Nation and State in the Horn of Africa* (London: Longman, 1980), 5.

56. B. W. Andrzejewski, "The Literary Culture of the Somali People," *Somalia in*

Word and Image, 35. See also Ali Jimale Ahmed, *Daybreak is Near . . . : Literature, Clans, and the Nation-State in Somalia* (Lawrenceville NJ: Red Sea Press, 1996).

57. Richard F. Burton, *First Footsteps in East Africa, or An Exploration of Harar* (1894; New York: Dover Publications, 1987), 81–82.

58. Lidwien Kapteijns, "Women and the Crisis of Communal Identity: The Cultural Construction of Gender in Somali History," *The Somali Challenge: From Catastrophe to Renewal?* ed. Ahmed I. Samatar (Boulder: Lynne Rienner, 1994), 212.

59. Samuel M. Makinda, *Seeking Peace from Chaos: Humanitarian Intervention in Somalia* (Boulder: Lynne Rienner, 1993), 18–21.

60. Catherine Besteman, *Unraveling Somalia: Race, Violence, and the Legacy of Slavery* (Philadelphia: University of Pennsylvania Press, 1999), 4.

61. For an overview of the history of modern Somalia, see David D. Laitin and Said S. Samatar, *Somalia: Nation in Search of a State* (Boulder: Westview, 1987).

62. Nevertheless, according to Ahmed I. Samatar, the restoration of a civic identity and identification with a nation-state is the answer to Somalia's political chaos. "The Somali Catastrophe: Explanation and Implications," in *Ethnicity Kills? The Politics of War, Peace and Ethnicity in SubSaharan Africa,* ed. Einar Braathen et al. (Houndmills: Macmillan, 2000), 37–67.

63. For a detailed account of the complicated history of Cold War politics concerning Ethiopia and Somalia, see Jeffrey A. Lefebvre, *Arms for the Horn: U.S. Security Policy in Ethiopia and Somalia, 1953–1991* (Pittsburgh: University of Pittsburgh Press, 1991).

64. Ahmed Farah Mohamed and Jasmin Touati, *Sedentarisierung von Nomaden: Chancen und Gefahren einer Entwicklungsstrategie am Beispiel Somalias* (Saarbrücken: Breitenbach, 1991).

65. Abdalla Omar Mansur, "Contrary to a Nation: The Cancer of the Somali State," in *The Invention of Somalia,* ed. Ali Jimale Ahmed (Lawrenceville NJ: Red Sea Press, 1995), 115.

66. Lévi-Strauss, "Saudades do Brasil," 19.

67. Jasmin Touati, "Der UNO-Einsatz in Somalia. Eine Zusammenstellung der Interessen der Vereinigten Staaten von Amerika und der Vereinten Nationen," in *Wüstenstürme: Der Krieg des Nordens gegen den Süden?* ed. Andreas Disselnkötter (Duisburg: Duisburger Institut für Sprach- und Sozialforschung, 1994), 59.

68. Touati, "Der UNO-Einsatz in Somalia" 60–62; Ruf, *Die neue Welt-UN-Ordnung,* 125–26, 160–61.

69. See, for example, Bettina Gaus, "Und dann entscheide ich," *die tageszeitung,* July 4, 1997, 11; Bettina Gaus, "Schritt für Schritt zur Militärmacht," *die tageszeitung,* December 14, 1996, 5; Horand Knaup, "Vorsicht, Helfer!" *Die Woche,* November 29, 1996, 8; Andreas Borchers, "Out of Africa," *Die Woche,* November 22, 1996, 8; Reymer Klüver, "Hunger ist nicht Schicksal," *Süddeutsche Zeitung,* November 16, 1996,

4; Daniel Stroux, "In Ostzaire kann am ehesten eine afrikanische Intervention helfen: Interview mit Rupert Neudeck," *die tageszeitung,* November 12, 1996, 10.

70. Rakiyah Omaar, "Töten und vergelten," *Der Spiegel* 35 (1993): 133.

71. Ulrich Menzel, *Das Ende der Dritten Welt und das Scheitern der großen Theorie* (Frankfurt am Main: Suhrkamp, 1992); Dieter Senghaas, *Von Europa lernen. Entwicklungsgeschichtliche Betrachtungen* (Frankfurt am Main: Suhrkamp, 1982). Beginning in the mid-1980s, Senghaas distanced himself from earlier positions and explored other models relevant to solving political and economic conflicts arising from globalization.

72. See introduction.

5. TOURISM

1. Ernest Hemingway, *Green Hills of Africa* (New York: Simon & Schuster, 1996), 6.

2. For detailed discussions of the different approaches to the study of tourism, see John Urry, *The Tourist Gaze: Leisure and Travel in Contemporary Societies* (London: Sage, 1990), 7–15; Martin Mowforth and Ian Munt, *Tourism and Sustainability: New Tourism in the Third World* (London: Routledge, 1998).

3. Dean MacCannell, *The Tourist: A New Theory of the Leisure Class* (New York: Schocken, 1989), 1; Urry, *Tourist Gaze,* 4.

4. MacCannell, *Tourist,* 178.

5. For variations in the interpretation of notions of authenticity, see Daniel J. Boorstin, *The Image: A Guide to Pseudo-Events in America* (New York: Harper, 1964); Dean MacCannell, "Staged Authenticity: Arrangements of Social Space in Tourist Settings," *American Journal of Sociology* 79.3 (1973): 589–603; Philip L. Pearce and Gianna M. Moscardo, "The Concept of Authenticity in Tourist Experiences," *Australian and New Zealand Journal of Sociology* 22.21 (March 1986): 121–32.

6. Malcolm Crick, "Sun, Sex, Sights, Savings and Servility: Representations of International Tourism in the Social Sciences," *Criticism, Heresy, and Interpretation* 1 (1988): 65–66.

7. See Maxine Feifer, *Tourism in History: From Imperial Rome to the Present* (New York: Stein and Day, 1986), 259–68.

8. Victor W. Turner, *The Ritual Process: Structure and Anti-Structure* (Chicago: Aldine, 1969); "The Center Out There: Pilgrim's Goal, "*History of Religions* 12.3 (1973): 191–230.

9. John J. Pigram and Salah Wahab, "Sustainable Tourism in a Changing World," *Tourism, Development and Growth: The Challenge of Sustainability,* ed. Salah Wahab and John J. Pigram (London: Routledge, 1997), 19.

10. Simone Abram and Jacqueline Waldren, "Introduction," *Tourists and Tour-*

ism: Identifying with People and Places, ed. Simone Abram, Jacqueline Waldren, and Donald V. L. MacLeod (Oxford: Berg, 1997), 9.

11. Abram, Waldren, and MacLeod, *Tourists and Tourism,* 8–9.

12. Alma Gottlieb, "Americans' Vacations," *Annals of Tourism Research* 9 (1982): 165–87.

13. The Lexis-Nexis database lists hundreds of articles reflecting the negative image of the German tourist.

14. All names have been changed to secure the privacy of the individuals.

15. The series was preceded by the pilot movie *Clarence, The Cross-Eyed Lion* (1965). The first of eighty-nine one-hour episodes was broadcast on January 11, 1966, the last one on January 15, 1969.

16. In one of his shows in the 1960s Grzimek claimed that a vacation in Kenya, including a safari, cost only DM 2,000. When Germans stormed travel agencies the next day, the industry was encouraged to accommodate the sudden demand.

17. See Helmut Ludwig, *Notiert in Kenia: Erlebnisse und Begnungen in einem Entwicklungsland* (1970); Regina Horstmann, *Ankomme Kenia morgen: Erlebnisse im Entwicklungsdienst* (1975); Hartmut Deckelmann, *Leben in einem Entwicklungsland: Beispiel Kenia* (1979); and Kurt Mikolaschek, *Im Herzen des schwarzen Kontinents: Erfahrungen und Reiseabenteuer eines Arztes in Kenia* (1989).

18. More specifically, the man is a member of the Samburu tribe. *Masai* is technically a linguistic term for speakers of this eastern Sudanic language, which include the pastoral Masai, who range along the Great Rift Valley of Kenya and Tanzania; the Samburu of Kenya; and the semipastoral Arusha and Baraguyu (or Kwafi) of Tanzania. Since the Masai are more widely known and have acquired quite a reputation for their charisma as mysterious warriors and noble savages, the publisher might have opted to use this term in the title to attract more attention to the book.

19. The novel was on the best-seller list of the weekly magazine *Der Spiegel* from January 1999 to March 2000; in spring and summer 1999 it held the second place for fourteen weeks. In the weekly *Die Zeit* the autobiography ranked first for several weeks in spring 1999.

20. The publisher did not share figures regarding the sales, but, in the wake of the frenzy about Hofmann's account, the book was exhibited in all major bookstores and likely drew a large readership.

21. Roughly 21 percent of all Kenyans are Kikuyus. Other groups are Luhya (14%), Luo (13%), Kamba (11%), Kalenjin (11%), Ksii (6%), Meru (5%), Mijikenda (5%), and the Masai (2%). Roughly thirty other groups, including Asians, Europeans, and Arabs make up 12 percent of the population. See Simon Baynham, *Kenya: Prospects for Peace and Stability* (London: Research Institute for the Study of Conflict and Terrorism, 1997), 24.

22. On decolonization and independence, see B. A. Ogot and W. R. Ochieng', eds., *Decolonization and Independence in Kenya, 1940–1993* (London: James Currey,

1995); David F. Gordon, *Decolonization and the State in Kenya* (Boulder: Westview, 1986); Keith Kyle, *The Politics of the Independence of Kenya* (New York: St. Martin's, 1999).

23. Kenyatta's ethnographic account of the Kikuyu people, *Facing Mount Kenya: The tribal life of the Gikuyu* (1965), is well known. Another key political figure during the early period of Kenyan independence was Tom Mboya. He gained attention in the United States in connection with a student airlift he initiated, geared at supporting Africans who wanted to pursue higher education in the United States. Mboya became the victim of political power struggles and was assassinated in 1969. For a bibliography of his writings, see David Goldsworthy, *Tom Mboya: The Man Kenya Wanted to Forget* (Nairobi: Heinemann, 1982), 295–99.

24. See Jennifer A. Widner, *The Rise of a Party-State in Kenya: From "Harambee!" to "Nyayo!"* (Berkeley: University of California Press, 1992); Ngugi wa Thiong'o, *Barrel of a Pen: Resistance to Repression in Neo-Colonial Kenya* (Trenton: Africa World Press, 1983).

25. Norman Miller and Rodger Yeager, *Kenya: The Quest of Prosperity* (Boulder: Westview, 1994), 131; Baynham, *Kenya,* 6.

26. A paper presented by the former mayor of Mombasa Najib Balala at a meeting of the Mombasa and Coast Tourist Association (MCTA) on June 19, 1998, asserts that the coast alone has "270,000 tourism industry related employees" (7).

27. In 1996, according to figures from the Kenyan government, provided by the Kenyan consulate in Frankfurt in summer 1998.

28. A blueprint plan for the development of the Diani area was designed in the mid-1970s. This plan, the realization of which would have produced an extraordinary model for tourism, included significant benefits for the local population. See "A Report to the Government of Kenya for the Development of Tourism at Diani" (prepared by Kenya Coast Planners Ltd., Nairobi, December 1975).

29. Figures are based on publications by the Kenya Association of Tour Operators (KATO), the Kenya Tourist Board, the Kenya Association of Hotelkeepers and Caterers (KAHC), and the Mombasa Coast Tourist Association (MCTA).

30. Comparable figures are also provided in Isaac Sindiga, "Tourism," in *Kenya Coast Handbook: Culture, Resources and Development in the East African littoral,* ed. Jan Hoorweg et al. (Hamburg: LIT, 2000), 223–25.

31. Alamin Mazrui, "Ethnic Voices and Trans-Ethnic Voting: The 1997 Elections at the Kenya Coast," in Marcel Rutten et al., *Out for the Count: The 1997 General Elections and Prospects for Democracy in Kenya* (Kampala: Fountain, 2001), 281.

32. Figures according to Statistisches Bundesamt.

33. Philipp Bachmann, *Tourism in Kenya: A Basic Need for Whom?* (Bern: Lang, 1988), 301.

34. Bachmann, *Tourism in Kenya,* 301.

35. See Eva Kurt, *Tourismus in die Dritte Welt—Ökonomische, sozio-kulturelle*

und ökologische Folgen: Das Beispiel Kenya (Saarbrücken: breitenbach, 1986), 23–65; Wilhelm Englbert Pompl, *Der internationale Tourismus in Kenia und seine Implikationen für die sozio-ökonomische Entwicklung des Landes* (München: Frank, 1975); Sindiga, "Tourism," 230–34.

36. Jaap Schoorl and Nico Visser, *Towards Sustainable Coastal Tourism: Environmental Impacts of Tourism on the Kenyan Cost* (Nairobi: Commissioned by the Netherlands Ministry of Agriculture, Nature Management and Fisheries, 1991).

37. Pompl, *Der internationale Tourismus in Kenia,* 276–84.

38. Kurt, *Tourismus in die Dritte Welt,* 70.

39. Christiane Schurian-Bremecker, "Kenia in der Sicht deutscher Touristen" (Ph.D. diss., University Münster, 1989), 350–54.

40. David Jerome Jamison, "The Brotherhood of Coconuts: Tourism, Ethnicity, and National Identity in Malindi, Kenya" (Ph.D. diss., University of Florida, 1993).

41. Johanna H. Schoss, "Beach Tours and Safari Visions: Relations of Production and the Production of 'Culture' in Malindi, Kenya" (Ph.D. diss., University of Chicago, 1995), 16.

42. S. E. Migot-Adholla et al., *Study of Tourism in Kenya: With Emphasis on the Attitudes of Residents of the Kenya Coast* (Nairobi: Institute of Development Studies, 1982), esp. 95–149.

43. Rosemary Jean Cadigan, "Sex, Power, and Adventure: Tourist-Beach Boy Relationships on the Kenyan Coast: A Proposal for Research" (Master's thesis, University of California at Los Angeles, 1998).

44. The founding of the association was announced in one of the national newspapers, *Daily Nation,* July 12, 1999, 4.

45. Tamara Kohn, "Island Involvement and the Evolving Tourist," in Abram et al., *Tourists and Tourism,* 15.

46. Jacqueline Waldren, *Insiders and Outsiders: Paradise and Reality in Mallorca* (Providence: Berghahn, 1996), x.

47. Five of the individuals who filled out questionnaires in the hotels in Kenya were Swiss. Due to rounding, percentage figures do not add up to 100 percent. Of the respondents 109 of 110 provided information on their age.

48. "Schulabgänger 1987," *Statistisches Jahrbuch 1989 für die Bundesrepublik Deutschland* (Stuttgart: Metzler-Poeschel, 1989), 345; "Schulentlassene 1996/97," *Statistisches Jahrbuch 1999 für die Bundesrepublik Deutschland* (Stuttgart: Metzler-Poeschel, 1999), 375. Some tourists also might have had an academic education and work now in professions that do not require such training.

49. "Bevölkerung im April 1998 nach Altersgruppen und Bildungsabschluß," *Statistisches Jahrbuch 1999 für die Bundesrepublik Deutschland,* 369.

50. Pompl, *Der internationale Tourismus in Kenia,* 270; Schurian-Bremecker, "Kenia in der Sicht deutscher Touristen," 158.

51. See Dieter Kleiber and Martin Wilke, *Aids, Sex und Tourismus: Ergebnisse*

einer Befragung deutscher Urlauber und Sextouristen (Baden-Baden: Nomos, 1995), 167–69, 185, 198–199; see also "Weltmarkt Sex," *Focus-Magazin*, January 9, 1995, 110–18.

52. Kleiber and Wilke, *Aids, Sex und Tourismus*, 157.

53. This can even be observed in the case of Thailand where the attraction of Thai prostitutes seems to be at least partially related to the different codes of Western versus non-Western sex industries. Jeremy Seabrook, *Travels in the Skin Trade: Tourism and the Sex Industry* (London: Pluto, 1996), 3. See also Dennis O'Rourke's 1995 film *The Good Woman of Bangkok*.

54. See Kleiber and Wilke, *Aids, Sex und Tourismus*, 245–79. Also Edith Kresta, "Wenn reisende Frauen vögeln," *die tageszeitung*, June 8, 1996, 18.

55. Kleiber and Wilke, *Aids, Sex und Tourismus*, 267, 278.

56. One hotel listed 80 guests in 57 rooms (23 double, 34 single occupancy); other hotels listed 73 guests in 37 rooms (36 double, 1 single occupancy); 110 guests in 56 rooms (54 double, 2 single occupancy); 270 guests in 170 rooms (100 double, 70 single occupancy). Another hotel listed 165 adults and 24 children.

57. According to a survey of the Forsa-institute, 10 percent of all 16- to 45-year-old tourists had sex with a stranger during their vacations of the last three years. "Sonne, Sand—und Mehr," *Süddeutsche Zeitung*, July 16, 1996, section "Reise."

58. Fifteen of the twenty-eight interviewees also filled out questionnaires, which were included in the evaluation of the 110 questionnaires.

59. Fourteen of the tourists traveled with a partner and were interviewed together. Two interviewees always traveled with their spouse, one traveled with her lover, and another traveled with a group of friends, but all four of them were interviewed without their partners.

60. Migot-Adholla et al. 108–9.

61. At the time, school fees for elementary schools were 4,000 KSh per year for KG 1 and 2 and grades 1–3, 7,000 KSh per year for grades 4 through 8. School uniforms were 1,500 KSh per year, books and materials amount to 6,000 KSh per year. In 1999, $100 equaled roughly 1,000 KSh. Basic monthly salaries for workers in the hotel industry ranged roughly from 3,000 KSh to 6000 KSh. The salary of a general manager, on the other hand, ranged from 150,000 to 180,000 KSh. While most basic food was relatively affordable, an average employee was paying 1,000 KSh and more for two rooms in a modest house or apartment building.

62. Peggy Piesche elaborates on the contradictions between declarations of international solidarity and the racism in East Germany in "Black and German? East German Adolescents before 1989: A Retrospective View of a 'Non-Existent Issue' in the GDR," in *The Cultural After-Life of East Germany: New Transnational Perspectives*, ed. Leslie A. Adelson (Washington DC: American Institute for Contemporary German Studies, 2002), 37–59.

63. Figures according to Statistisches Bundesamt, Wiesbaden. For the year 2000,

the Embassy of the FRG in Nairobi recorded 141; for the year 2001, 284 marriages between Kenyans and Germans.

64. Figures provided by the Swiss Office Fédéral de la Statistique.

65. I would like to thank my daughter Milena, who was a great help in recording the data.

66. The breakdown is as follows: special license: 5,000 KSh; certificate: 100 KSh; certified copy: 100 KSh; registration fee: 50 KSh; office ceremony fees: 1000 KSh; 5,000 KSh for outside ceremonies.

67. The licenses were not all in chronological order but were organized according to the month of the event. Therefore, I organized the statistics following the order of the file folders.

68. Ten German men and four German women were retired; one man and one woman from non-German-speaking countries were also retired. Three tourists did not provide information on this subject.

69. Compare "Durchschnittliches Heiratsalter nach dem bisherigen Familienstand der Ehepartner," *Statistisches Jahrbuch für die Bundesrepublik Deutschland 1999,* 69. Regarding the U.S. context, see "Marriage—Age Differences of Bride and Groom, by Age: 1985," in *Statistical Handbook on the American Family,* ed. Bruce A. Chadwick and Tim B. Heaton (Phoenix: Oryx, 1992), 18.

70. "Weltmarkt Sex," *Focus Magazin,* January 9, 1995, 110–18.

71. The "Verein deutscher Frauen in Tunis" is but one indication for the existence of this phenomenon in other countries. See Renate Fisseler-Skandarani, "Ja, das muß doch Liebe sein . . . ," *die tageszeitung,* October 11, 1999, 18.

72. Rosemary Breger, "Love and the State: Women, Mixed Marriages and the Law in Germany," in *Cross-Cultural Marriage: Identity and Choice,* ed. Rosemary Breger and Rosanna Hill (Oxford: Berg, 1998), 131.

73. Breger, "Love and the State," 131–32.

CONCLUSION

1. In "German Colonialism: Another *Sonderweg?*" Russell A. Berman argues that the main differences lie in the historical belatedness of German national unity, the fact that German colonialism ended early, and that German colonialism was distinguished by "a predisposition to grant at least relative legitimacy to local cultures" (33).

INDEX

In the *Texts and Contexts* series

Affective Genealogies
Psychoanalysis, Postmodernism, and the "Jewish Question" after Auschwitz
By Elizabeth J. Bellamy

Sojourners
The Return of German Jews and the Question of Identity
By John Borneman and Jeffrey M. Peck

Impossible Missions?
German Economic, Military, and Humanitarian Efforts in Africa
By Nina Berman

Serenity in Crisis
A Preface to Paul de Man, 1939–1960
By Ortwin de Graef

Titanic Light
Paul de Man's Post-Romanticism, 1960–1969
By Ortwin de Graef

The Future of a Negation
Reflections on the Question of Genocide
By Alain Finkielkraut
Translated by Mary Byrd Kelly

The Imaginary Jew
By Alain Finkielkraut
Translated by Kevin O'Neill and David Suchoff

The Wisdom of Love
By Alain Finkielkraut
Translated by Kevin O'Neill and David Suchoff

The House of Joshua
Meditations on Family and Place
By Mindy Thompson Fullilove

Inscribing the Other
By Sander L. Gilman

Antisemitism, Misogyny, and the Logic of Cultural Difference
Cesare Lombroso and Matilde Serao
By Nancy A. Harrowitz

Opera
Desire, Disease, Death
By Linda Hutcheon and Michael Hutcheon

Man of Ashes
By Salomon Isacovici and Juan Manuel Rodríguez
Translated by Dick Gerdes

Between Redemption and Doom
The Strains of German-Jewish Modernism
By Noah Isenberg

Poetic Process
By W. G. Kudszus

Keepers of the Motherland
German Texts by Jewish Women Writers
By Dagmar C. G. Lorenz

Madness and Art
The Life and Works of Adolf Wölfli
By Walter Morgenthaler
Translated and with an introduction by Aaron H. Esman in collaboration with Elka Spoerri

The Nation without Art
Examining Modern Discourses on Jewish Art
By Margaret Olin

Organic Memory
History and the Body in the Late Nineteenth and Early Twentieth Centuries
By Laura Otis

Crack Wars
Literature, Addiction, Mania
By Avital Ronell

Finitude's Score
Essays for the End of the Millennium
By Avital Ronell

Herbarium / Verbarium
The Discourse of Flowers
By Claudette Sartiliot

Atlas of a Tropical Germany
Essays on Politics and Culture, 1990–1998
By Zafer Şenocak
Translated and with an introduction by Leslie A. Adelson

The Inveterate Dreamer
Essays and Conversations on Jewish Culture
By Ilan Stavans

Budapest Diary
In Search of the Motherbook
By Susan Rubin Suleiman

Rahel Levin Varnhagen
The Life and Work of a German Jewish Intellectual
By Heidi Thomann Tewarson

The Jews and Germany
From the "Judeo-German Symbiosis" to the Memory of Auschwitz
By Enzo Traverso
Translated by Daniel Weissbort

Richard Wagner and the Anti-Semitic Imagination
By Marc A. Weiner

Undertones of Insurrection
Music, Politics, and the Social Sphere in the Modern German Narrative
By Marc A. Weiner

The Mirror and the Word
Modernism, Literary Theory, and Georg Trakl
By Eric B. Williams